Sport and Violence

Sport and Violence:
A Critical Examination of Sport

Lynn M. Jamieson
Thomas J. Orr

AMSTERDAM · BOSTON · HEIDELBERG · LONDON · NEW YORK · OXFORD
PARIS · SAN DIEGO · SAN FRANCISCO · SINGAPORE ·SYDNEY · TOKYO
Butterworth-Heinemann is an imprint of Elsevier

Butterworth-Heinemann is an imprint of Elsevier
Linacre House, Jordan Hill, Oxford OX2 8DP, UK
30 Corporate Drive, Suite 400, Burlington, MA 01803, USA

First edition 2009

British Library Cataloguing in Publication Data
A catalogue record for this book is available from the British Library

Library of Congress Cataloging-in-Publication Data
A catalog record for this book is available from the Library of Congress

ISBN: 978-0-7506-8405-7

For information on all Butterworth-Heinemann
publications visit our website at elsevierdirect.com

Printed and bound in Great Brittain

09 10 11 12   10 9 8 7 6 5 4 3 2 1

los TTS TS
30/3/12
£32.99

Dedication

This book is dedicated to our families who have been on the forefront of experiencing sport first-hand with its accomplishments, disappointments, and dangers.

Living among some of the greatest relatives I could ever hope to have, I wish to thank my family for being the supportive and active people they have been all my life. An early bout of polio could have ended much of my sport involvement for life if it hadn't been for my mother and father, and extended family who would not allow that to become a disabling condition. On all sides of my family are those who have ventured into the dangerous and intoxicating world of sport – through dedication to helping children, to actual personal accomplishments themselves. Because of them, I learned to play baseball in the streets, swimming in the lakes, fishing in the ocean, and developing a dedication to recreational sports.

Lynn Jamieson

"To produce a mighty book, you must choose a mighty theme. No great and enduring volume can ever be written on the flea, though many there be that have tried it."

Herman Melville, my ancestor and author of the classic Moby Dick novel has passed this advice forward to myself and the world in this quote. The dynamics of the sport environment has proven to be a very worthy topic, and has provided a rich amount of material that investigates the actions, thoughts and behaviors of people as they navigate their way through a social environment that we have come to know as sport.

By avoiding the study of flees, I have instead had to navigate the deep blue waters of research into finding the causes, roots and solutions to a social problem that has become figuratively as large as the mythical Moby Dick, that my great-great-great uncle was in search of.

Tom Orr

Violence impacts societies and people. Often times that impact is tragic, devastating, and senseless. In thinking, researching, and writing on violence

I am sadly reminded of those close to me that have lost their life at the hands of another for the meaningless sake of fun or disagreement. To Nailah Oliani Franklin, who came into the community center I once supervised to volunteer full of joy and excitement. However, who left this world many years later while beginning a successful career through a vengeful act of murder. Because you gave myself, the center, and the youth of Douglass Community your endearing love, committed service, and unyielding effort you will never be forgotten. Also, to Laquentin Renaldo Porter-Hughes, who was the first youth I ever worked with as a volunteer when I walked into the Douglass Community Center. You initiated my path in leisure service provision as a youth but also signaled the change in path to leisure research when you were shot while holding your daughter on New Years Eve as an adult. Thank for you helping me make the decisions that I am most proud of.

Rasul Mowatt, Guest author

Epigraph

They came to play, have fun, laugh, and run
And although they were fierce, the real show had begun
and to their surprise
Right before their eyes stood two of their parents
Who were acting unwise.
By yelling and screaming, the fun has been ended
And having some fun had to be on the run.

Table of Contents

Foreword

It is not often that one is inspired to write a book that reads like a novel but is fully based on truth. This book is inspired by a growing concern about real experiences that began primarily when a seven-year-old child was viewed being kicked by his father on a flag football field, when an adult touch football player decked an official, when post-game rioters damaged a city's football field, when a volunteer coach shouted a racist epithet at a five-year-old baseball player, when parents bribed a coach to play their child over another, when an irate teammate damaged a fellow hockey player's car, when a hazing initiation rite for a boy's soccer team involved placing a choke collar on a freshman player and running him through an electrified invisible fence, when a high school athletic director claimed there were no written policies on hiring and supervision of their coaches, and when parents of an under 12 girls fast pitch team barricaded officials in a room after a hotly contested national game. This listing, while only a small subset of the full range of observations, represented a cadre of ongoing interactions that are similar to what is happening in every sector of sport around the world.

The inspiration grew when it was realized that children were playing games that mimicked professional teams, that parents became agents for their children, that children were being exploited by organizations, that children were younger and younger when starting sophisticated sports, that injuries were rising in younger players, that reports of abusive behaviors on the part of adult role models were becoming criminal, that children were quitting involvement because it wasn't 'fun' anymore, and that a majority of states developed anti-hazing and anti-sport violence laws. It became evident that something needed to be done to counteract the continual problems arising in all phases of the sport experience. Indeed, it was time to provide facts and solutions to an increasingly pervasive social problem. In addition, it was becoming evident that regardless of the number of organizations that held regulatory influence over sport, violent acts were becoming more a part of mainstream experience regardless of age, gender, ability, race, ethnicity, religion, and other differentiating factors.

This inspiration, now complete in a text that examines these social phenomena from theoretical and realistic perspectives, now has become a call to end sport violence around the world through improvements in coordination of programs, through collaboration of regulatory agencies and organizations, through the development of local, regional, state or provincial, and national policies that return the sport experience and its ultimate enjoyment back to players in all categories of play. It is realized that the key responsibility for improvement rests with public and private sector cooperation at all levels to improve oversight and leadership of programs that occur on community property. Further, it is important to continually encourage large-scale national organizations to continue their individual efforts to provide positive athlete role-modeling and mentorship that give players an opportunity to emulate the positive features of sport. Finally, national entities are encouraged to unite and provide guidance and incentives to end the cycle of violence that threatens to erode important experiences in active living and sport involvement.

Written from experience and from the heart, it is hoped that this book will serve as an inspiration to others as they focus on organizational leadership, training and education of sport specialists, oversight of sport volunteers, support for positive outcomes for players and participants, and ultimate enjoyment of skill development, spectatorship, and FUN.

Lynn M. Jamieson, Re. D.
Professor
Indiana University
Department of Recreation, Park, and Tourism Studies

Recreational sport supervisor, physical educator, coach, player, official, judge, park and recreation administrator, college and university educator and administrator, consultant, concerned parent.

Preface and Acknowledgment

The development of this text was conceived as a critical analysis of a social issue that is plaguing the enjoyable pursuit of sport for its own sake. Research involved years of collection of research articles, analysis of cases, exploration of sport structure, experience, and finally concern. It is a major thesis of this text that those who professionally prepare themselves to enter into the sport world, whether as an administrator, coach, player, adult role model, official, teacher, volunteer, fan, investor, or other interested party should be familiar with the problems that occur in the sport environment.

Our research has shown that most problems surrounding the sport environment, while endemic to societal issues, are for the most part, avoidable. In most cases, and upon further analysis, improved sport programming and facility administration can greatly reduce incidences of violence that occur. With this in mind, this text is unique in that it provides an approach to the reader that allows for critical analysis and solutions to be developed. This is accomplished in several ways. Each chapter contains not only textual content, but also actual sport experiences called Sport Stories and Feel Good Cases. Using this technique, the reader may experience one's triumphs and challenges as context is being explained.

Each chapter also covers much background information that can be further researched. Tables contain information that provides a resource that may be helpful in establishing a sound organizational structure around sport. The initial portion of the text contains an analysis of the key problems associated with sport and violence, its history, and status. In later chapters, societal factors and issues are more thoroughly represented, and in the final portion of the text, solutions and approaches are discussed that may provide a springboard for change.

This book differs from many texts that explore sport and leisure in the sense that it is a critique that contains a call to change. The content of each chapter represents a global view of issues, not just issues apparent in one country. It is also a text that provides real experiences so that the reader is armed with facts and intention to make change. The audience for the book can include upper division students and also graduate students desiring in-depth study of a topic. This is also a book that can assist an administrator to organize a safer and civil sport experience.

Of course, an undertaking such as this text could not have been successful without the help from many people. Many family members provided Sport Stories since we all have come from families immersed in all levels of sport. Also, special thanks to family members who provided support to us during our efforts to complete the deadlines and collect the information. Each of us has special thanks as noted below.

From Lynn Jamieson – Thanks to my family – Steve, my husband – whose 9 high school letters and abilities never cease to amaze me. To Byron and Ben who have experienced firsthand the crazy world of sports and parental pressures, and violence. This book has been a quest – for the development of better policies to live by that ensures a safer environment for future sports enthusiasts. Thanks for all your support.

From Tom Orr – I would like to thank my family for their support and love throughout my lifetime. I would like to thank my wife Matty, and my children Lyndon, Jocelyn, & our baby Ellen Annette Orr for the joy they have given me while writing this book. Finding balance in my own work and life commitments while writing this book has been a practical reminder of the difficult tasks and choices of priorities we have of being a part of a complex world full of individual and social obligations. Hopefully our perspective as "Doctors of Leisure" will allow others to find a better way to approach their own recreation and leisure pursuits so that we can all find them a remedy to our problems and not just another stage to display our inability to get along with each other in life, and sadly, while we "play".

From Rasul Mowatt, Guest Writer – To my family, mentors, and friends who stood by me throughout the ordeal of research on leisure related violence. To Akins Adolfo Timothy Butler, Amili Cheo Rhodes, Anthony Martin Neal, Betty Shabazz, El Hajj Malik El Shabazz Omowale Malcolm X, Fundisha Kummba Pinkington, Kevin L.S. Andrew Moore, LaQuentin Hughes, Maria (Briana), Nailah Franklin, Martin Luther King, Jr., Patrice Lummumba, the numerous victims of lynching, and so many others who touched my life, yet met their violent end at the hands of another.

Introduction

In the past half century sport has emerged as a major factor in shaping American culture. Coupled with the pervasive presence of television and instant reporting of events across the globe, sport has become the spotlight for all that is common across cultures. Conversely, sport has also become a pivotal issue when one examines America's values, priorities, ethics, lifestyle and well-being. While we are consistently bombarded with media images in sport over television (e.g.) bullying, physical assault, upstaging, etc., the actual behavior of millions of boys and girls as sport participants across the globe is often marked by good behavior. Yet when the purest context of sport is compromised by national ideology, greed, or other untenable motives, sport becomes the face of these motives. The price of winning is then paid for by egregious violations of rule, policy, law, and ethical canons held dear when amateur sport was born in the first Olympiad. Violence in sport is clearly an issue of contemporary concern. This book presents a clarion call for action.

The authors set the table for the careful examination of sport as a *public good* and create awareness of the seminal issues and forces related to the problems of sport violence. They offer vivid perspectives on the management of the sport experience and environment, the role of sport in society, policy perspectives and a glimpse of the impact of sport on family dynamics. While this book is not prescriptive it provides clear insight into the root causes of sport violence. The consequential nature of engagement in sport today poses grave danger to the health and well-being of those who seek enjoyment, development of their physical capacities, a social or leisure outlet or a lifetime pursuit. Behavior by others during the course of a game that compromises the nature of the game is of paramount concern. Violation of universally accepted virtues when interacting with another human being during engagement in sport is deeply disturbing and disruptive. Is winning really the only thing? Must we win at all costs? Is the humiliation or degradation of my opponent essential to the game? These and many other questions are at the apex of this important work by the authors. All athletic administrators, coaches, public officials, parents and sponsors of sport should read this book and become part of the solution, not parties to the perpetuation of violence in sport. In that regard the words of Robert Herrick should guide us the in pursuit of solutions.

Each must in virtue strive for to excel; *that man lives twice that lives the first life well.* Robert Herrick

David M. Compton, MS, MPH, Ed.D.,
Professor and Chair, Department of Recreation,
Park, and Tourism Studies, Indiana University

CHAPTER 1

Our Violent Society – Nationally and Globally

"A sense of identity can be a source not merely of pride and joy, but also of strength and confidence. It is not surprising that the idea of identity receives such widespread admiration, from popular advocacy of loving your neighbor to high theories of social capital and of communitarian self-definition. And yet identity can also kill - and kill with abandon. A strong-and exclusive-sense of belonging to one group can in many cases carry with it the perception of distance and divergence from other groups."

(Sen, 2006, p. 1)

As we approach the phenomenon of violence in sport, we need to take into consideration that sport is merely a reflection of society, one lens by which we define what that society stands for and creates as an image for itself. In examining the topics we have chosen to share in this book, we examine how societies reflect their particular identity to the world. That is to say that sport is one of the ways that we are introduced to a nation and its citizens. It is a positive reflection, for the most part, but the phenomena that surround the violent aspects of sport reveal a great deal of the underbelly of a society's character, and herein, reflect on all of those who participate either directly or indirectly in the sport experience. One could suggest that all individuals are affected by what happens in the sport environment whether they directly engage in the sport itself, view the sport, or remain aloof to any participation whatsoever. This is due to sport's maximum visibility in media and imagination. In this book, we examine the epidemic of sport violence to provide an understanding of the many ways it permeates through the entire sport participation continuum, provides the backdrop for much criminal activity,

CONTENTS

and in the end, leaves a path of disappointment and frustration. This chapter provides an introduction to what sport violence means, the nature of its origins and the backdrop from which it develops. Subsequent chapters will go into greater depth about our historical roots, causal factors in sport violence, sociological factors, roles and solutions.

WHAT IS SPORT VIOLENCE?

In the United States, but certainly not restricted to this setting, the concern for increased incidences of altercations, criminal activity and even death during and around sport venues has been well documented. Violent episodes between players, spectators, revellers and officials within and outside the contest have raised the specter of curiosity and questions as to why these incidents occur and what can be done. In addition, the events have resulted in increasingly strict actions taken to provide remedy through the courts, incarceration and other means to treat these as criminal acts. One of the most publicized events in the United States in recent years was the pummelling death of a father of a recreational hockey player, and this report galvanized people to begin investigating root causes. The phenomenon is not restricted to the highest levels of competition but seems to permeate all levels of sport participation along the entire continuum from start to top accomplishment. In addition, incidents have been occurring around the world in many cultures and in many forms (Coakley & Dunning, 2000; Tomlinson, 2007). It is the intent of this book to articulate a perspective toward sport violence that helps the reader to not only understand ways to avoid violence personally, but also to provide solutions from an organizational standpoint. It is also the major premise in this book that sport violence episodic behaviors have their roots in the home and organizational structure surrounding sport, and as such, solutions must begin in those two venues.

As a backdrop, school violence has caught the attention of many administrators who cannot understand why a young person would go to the lengths that he/she would to make a statement about issues that are later revealed once the individual is either incarcerated or pieced together after he/she dies. Time Magazine shared the backgrounds of several young students who have either successfully or unsuccessfully planned killing strategies – stimulated by the most notable of which was a commando-style raid by two students on Columbine High School in 1999 that ended in the death of several fellow students and the perpetrators themselves (McCarthy, 2001). Fortunately, most of the efforts were foiled by advanced surveillance; however, those that were carried out were studied more fully. Andy Williams killed two fellow students in Santee and wounded 13, and was revealed to have been bullied mercilessly by these and other individuals. It pointed to lack of adult supervision by two parents and even being dared by friends to "pull a Columbine".

In looking at many of the situations that caused this and similar debacles, the unhappiness of these students was documented, and studies that began revealed methods to create a safer school environment. Notwithstanding, the background of frustration and violence provides an intricate tapestry with which sport violence may be better understood – in that many of the incidences occur due to frustration, deep unhappiness and neglect. According to the *Time* (2001) article, understanding students could better alleviate even the most difficult of situations.

It is important to note that "violence has always been a fact of human existence, in every civilization." (Spinrad, 1979, p. 240). It is the way in which we address violence that differs – for example, many sport activities within the playing setting really are acts of controlled violence and are acceptable; however, if these same acts occurred on the street, they would be considered criminal and at the very least, deviant behavior (Shillito, 2004; Reshef & Paltiel, 1989). Molina (1999) refers to the prevalence of violence in culture and the notion that continuous existence may cause youth to become hardened to the consequences brought on by violent acts. Our dilemma has been – What constitutes acceptable behavior and what constitutes violence that should be viewed more as unacceptable, or criminal, behavior? In this text, attempts are to be made to differentiate these and provide approaches to mitigate those behaviors that are deemed criminal, either in intent or as a result of accident.

DEFINITIONS

But first, we must explore working definitions and premises for this text so that we understand the complexity of this phenomenon and the degree to which we all can address the solutions made necessary by these unfortunate acts. For the purpose of definition, the following background definitions are offered to culminate in an operational definition of sport violence. This will allow for an understandable framework to the phenomena of issues that exist in sport today.

We start with the term sport and then violence as well as combining the two terms together to form this approach to understand the nature of these pervasive phenomena. Definitions of sport vary but include the following:

1. Sport – "an activity, experience, or business enterprise focused on fitness, recreation, athletics, or leisure" (Pitts, Fielding, and Miller, 1994, p. 15).

2. Sport Management – "the total process of structuring the business or organizational aspects of sport." (Mull, Bayless, Ross, and Jamieson, 1997, p. 7).

3. Recreational Sport – "playing cooperative or competitive activity in the game form" (Mull, Bayless, and Jamieson, 2005, p. 7).

4. Athletic Sport – located within the recreational sport continuum as it pertains to the entire sport experience of athletes and spectators, defined as "directing individuals toward a margin of excellence in performance that can be identified as wanting and needing to win." (Mull, Bayless, and Jamieson, 2005, p. 10).

5. Professional Sport – "a system where the very best are brought together to participate at the highest level" (Mull, Bayless, and Jamieson, 2005, p. 10).

Violence, according to Spinrad (1987, p. 238) is "use of physical force to destroy or coerce; conflict; brawn over brain; disorder". When we combine the terms sport and violence together, we have the following:

■ Contact or non-contact behavior which causes harm.

■ Occurs outside of the rules

■ Unrelated to the competitive objectives

■ Use of excessive physical force causing harm or destruction (Coakley, 2001)

This definition is expanded for the purposes of our book to include the following operational features:

Sport violence is any behavior that causes either physical or psychological injury related to either a direct or indirect result of a sport experience. Therefore, our definition points to the diffusion of violent acts resulting from one's direct or indirect involvement in sport. Sport violence, therefore, can occur in the home, school, workplace, recreational site, at events and many other venues due to the sport contest or involvement itself. While we are very aware of well-publicized violent events occurring during a sport contest, we have become more aware of the insidious nature of violence that occurs because of a sport.

It is fitting to also describe the nature of sport in terms of how it is delivered. For the purposes of understanding much complexity surrounding the role of sport in every society at all levels, there are many differences that exist. The following description and subsequent explanation will be the way sport systems are identified for all cases: as a *loosely coupled, semi-autonomous, autopoietec system.* Separating the parts of this description, one may better understand how we can regard this more completely:

1. Loosely coupled – This term comes from Hirschhorn (1994) who developed this concept for many organizations that have elements with high autonomy where actions of one sector may have little relevance or impact on another sector.

2. Semi-autonomous – Partially self-governing or having the powers of self-government within a larger organization or structure (Answers. com, 2009).

3. Autopoietec – A systems theory that deals with the idea of self-organization or one that remains stable regardless of constant matter pouring through it (Luhman).

To understand the concepts as they may be combined, sport delivery systems seem to consist of organizations that are loosely coupled, that in some way remain linked together even if they are semi-autonomous in their delivery of service. The delivery itself is affected by many external influences such as that of regulatory bodies within and outside of a specific sport, administrative structures that serve as contractors and the playing experience itself with its constraints and consequences. Even so, the system remains somewhat self-contained and growth-oriented. As we move through the text, the challenges placed on managing a system such as this requires that the system is protected and that those who lead it are able to monitor and protect it from imploding during problems. These problems can include issues of destabilization through budget cuts, leadership gaps and controversy. Of course, the issue of sport violence is a continuous assault on sport delivery systems, and the manner in which efforts to protect the system occur is crucial to the continued stability of sport delivery itself. That said, the types and breadth of issues prevalent in sport violence continue to erode the ability to manage the system. In a loosely coupled system, one incident of sport violence reverberates throughout a much wider system of sport delivery, but it also affects community and society.

Therefore, sport violence is the use of physical force or coercion within or outside of the playing venue either directly or indirectly the result of frustration over an event associated with the playing environment. This definition includes conflicts that may occur between players, and it also includes conflicts that arise from one or a combination of the following:

1. Player: One engaged in a sport experience.

2. Coach: Volunteer or paid leaders of sport teams.

3. Referee/official: Those who regulate game, contest situations.

4. Fan/spectator: Those who observe practices, games or contests either in person or through media.

5. Volunteer: One who serves in a number of roles to help support a sport delivery system and include helpers at events, board members, coaches, parent representatives.

6. Administrator – An individual or group of individuals having direct or indirect authority over the sport environment.

7. Parent/guardian/family – Those related to a player or players.

8. Adult role model – Coaches, teacher, recreation leader, athletes, or anyone who has direct or indirect influence on a player.

9. Business associate – One involved in investing, donating, or supporting the sport with a monetary exchange.

10. Criminal – One who breaks rules to the extent that he/she may be brought up on charges.

11. Terrorist – One who commits crimes for the purpose of giving exposure to a particular ideology, issue of concern, or grudge.

Table 1.1 shows some of the actual types of problems occurring with each category of sport participant that have received attention by the media or been experienced through observation. These incidents have occurred with a frequency that appears to reveal the ultimate acceptance of sport violence as a part of the normal business as usual aspect of sport; however, penalties and concerns have been increasing, and until the social issue of sport violence is more comprehensively addressed, incidents such as the ones described may be the cause of activities to be cancelled.

Regardless of the types of conflicts that may occur, if there is a relationship of the violent event to the sport activity, venue, or spillover from same, the act is considered sport violence. We then address the types of behaviors that can fall into the realm of sport violence as follows:

1. Direct injurious actions between people: These may occur within and outside of the sport venue as a result of reactionary or intentional intent to harm or injure.

2. Sport injury that occurs as a result of drugs use, overuse and over coaching: This is a broad category of abuses that may be the result of failing to observe the problems associated with the ingestion of a wide

Table 1.1	Violent Episodes Committed by Those in the Sport Environment
Role	**Incidences**
Player	Drugs use, domestic battery, weapon possession, sustaining and giving injuries, fighting, temper tantrums, illegal gambling, attacking rival player, obscene gesture, altercations, violating conduct code, sideline clearing brawls, throwing pitches, being robbed, disorderly conduct, flagrant fouls, murder, driving while intoxicated, involved in shootings, arguing call and spitting seeds, vandalism and destruction of property, pranks, illegal dog fighting, lack of respect for referees, hazing, accidental injury, intentional injury, off-field conduct, larceny, kicking opposing player, improper on-court conduct, beaned by 90 mph ball, pranks and assault of officials.
Coach	Brawls, harassment, sexual harassment, sexual assault, being stalked, physical assault and battery, threatened, vandalism, attacking fans, bribing player to keep autistic child from playing three innings as required by league, criticism of official, fired over dirty play, decking opposing player, hazing, coercion of playing through injury, off-field conduct and hitting players.
Referee/official	Game fixing, unnecessary technical foul, baiting players, protected by French government actions, incompetence and inconsistency.
Fan/spectator	Illegal acts, pelting players with debris, kidnapping, attacking school coach, grabbing professional player and choking, burning couches and mattresses, streaking, charged in brawling, allowing hazing rituals, stalking, off-field conduct, bribery, intimidation of referees, death over jersey, killed by police, killed by stampede, assault, threatening and detainment of officials.
Volunteer	Theft, hazing, hacking information from French doping lab, cheerleader trampled by football team.
Administrator	Reschedule of practices due to fires, acts of omission and commission, mismanagement, manoeuvring and manipulation, permitting continuance of discrimination, making unacceptable remarks and perpetuating inequality.
Parent/guardian/family	Manslaughter, beatings, permitting hazing, poisoning players, murder contract, stalking, pressure, child abuse, threatening, bribing, buying coaches, promoting inappropriate conduct and permitting inappropriate conduct.
General citizen	Terrorism, hazing, permitting illegal acts, murder, shooting, hero, suicide of former player, killed by robbers, bombing at Olympics.
Business associate	Trainer released from prison, shoving, rigging and making improper payments to player.
Criminal/terrorist	Stray bullets, using field for terrorism, threatening large gatherings of sport enthusiasts.

variety of performance-related additives, or the consistent failure to observe or understand the way in which constant overuse in training can be harmful particularly during certain developmental periods.

3. Hazing and all forms of initiation activities that single out an individual or group – Activities that tend to isolate a group of people in order to test loyalty to the group through a series of humiliating experiences that go on for an initiation period.

Table 1.2		High Visibility Youth Sport Violence Episodes
1.	Atlanta	Shooting occurs after an argument between a coach and parent.
2.	Georgia	Coach gives his 10-year-old Midget football players Lasix to make weight.
3.	Chicago	Mary Pierce keeps bodyguard since 14 to protect her from father.
4.	Florida	Barroom-type brawl between parents during 11–12 year football game.
5.	Sterling, NJ	Father of high school soccer player punched out son's opponents.
6.	Cleveland, OH	Parent attacks coach of his son's hockey team, coach dies.
7.	Reading, MA	Seven-year-old flag football player caught choking members of opposing team.
8.	Allentown, PA	Argument between coaches and referee in 11–12 year old game, hospital.
9.	Wilmington, DE	Ten-year-old baseball player slugs umpire who made a call against him.
10.	Allentown, PA	Mother of 9-year-old physically assaults opposing coach after game.
11.	Kansas City, MO	Coach breaks jaw of umpire after disputing call.
12.	Florida	Coach breaks both arms of football player on his time after dropped pass.
13.	Texas	Brawl with all erupts during high school sectional soccer match.
14.	Charleston, WV	Umpire ejects female player for cursing in co-ed church team after prayer.
15.	Galveston, TX	Coach, also full time police officer offers pitcher $2 to hit next player.
16.	Tamaqua, PA	High school basketball player gets five years after intentional elbow.
17.	San Antonio, TX	Father arrested for sharpening buckles on son's football helmet.
18.	Albuquerque, NM	Brawl over tiebreaker during eight-year-old boys soccer charity match.
19.	Hamilton Twp, NJ	Father breaks nose of his 10-year old's coach with hockey stick.
20.	Staten Island, NY	Former Texas Ranger father puts referee in chokehold following dispute.
21.	Texas	Policeman gives ticket to referee who threw him out of game.
22.	Pennsylvania	Two soccer parents are arrested for disorderly conduct and assault.
23.	Amherst, MA	A mother charges the field and slaps referee, got arrested.
24.	Greensboro, NC	Fifteen-year-old slams opponent into boards and paralyses him.
25.	Chicago, IL	Little League umpire is assaulted, receives four stitches, after balk call.
26.	Sturgeon Bay, WI	Recreational league hockey player throws skate at referee, injuring him.
27.	New Jersey	Recreational league basketball official needed 21 stitches to repair cut.
28.	San Diego, CA	Father given 45 days for murder threat of son's Little League manager.
29.	Los Angeles, CA	Soccer player kicked goalkeeper in face, fractured cheekbone.
30.	Cleveland, OH	Youth basketball game of seven to eight-year olds, referee slashed coach with knife.
31.	Fayetteville, GA	Youth plants forearm to back of official's head that sent him to his knees.
32.	Fort Worth, TX	Player smashes aluminum bat into umpire's face.
33.	Albuquerque, NM	High school coach struck daughter at softball game, gets felony abuse.
34.	Riverside, CA	Basketball player's teammate punched him in eye and destroyed sight.
35.	Carlsbad, CA	Ray Knight punched man after altercation at 12-year-old daughter's game.
36.	Cincinnati, OH	Sixteen-year-old charge with inciting riot in stands with two rival team fans.
37.	Orange, NJ	Father of 11-year-old wrestler sentenced one year for punching referee.
38.	Doylestown, PA	Father and son confront referee after wrestling match, then punch those who try to break it up. Tournament postponed two days.
39.	Columbus, GA	Enraged mother leaps from stands and chokes teenage umpire over call.

4. Intimidation in the form of verbal and the suggestion of physical injury – The suggestion or threat of injury in order to psychologically impair another individual or group.

5. Intentional sport injury – A direct act intending to hurt another to deprive that person of continuing play. An injury that is pre-meditated for this purpose and not viewed as an accident.

6. Injury as a result of improper or inappropriate overuse – Over time the onset of injury that is incurred through failure to handle stress and strain in exertion. This occurs usually from someone who does not know or disregards what is best for the player in order to win.

7. Child abuse through threats of consequences of non-performance according to parental expectations – Parental pressure or that of other adults that creates a victim rather than a stable player.

8. Fan/Spectator activity – Any activity that causes injury, damage or interruption of game activity.

9. Adult role model behavior that causes psychological problems – Any issue, action, or behavior that creates fear, apprehension, or injury to another person, particularly an individual who can be manipulated or overpowered.

10. Acts of omission that create dangerous environments – Any failure to properly regulate activity or fix hazards that may cause injury.

11. Political activity that creates pressure to perform and succeed – External pressure brought on by individuals with power, responsibility and money that creates a feeling of being threatened or coerced to succeed.

12. Overemphasis on winning that results in emotional contagion – The clash of individuals in a crowded situation that results in injury or other problem.

13. Gambling associated with sport – Illegal activity based upon betting that causes a third tier participant that has a stake in the outcome of a game or contest.

14. Media reporting that influences viewers – Broadcast or print media with a slant that causes a certain perspective or attitude in sport viewing.

15. Sport role model's negative activities that influence fans and viewers – Negative actions by those who have attained celebrity status.

16. Inappropriate sport organizational structures that promote pressurized sport involvement – A systemic situation that promotes winning at all costs instead of a developmental approach to sport.

17. National ideologies that fail to provide a safety net for violent occurrences – The nationalism or identity of a nation that directly or indirectly influences the escalation of violence in sport.

18. Sport terrorism – Any act of exertion of power resulting in an attack that focuses on a sport environment.

The above list does not tell the full picture, but it does address the way in which sport violence permeates our society through and occurs as a result of many factors. Simply stated, what occurs in a playing event can also radiate to events outside of the environment that are attributable to the sport experience. The aspects of which this becomes a societal problem is the manner in which sport is a pervasive part of practically everyone due to the fact that it attracts players and viewers in greater number than other activities.

THE VIOLENT SPORT ENVIRONMENT

Instances of sport violence occur in the most basic of instructional programs all the way up to professional sport and beyond. There is also no evidence to suggest that it is not confined to one group, gender, age, or culture. A series of composite examples of the more widely publicized events include:

1. Girls Tennis Father – Poisons fellow teammates of his daughter, one dies.

2. Boys Hockey Father – Kills coach of his son's hockey team.

3. Girls Cheerleading Mother – Pays contract to kill mother of star cheerleader.

4. Under 12 girls Baseball Parents – Barricade umpires in room after national contest.

5. Professional player – Illegal dog fighting operation operated from home.

6. Olympic player – Loses medals for illegal drug use.

7. Fan – Throws beer on basketball players.

8. Volunteer coach – Abuses player on team.

9. Recreational player – Decks official.

10. Parent – Decks coach.

Sport violence occurs in every type of active environment whether it is operated by the local recreation program or the Olympic committee. In fact, more instances of sport violence occur in what might appear to be innocuous environments such as the local playing field, gymnasium, courts, backyard, open area, as opposed to well-publicized and highly organized sporting events and aftermaths of contests. It is a pervasive activity that strikes when one least expects it, even though most events are preventable when considered in hindsight.

It appears that no sport or group is immune to the possibility that a violent event will erupt within and outside of the game. It is also suggested that the most widely publicized problems are just a tip of the iceberg when exploring the underlying reasons why they occurred. It is also suggested that many of these events could have been prevented with early intervention into the underlying threats to the proper conduct of the sport.

With this in mind, the following list includes places where sport violence has occurred:

1. Site of actual contest, practice and preparation.

2. Sites adjacent to actual contest, practice and preparation.

3. Sites associated with sport organization such as homes, social events and travel venues.

4. Sites not directly associated with sport venues such as home, casino, theatres, dormitories etc.

5. Hazing sites associated with initiation activities such as locker rooms, remote areas, backyards and parks.

6. Organizational offices where meetings and pre-planning are held.

7. Business establishments that are gathering places for large groups of fans or viewing audiences.

8. Universities.

9. Anywhere.

Table 1.3 lists actual places where incidents of sport violence have occurred, and Table 1.4 shows organizations that provide sports programs. This information was a collection through an analysis of news reporting over a five-year period.

Table 1.3	Sites Where Sport Violence Occurs
Site	**Jurisdiction**
Parks	Cities
Fields	Schools, cities and private business
Schools	Schools
Recreation centres	Cities and private business
Bars	Private business
Restaurants	Private business
Streets	Cities
Churches	Non-profit organizations
Homes	Private owners
Courts	Cities, schools and private business
Gambling venues	Private enterprise
Parking lots	Cities
Universities	State and private enterprise
Hotels	Private enterprise
Alleys	Cities
Locker rooms	Schools, cities and private enterprise
Hallways	Everyone's
Everywhere	Everyone's

KEY EXAMPLES

In this book, the reader will be presented with a myriad of examples of precursors and actual sport violent episodes to illustrate points and provide solutions. In this chapter, several representative examples are described here to further support the contention that sport violence is a common occurrence and spans all ages, gender, cultures, locations, abilities and sports. The authors have collected many personal and reported examples, and those included here are personal experiences that form the reason for this book.

Table 1.4	Organizations Influencing Sport Programs
Organization	**Sport Purpose**
Public	Public sector provides for all
Private not for profit	Provides for membership and paying individuals
Private for profit	Provides for membership and paying members
Schools	Provides education for all
Other	Use many of the facilities owned by those above

1. Stalking – A mother of a rival teammate parks her car behind a soccer goalkeeper at a club game that her son is not enrolled in, and watches her son's rival as he plays, later reporting back to her son about what he did.

2. Bribing – Parents give players soccer bags during the weekend that a closely contested effort to achieve starting goalkeeper ensues between two teammate rivals, one of whom is their son.

3. Fighting – Two parents fight at a hockey tournament after one team wins. The fistfight involves police and arrests.

4. Vandalism – One teammate gets mad after practice and damages another teammate's car to the tune of over $4000. The perpetrator is not dismissed from the team.

5. Abuse – A father who is a volunteer coach for a flag football team stands over his crying son (seven-year old) and kicks him to get up. This was in front of parents, spectators and players of two teams.

6. Injury – A soccer player sustains a concussion in a game that later brings on epilepsy that cannot be fully treated by medication.

7. Anger – Parents barricade umpires who have completed the calling of a championship fast pitch under 12-year-old girls team. Police have to escort the umpires out.

8. Mismanagement – Referees fail to closely call a game that starts off with intentional injury attempts, resulting in a major fight that ends the game and yields injuries to both teams.

9. Revenge – Players on teams in a league focus on a hockey member of one team and attempt to injure him at every game.

10. Manipulation – Parents of a player are investors at a sports complex where the coach works. This results in that player gaining favored positions regardless of skill.

11. Death – A hockey player died after being back checked into the boards at a league hockey game.

What are the issues of concern?

As a framework for operation, four items are discussed in this section: ideology, reflection on society, sport ethic – hubris and societal problems. While these items are not the only issues that are prevalent when looking at sport and violence, they provide a reasonable framework to discuss other issues more in-depth. It is important to understand the international perspectives prevalent in sport violence, particularly when understanding pluralistic societies that feature many cultures, as well as more dominant cultures within other countries. Further, according to Hardcastle (2008), the actions inherent in sport violence are causes for disenchantment, as seen in changes in rules and regulations, management aspects, consequences and other factors.

Ideology

A country's ideology refers to "the body of doctrine, myth, belief etc., that guides an individual, social movement, institution, class, or large group" (Flexner, S.B., Ed., 1987, p. 950). In other words, the belief systems that create a country's identity, or personality, form an ideological framework for many activities that form a cultural or sport atmosphere. We can refer to a country's cultural domain through its activities and visibility to the world. In sport, this ideological domain can vary according to the societal norms and myths that are ascribed to the country's personality. Essentially, that domain consists of social constructions of groups that form according to common interests in particular phenomena, in this case sport. This bonding or joining is predicated on the country's ideological domain; hereby defined through the way in which a country's citizens are influenced to participate (Maraniss, 2008; Wilsey, 2006). For example, in mainland China, there is a high expectation that citizens will participate in daily exercise through calisthenics, tai chi, or other solitary pursuit. In that regard, one may view many citizens exercising early in the morning as a part of being influenced to meet their duty as a citizen. Part of the duty is to build individual strength – thus accomplished through the daily exercise regimen that is expected of all. In the United States, the major power structure is based on money and power; therefore, those who participate in sport either engage in a social structure that conforms to the norms of capitalism and individuality or they rebel and become a part of a marginalized or excluded category that does not meet the social norm. Often acts of violence in schools are committed by those who feel excluded by sport participants (i.e., those who are perceived to be "in power" and due to repeat the dominant social system that defines the United States) (Hughes & Coakley 1991; McCarthy, 2008). In other countries, that definition may vary considerably – for example, in Sweden, volunteerism and sociability are valued to such an extent that social groups form with very little instigation from anyone. These socially adept groups are willing to take considerable time to be involved in sport clubs, and they also are rewarded with a national policy that provides incentives to the clubs that are formed.

Of recent note, the role of China in delivering the Beijing Olympics gave the world an amazing look at the culture and ideals of this powerful nation particularly through the delivery of the opening and closing ceremonies. The spectacular availability of over one million volunteers acted in unison to depict what appeared to be technologically-enhanced computer keys. After the completion of the number, the people under the boxes all waved. The ideology of China as one people united was palpable, revealing its strength by this and many other demonstrations during the Olympic event.

From the ideology, government policies may develop to reflect the ideology of a particular country. In some countries this ideological domain represents control and direction, while in others, a looser framework is provided to encourage and support concepts without dictate. From governmental policy, social policy evolves as a result of describing the social interactions of groups, within and among the various socially constructed roles. It is these constructions that further define the cultural norms of a society. According to some researchers, this social policy can be manifested in gender relations, the development of leisure norms, and the reflection of traditions of home, work and leisure (Kay, 2000; Coulter, 2000; Yule, 1997). In addition, social policy supports a national policy framework (2000). In this context, reports of misuse of sport for commercial, financial and political gains can diminish overall goals to provide value through sport. Therefore, Coulter (1995) alludes to the value of leisure policy to define how to address quality of life through all of the mechanisms available and to address the misuse of sport through stronger measures to mitigate its negative aspects. Some of these positives include the development of bridges across countries as was experienced in the change of South Africa in its ending of apartheid, and also the way in which sport operates to deal with fairness, rules and excellence (Keech, 1999). Sport also may reflect the dominant power structure, but it can also alter this through broader schemes that include active living and concern for the general health and well-being of citizens. Sport, however, may also reflect the dominant society in the creation of cultural policies of exclusion (Evans, 1999); however, policy may make provisions for general social welfare to mitigate exclusionary frameworks (Coulter, 1995).

Reflection on society

Wilcox (1994), in *Sport in the global village*, describes sport in the United States as the "nation's dominant system of cultural values" (p. 73). In revealing alarming trends as paramount to noting the issues, it is noted that sport holds control over most with the expectation placed on young people to participate, the issues experienced on college campuses where athletes play but may not succeed academically. The role of the media is also noted to overemphasize sport and influence many who are involved with sport delivery systems.

As such, sport is a reflection on society in the sense that it is one of the ways that a country portrays its ideology and goals. Because of the highly dynamic and visible aspect of sport, its media appeal and the sheer numbers of participants who engage in sport from the time they are in preschool through times when they are into their 80s, 90s and 100s, sport involvement depicts a culture that shows more dedication, commitment and perseverance than many other leisure pursuits. In the media coverage that follows, regardless of the level of the sport skill level, everyone becomes aware of detailed accounts of sport stories regarding coaches, referees, players and fans. More recently, within the last decade, more stories abound that cast a shadowy light on sport involvement: parents killing parents, fans looking ugly, undue pressure placed on kids, cheating, stalking, intimidation and many forms of reckless out of control episodes. Coverage of these events' results has been extensive, and the resultant impression is that a societal issue is present.

Of course, sports are also a positive reflection on society as well. Of particular note is the national policy on sport in Sweden which is fully based on volunteerism and the formation of clubs in which volunteer leaders engage in the development of many sports. According to the Swedish Sport federation, if you have two Swedish citizens in one room, they will form a club. Therefore, there are millions of volunteers who are supported through the national policy to lead and accomplish sport and social goals (Oloffson, 2008; Nathanson, 2007; Roddy 2004; Schwarz & Tait, 2006).

Coakley (2007) notes the value of sport participation for youth as being well documented, particularly if the participation occurs "with the explicit teaching of (1) a philosophy of nonviolence, (2) respect for self and others, (3), the importance of fitness and control over self, (4) confidence in physical skills, and (5) a sense of responsibility" (p. 149).

Sport also may be based on a country's political partisanship; for example in Israel, the society was formed by immigrants who had a particular religious ideology (Reshef & Paltiel, 1989). The institutionalization of sport also reflects that partisanship toward that ideology in the manner in which it is conducted, and in the power structure that supports and retains it. With sport clubs considered as a mechanism to spread Zionism, the evolution of sport in Israel is also a recounting of historical events that developed through increased metamorphosis of Israel's political intent. It is difficult to separate the ideology from the nature of participation in this country, and the utility of sport to demonstrate support for or disaffection with the power structure has been of paramount value to the social structure that has emerged through sport involvement (Sorek, 2005; Rainey & Hardy, 1999).

Sport and hubris

Much has been written about hubris, or the ego attached to sport accomplishment. Most athletes aspiring to succeed are conditioned to a sport ethic that deals with differentiating oneself from others in the pursuit of excellence. As athletes climb the success ladder, an egocentric personality develops that tends to make individuals feel separate from the rest of the population. This often leads to athletes feeling special, above the law, and able to get away with behaviors that would not be condoned in others (VonRoenn, Zhang, & Bennett, 2004).

Coakley (2007) refers to the development of this ethic as insulating the player from schoolmates, the public and other groups to the extents that they feel above the law. In these cases, deviant behavior can develop above and beyond what is normally accepted in the sport environment. Such behavior manifests itself in many ways – from pranks gone wrong, to a sense of entitlement that may result in rape or battery, to vandalism, intentional injury, substance abuse, bullying and other behaviors.

Societal problems

Sport violence is not an isolated incident but one that is influenced by societal norms. It is the contention within this text that different nationalities exhibit different forms of violent sport behaviors, and some are very subtle while others are very visible. Suffice it to note that there are examples of categories of sport violence in every developed country in the world as well as developing countries influenced by what is seen on the Internet and through media. Further, to the extent that sport participation represents a utilitarian purpose to promote and project a national image, political strength, or other issue, sport is seen as extremely powerful in conveying a variety of messages.

The extent to which the value of sport is seen as raising the level of a country's economical domain is well documented for those who study the Olympic movement and those who use sport to attract tourist number to their country. In addition, sport is used as an intervention to provide youth with positive alternatives in the way that time is used.

A BRIEF TOUR OF THE WORLD

Countries

Whether it is a highly developed country like the United States or a developing country such as Kyrgyzstan, sport violence or violence associated with sport is commonplace in many countries. While the reasons for it may depend on the differences defined by the ideology of the country, many of the outcomes are the time – fear, hurt, disappoint, cruelty, injury and other factors. Sport violence occurs because of a lack of regulation and also an encouragement that may spur the necessity due to attracting more viewers or improving the role of the country on the international sport scene. The following issues have been unearthed through a study of several countries and their violent sport involvement.

Australia	Development of strong ties with neighborhood clubs causes strong rivalries that can result in taunting, intimidation, fights and vandalism between rival team fans.
Israel	Close connection of sport to the ideology of Zionism creates stresses in soccer.
England	Hooligans en masse create problems for overcrowded facilities.
United States	Parent wars result in injury and death.
Thailand	Youth Thai-boxing results in exploitation and gambling.
Canada	Hockey violence occurs due to intentional injury.
South America	Rabid fans identify with players win–loss records to the extent that players have been killed after losing major contests.
South Africa	Apartheid caused this country to be banned from international activity until it ended.
China	Controversies regarding talent identification at an early age and regulatory issues involves close scrutiny from the international community.

These are but a few of ways that countries display themselves – ways that create controversy over the many positive accomplishments of the thousands of elite athletes, the millions of aspiring athletes and the untold number of those who wish to recreate by choosing a sport or a series of sport experiences.

Regardless of the country, the above issues have been researched and entered into the media as various incidents are cause for concern. More notably, many of these incidents do go unpunished depending on the type of law enforcement that may occur.

Other countries have sport policies that may be a hardship for families and athletes. These are supportive policies; however, criticisms of the process of disseminating the policies throughout all service delivery systems include the difficulties concerning access, varying needs and interests of prospective participants, affordability and potential exclusion of major groups.

Policy approaches

The study of policy development has occurred in Europe and the United States. Much of the study was initiated through Trim and Fitness International which contains all Olympic organizations who also participate in a "Sport for All" principle. Heralded by Pierre de Coubertin in the early 1900s, Sport for All did not develop fully until then 1984 Olympics in Los Angeles, California with the start of the Sport for All Symposium. This symposium featured reports from those who advocated for sport opportunities for all citizens. Funding mechanisms, stimulated initially by national and international competitions, were used to develop a better-rounded base of sport in each participating country. These participatory programs have been designed to reach them grass roots of society, to identify those excluded from sport participation, and to encourage increase in sport and fitness activity through various programs (U.S. Department of Health and Human Services, 1999). Referred as disported *Para tous, le sport pour tous*, Aussie sport and other names, these programs have grown in each nation due to the development and expansion of policy guided by research, strategic planning and campaigns. Throughout this text, there will be many references to these programs; however, a few examples are shared here to note scope and range of programs in each continent.

Australia	Active Australia features ways that governmental, educational and club sports thrive in each state and locale.
Scotland	Sport Councils effected through governmental funding; provide local programs for all ages.
Sweden	Sport Federations are assisted by governmental funds to fuel a giant volunteer network that provides leadership for sports and social exchange.
South Africa	A white paper in the mid-90s gave way to a trust to fund sport programs as a result of the ending of apartheid. Given five years to enact total integration of sport between blacks and whites, this policy helped to reintroduce South Africa to the international sport competition.
Singapore	Sport Councils provided through the government enact program for the public through a philosophy that if there is a solid base of activity, there will be eventual sport prowess on the international scene.
Canada	Active Canada, enabled through the government is delivered through each province to local organizations. This program features specific campaigns to help Canadians become more active and healthy.

TAFISA has over 150 countries involved in sport for all projects; however, this sampling shows the range and breadth of potential sport influence nationally and internationally.

Policy development

Government policies vary country to country; however, in several studies, one can see commonalities (Jamieson and Pan, 2000; Houlihan, 1997; DaCosta and Miragova, 2002). Through comparative analysis, it has been found that policy emphasizes traditional sport, excluded populations that (Theberge, 1989) need additional support, overall fitness measures of the population, cultural norms to be protected, venues through which sport and fitness efforts may be delivered, issues with training and funding, outcome assessment and concerns with deviance such as drugs use, violence, gambling and other mitigation. References to such policy will be made throughout the text to note the international efforts and specific problems in each country with respect to violence in sport.

Where organizations fit in

Each country has a network of organizations that provide for sport. While each country varies in its approach, the mention of typical organizations will be helpful as such are referred to throughout the text. These organizations may vary in type and the way they are configured in an organizational chart, but the process of what they do is very similar throughout the world.

NGOs National governing organizations exist in most countries to represent a particular sport or a combination of sport efforts. These organizations provide specific regulatory controls over a sport, contribute to the betterment of sport and also address concerns with respect to the development of programs and events for aspiring and accomplished sport participants. Developing countries have these organizations often aiming at introduction of general and specific sport experiences in a country; whereas, developed countries have sport-specific organizations that form a federation for general sport policy as well.

National Through ministries of sport, education, tourism, environment and other nomenclature, national policy is initiated to govern the country in a continuum that ranges from flexible to directed mechanisms. Depending upon how the country is ideologically organized, these ministries coordinate activities that lead to policy development and strategic direction for the country. Working through two to three levels of government, policy is influenced through top down or bottom up or both.

Provincial/State A second level of government exists as a state or province or district. This level contributes to the development of more regional policy, influences national policy and has more specific direction for local policy.

Local Leisure Service Delivery At the local level, sport and leisure service delivery occurs. Through this mechanism, often consisting of a network of public, private and commercial operations that provide a framework of educational, governmental and club activities, national and regional policies are reflected in part depending upon the comprehensiveness of the organization.

There is a solution

Before embarking on the process for solving a pernicious problem, we can draw on the following anonymous aphorisms provided in the *Speaker's Lifetime Library*:

Violence is self-destructive.

Violence is as American as apple pie.

Don't start a fight if you're not prepared to finish it.

Violence on behalf of the right side can make it the wrong side.

People who live in glass houses shouldn't throw stones.

When there is an epidemic of violence, nobody can consider him/her immune. (Spinrad, 1987, p. 239)

With this in mind, we will address not only the process and root causes of sport violence, but, more importantly, there are solutions that must be explored and if so, the problem of sport violence is correctable. Focus in this text will be on three major areas, or those that can be taught in a – classroom – management, training and the role of sport. It is a mission of the authors to not only correct the problem through improved curriculum and educational processes, but also to raise the awareness of participants, viewers and related groups as to their responsibility in mitigating violent episodes that they witness during the course of fulfilling their roles as players, officials, administrators, spectators, role models, coaches, volunteers, media personnel and many other groups.

Management of the sport environment

The dynamics of sport are such that specific managerial roles must be present. It is the contention of the authors that most issues of sport violence may be contained through proper management of the sport environment.

Whether it is facility security, parent education, referee orientation, rule development, selection of staffing, sport development or program organization, legal issues can point to lack of appropriate supervision, facility hazards, inadequate control and other factors that cause a situation to erupt.

Training

In all cases regarding violent episodes, lack of training has been a key to the escalation of sport violence. It can start with parental influences that are based on ignorance to adult role models who are not aware of the intricacies of sport development. It can also be gaps in administrative development dealing with volunteers and pressure groups, and it can be political lack of awareness of the issues at hand. Regardless of the levels of training needed, a more enlightened process is indicated.

The theme throughout this text includes the need for specific training that starts with community education and ends with professional development of all those associated with a sport environment.

Rethinking role of sport

Starting with the contention that no sport experience is worthwhile if it contains the elements of sport violence that are in existence today, it is time to rethink the role of sport in society. Regardless of nation, sport is a dominant feature within society – it reflects the nature of a populace, and it defeats efforts to improve national image when it exists.

TOWARD POLICY – AN INTEGRATED APPROACH

A policy is enacted by a government to respond to issues that need control or direction. It may occur at any level or jurisdiction; however, every country has established national policy on many matters. In the sport world, over 100 countries have some national policy on sport, leisure, tourism, health and environment. Those that do not are often the result of being a developing country without the need to direct intervention for this portion of citizens' activities. One of the most highly developed countries, the United States, does not have a central policy on sport; however, it has a loosely coupled system that includes Olympic Development, regulatory bodies for colleges and universities, secondary schools and individual sport regulatory bodies that affect the offering of sport on the community level. All of these groups interact in some way in a fragmented system that often results in violent acts.

As noted, government policies develop as a result of the ideology of a particular. Many sport policies have been influenced by the Olympic ideological domain and not the needs of a particular populace. In some countries this ideological domain represents control and direction, while in others, a looser framework is provided to encourage and support those concepts without dictate. Regardless of how a country rules, a sport and leisure policy that encompasses national well-being, traditions and excellence is important. A policy that integrates all sport efforts will be more effective than one that is a series of fragmented organizations looking out for special interest. This text stresses ways that those who read it may change their way of thinking and become involved in an important movement for change. Policy development is important to recognize socialized culture and the way that it plays out in the social constructions of sport, leisure lifestyle, work, education and many other parts of daily living. By tracking how people interact, one is able to discern how the culture may benefit from a structure to facilitate and enable maximum enjoyment and aspirations. The impact of a change in social policy, ergo, the end of apartheid in South Africa, opened many doors for both blacks and whites who were restricted under the old system. These changes manifested themselves most visibly in sport participation and the opening of new doors to excellence and accomplishment, as well as health.

In order to affect policy a country must study the issues of concern such as needs of the citizens, goals of the government with regard to national pride, sport infrastructure that exists and is further needed. Major studies, organizational coordination and local service review must take place in order to deliver coordinated sport services. Often policy development of this kind takes years to effect; however, in some countries it has been accomplished in less than five years as in the country of South Africa. This country ended apartheid and set on a five-year course to completely restructure sport and sport education delivery to be inclusive of all parts of the newly merged power structure. They succeeded in developing an impressive system between 1995 and 2000.

Toward change in family dynamics

It would be irresponsible to omit a key causal concern that affects the sport violence continuum, and that is the way in which children are brought up in this world (Hartley, 1990). The role of the parent, regardless of country, is a child's more singular influence. Enlightened parents who can effect a positive environment and be a positive role model with sport involvement are keys to changing the unfortunate sport situation in which we find ourselves. No amount of exploitation of the child will be effective if parents have a good grasp on what is important to their children. They are the key to the future of a safer environment. This social issue will change if parent and adult role models want change; furthermore, change will be effected with improved adult education that starts with parenting skills, volunteerism, professional development and policy support.

SUMMARY

In introducing us to the world of sport violence the key factors in this chapter are to define our terms and identify the ways in which sport violence manifests itself as a social problem in contemporary society. Although it has existed in most nation's early history, the visibility of sport violence and those who perpetrate it are different today. We see much of this through parents and adult role models who cause a mimicry of actions. In addition, we see extreme pressure placed on youth to perform well for an athletic scholarship that will never arrive. Indeed, the overemphasis on sport, started at an earlier and earlier age is a tragedy that results all too often in broken hearts, broken dreams and broken families.

REFERENCES

Calhoun, R., 2007. Interview with R354 Sport and Violence class students, Indiana University.

Coakley, J., Dunning, E., 2000. Handbook of Sports Studies. Sage, London, p. 570.

Coakley, J.J., 2001. Sports in Society: Issues and Controversies, 9th edn. McGraw Hill Higher Education, Hightstown, NJ.

Coakley, J.J., 2007. Sports in Society: Issues and Controversies, 9th edn. McGraw Hill Higher Education, Hightstown, NJ, p. 676.

Coalter, F., 1995. Compulsory competitive tendering for sport and leisure management: A lost opportunity? Managing Leisure 1, 3–15.

DaCosta, L., Miragova, A. (Eds.), 2002. Worldwide Experiences and Trends in Sport for All. Meyer & Meyer Sport Ltd, UK, p. 792.

Davidson, P., 2007. Research review: research into sport events. Australasian Parks and Leisure, 10–11.

Evans, T., Thamel, P., 2009. Barely teenagers, already groomed for stardom. *The New York Times*, Sunday, January 4, 2009, Sport Sunday, p. 1.

Flexner, S.B., (Ed.), 1987. The Random House Dictionary of the English Language, Second ed. Random House, New York, NY.

Hardcastle, J., 2008. *Sports Violence*. Ezine articles. http://ezinearticles.com/?Sports-Violence&id=290850&opt=print. Retrieved 8/26/08.

Hartley, G., 1990. Athletic Footwear Association. American Youth and Sports Participation. Athletic Footwear Association, North Palm Beach, FL.

Hirschhorn, L., 1994. Leading and Planning in Loosely Coupled Systems. CFAR, Philadelphia, PA.

Houlihan, B., 1997. *Sport, Policy, and Politics*. London Routledge, p. 313.

Hughes, R., Coakley, J., 1991. Positive deviance among athletes: the implications of overconformity to the sport ethic. Sociology of Sport Journal 8, 307–325.

Jamieson, L.M., Pan, Z., 2000. Government policy on Sport for all: developed and developing countries. Journal of the International Council for Physical Education, Recreation, Sport and Dance XXXVI (4), 16–20.

Kay, T., 2000. Leisure, gender, and family: The influence of Social policy. Leisure Studies 19, 247–265.

Keech, M., Houlihan, B., 1999. Sport and the end of apartheid. The Round Table 349, 109–12.

Luhmann, N., 1995. Social Systems. Stanford University Press, Stanford, California.

Maraniss, D., 2008. When worlds collided. *Sports Illustrated*, 108(22), 53–60.

McCarthy, M., 2008. Sports also paying a price amid struggling economy. USA Today, 1–2B.

McCarthy, T., 2001. Warning: the legacy of Columbine. Time, 23–25.

Mull, R.F., Bayless, K.G., Jamieson, L.M., 2005. Recreational sport management, 4th edn. Human Kinetics, Champaign, IL, p. 354.

Mull, R.F., Bayless, K.G., Ross, C.R., Jamieson, L.M., 1997. Recreational Sport Management, 3rd edn. Human Kinetics, Champaign, IL, p. 334.

Nathanson, K., 2007. Turn it around, team. Indiana Daily Student 140 (70), 5.

Oloffson, K., 2008. Long live the swimmer. Inside 3 (2), 12–14, 20–21.

Rainey, D.W., Hardy, L., 1999. Assaults on Rugby Union referees: a three union survey. Journal of Sport Behavior 22 (1), 105–1132.

Reshef, N., Paltiel, J., 1989. Partisanship and sport: the unique case of politics and sport in Israel. Sociology of Sport Journal 6, 305–318.

Roddy, D., 2004. *This Sporting Life*. Pittsburgh Post-Gazette. http://pittsburgh post-gazette.com/pg/04340/421600.stm.

Schwarz, E., Tait, 2006. All together now. Australasian Leisure Management 48–50, 51.

Sen, A., 2006. Identity and Violence: The Illusion of Destiny. W.W. Norton and Company, New York, p. 215.

Shillito, P., 2004. Violence: a rising sports trend. The Orion Online. California State University, Chico.

Sorek, T., 2005. Between football and martyrdom: the bi-focal localism of an Arab–Palestinian town in Israel. The British Journal of Sociology 56 (4), 635–661.

Spinrad, L., Spinrad, T. (Eds.), 1979. Speakers Lifetime Library. Vol. 1. Parker, West Nyack, NY, p. 256.

Theberge, N., 1989. A feminist analysis of responses to sports violence: Media coverage of the 1987 World Junior Hockey Championship. Sociology of Sport Journal 6, 247–256.

Tomlinson, A., 2007. The Sport Studies Reader. Routledge, London, p. 470.

U.S. Department of Health and Human Services, 1999. Promoting physical activity: A guide for community action. Human Kinetics, Champaign, IL, p. 386.

VonRoenn, S., Zhang, J., Bennett, G., 2004. dimensions of ethical misconduct in contemporary sports and their association with the backgrounds of stakeholders. International Sport Journal 3, 37–54.

Wilcox, R., 1994. In: Ralph, C., Wilcox (Eds.), Of fungos and fumbles: explaining the cultural uniqueness of American sport, or a paradoxical peek at sport: American style. In Sport in the Global Village. Fitness Information Technology, Inc., Morgantown, WVA, p. 521.

Wilsey, S., 2006. The beautiful game: why soccer rules the world. National Geographic 209 (6), 42–69.

Yule, J., 1997. Engendered ideologies and leisure policy in the UK: Part 2: Professional ideologies. Leisure Studies 16, 139–154.

Case Study 1.1

A coach of a prominent girls' gymnastics team has been preparing the competitors for their national competition. In the process of doing so, practices have extended to three hours per day, on a daily basis with no days off. The national event is now one week away, and one of the gymnasts sustains a hairline fracture of the tibia bone. Doctors recommend she rest and place her in a portable cast for one week with the cast due to be taken off one day before the national competition. The coach knows that a decision needs to be made as to whether or not the gymnast will compete. If she does not compete, an alternate will be able to replace her; however, this alternate has had severe emotional problems stemming from bulimia, and the coach is concerned about her stability if she competes on such short notice. If the coach selects the second alternate, it is probable that the team will lose due to consistently lower scores performed by this alternate, enough to reduce the team to second place.

If the coach has the injured gymnast compete, the team is relatively assured of a first place win. The coach knows that the competitor will be able to withstand the stress for the competition but is aware that the competition may cause greater injury, thus preventing any further competition.

What would you do if you were the coach? Would you forego an almost assured first place in the upcoming competition or would you play the gymnast knowing that would assure first place but end the career of the gymnast?

SPORT STORIES 1.1

I grew up in an all black neighborhood where everyone knew everyone. We all attended the same schools and we all played on the same sports teams. Our coach would be someone we knew from our community or it would be someone from another neighborhood who probably knew someone from our community. I had been playing sports for the recreation centre since I was seven years old and had the same coach all the way until I was twelve. One day my coach has gotten arrested, and the manager of the recreation centre brought in two Caucasian males to be our coaches. One day at practice, one of my friends and one of the coaches got into an argument because of some name calling. The coach told my friend to leave, however, he didn't want to so he decided to take matters into his own hand. He took off his helmet and hit the coach in his knee. At this time the coaches called off practice and went to file a report to the recreation centre. After that day we never saw the coaches again and we couldn't finish the season.

Calhoun, R. (2007).

CHAPTER 2

A History of Leisure, a History of Violence: Our Violent Society, a National and Global Historical Perspective

"That [people] have an enormous need to debase other [people] – and only because they are [people] – is a truth which history forbids us to labor."
(Baldwin, 1972, p. 392)

"History, despite its wrenching pain, cannot be unlived, but if faced with courage, need not be lived again."
(Angelou, 1993, p. C5)

History leaves footprints that can be backtracked as evidence of its pathway. In history ("effective history"), according to Foucault (1977b), the decent of "man" is documented. During this decent, certain points emerge not as a matter of the marking of triumph, but as notations of what progression in the descent of a society is being viewed. Through vestiges of older texts, artifacts, and even photography and other imagery, we are able to discern a sense of how people lived in the past. Peoples' leisure and ways of recreating are some of the aspects of life that can be gleaned from looking onto pottery, or photography, or a passage in a diary. This chapter serves as a discussion of the manner that history could inform us as leisure researchers, professionals, students, and enthusiast about the elements and evidence of violence in societies, both past and present in Western Civilization.

As Jantzen (2004) noted, "as the twenty-first century proceeds, the pace of violence increases," how would looking in to history assist leisure researchers today (p. 4)? Imbedded in the Western psyche is this penchant for

CONTENTS

violence and within this psyche more than others is the need to venture down a "path of healing… [and away from] its death dealing structures" (p. 4). Allison (2000) stated that, "issues of justice and injustice have only been tangentially addressed in the leisure literature," thus implying that adopting a social justice paradigm in research ought to be our position (p. 2). A social justice paradigm focus is on how a promotion is sought for the "fairness in the distribution of goods…and expressing our experience, feelings, and perspective on social life in contexts where others can listen" (Young, 1990, p. 37). A social justice paradigm recognizes the differences in "the social, cultural, historical and political histories of oppressed groups," while identifying "five conditions that [are shared]: exploitation, marginalization, powerlessness, cultural imperialism, and violence" (Allison, 2000, p. 3). While four of the conditions have been explored to varying levels in the leisure literature, it has been recognized that "the role of violence in constricting leisure choices has yet to be thoroughly explored" (Allison, 2000, p. 4). Through social justice paradigm there is much we could learn from the critique that researching violence in history could uncover.

The historical past is a difficult realm to venture in, especially for leisure researchers who concentrate on demonstrated human behavior. The subject matter has occurred in the distant past and is more than likely unattainable for confirmation and or follow-up. In particular, violent behavior of the past is even more problematic due to the inherent bias that one automatically registers the subject matter. Denied the ability to interview the actors of a scene due to the sheer issue of time, analyzing leisure related violence in history is an undertaking that places the researcher in a position of critique. The content remains frozen in the state and perspective that it has been unearthed in. However, once unearthed, "history becomes 'effective' to the degree that it introduces discontinuity into our very being…this is because knowledge is not made for understanding; it is made for cutting" (Foucault, 1977b, p. 154).

HISTORICAL INTERPRETATION

Violence typically involves social interaction, what is committed by one person on to another. As a result, control and power are brought into a discussion of violence. If this degree of control and display of power becomes systematic, then it becomes a fabric of a culture and society. This relationship between people and between people and the state/society, based on violence, can also "disrupt the ability to find continuity and meaning" due to its impact on memory (Pohlandt-McCormick, 2000, p. 24). In researching the historical past, commentary on the present can be useful and determining the possible course of the future. The historical past is thus an area of study that leaves much of its inquiry to interpretation.

Schwandt (2000) structures the basic ways of interpretivism as having the following features, "…view human action as meaningful…[make] an ethical commitment in the form of respect for and fidelity to the life world…" and the emphasis on the "human subjectivity to knowledge without sacrificing the objectivity of knowledge" (Schwandt in Denzin and Lincoln, 2000, p. 193). According to Schwandt (2000), qualitative/interpretive inquiry is a place "where issues of what it means to know the world are explored" (Schwandt in Denzin and Lincoln, 2000, p. 190). All things in the world are laden with meanings from the originators, the creators, the appropriators and eventually the researchers who come in contact with that which makes up the world. The aim in interpretive research is a sort of divining of those meanings in the hopes of making some sort of newfound pool of information that future researchers could draw upon.

Leisure is interwoven to a great extent into Western society. As a strong component of the popular culture of most Western countries, leisure is often expressed through various examples of activity. Due to this ambiguous expression, leisure has been and can be expressed as an activity that is not solely on some grassy field as some competitive game or sport. Within the expression of leisure as an activity, "the story of one's life is always the story of one's life in relation to others and in relation to meaningful places created and contained in one's surroundings" (Stokowski, 2002, p. 373). I envision leisure as a tool that can be shaped by the whim of a society. In my estimation the people of a society determine what activities are to be chosen, constructed, performed, and valued. However, leisure is a concept in the literature whose meaning has been challenged and altered; yet certain understandings of this concept have endured throughout time. Leisure conceptually has come to be linked to specific allocations of time, an activity in operation, and a state of mind (Jackson and Burton, 1999; Russell, 2002). Further, many discussions have been centered on leisure being of benefit to an individual, society, and as being "good" in nature (Driver, 1992).

SUBJECTIVITY, AGENCY AND MEANING OF VIOLENCE

Theories are developed to reveal and determine the nature of a thing (or things) and its relationship with other things. However, in interpretation the reason why is explored and discussed. In historical interpretation, the aim is

"to reveal subjectivity, agency, and meaning" (Martin, 1997, p. 2). Subjectivity seeks to provide the "ability to know and understand what it is like to be another" (Hexter, 1971, p. 207). As leisure researchers we investigate, analyze, and discuss human lived behavior. The experiences of others provide information as to the nature of leisure. Subjectivity is the examination of past-lived experience.

Agency provides a snap shot on the intent of behavior, how and possibly why did a person go about their perceived set of actions to achieve an end? In addition, in examining agency the resources pulled together to achieve that end are of importance. In the act of mustering a certain level of resources to enact a behavior and achieve an end also, demonstrates the amount of value the behavior and end is worth to the individual or group.

In regards to meaning, ambiguity resides the most in the act of interpretation. Meaning is the value that agency reveals. How did people interpret their own actions? What were the ways that they expressed their involvement in an act? How do they articulate themselves and their relationship with an activity? Meaning is also the ways that we facilitate our interpretations in the course of subjectivity. According to Schwandt (2000) "sociohistorically inherited bias or prejudice is not regarded as a characteristic or attribute that an interpreter must strive to get rid of or manage in order to come to a 'clear' understanding" (Schwandt in Denzin and Linclon, 2000, p. 194). In order for us to understand the lived experiences of those in the past we must mentally link our own lived experiences to the ones we are examining in the past in order to grasp, as best as we can, meaning.

Historical interpretation is the peering into moments of the past to make sense of their existence and impact on today. In the course of this chapter the discussion on the relationship between leisure and violence in history will be in four main sections utilizing only a few examples from history to provide a frame for this discussion. In **Feasts, Festivals, and Rage**, the aim is to briefly examine societies of antiquity to gauge the nature of those feasts and festivals for their possible role in shaping foundations for violence. The section on the **Role of Sport in Culture** will extend the previous section's discussion on feasts and festivals into the more specific area of sport and the ways that sport more articulately highlighted the presence and preference for violence. **Violence in Contemporary Society** seeks to broaden our perception of leisure as well as violence to question the impact of violence on today's society. Lastly, this chapter will conclude with an exploration of **Theories/Approaches on the Growth of Violence in Cultures** and what this could mean for future research endeavors as well as the future of societies.

FEASTS, FESTIVALS, AND RAGE

An "effective history" centers itself on "events in terms of their most unique characteristics and their most acute manifestations," for embedded in events are intricate details of human thought and action that could be overlooked by general chronological and situational analysis of history (Rainbow, 1984, p. 88).

Festivals or feasts are the oldest forms of events in human history. They are highly community driven. Both the word feasts and festivals are interchangeable in origin. Traditions are reinforced and passed down from one generation to another through these celebrations. Many festivals or feasts are religious, social or cultural identifying in origin and practice.

GREEK FESTIVALS OF VIOLENCE AND COMING OF AGE

According to Goff (1999) in Ancient Greece, a "healthy community is preserved and reproduced by representations of violence, particularly of violence with a sacrificial profile" as depicted in the play, *Iphigeneia in Tauris* (p. 109). Goff (1999) further noted that Greek tragedy typically takes festivals of ritual to cover for their true form; sacrifice is none other than a "glorified murder" (p. 109). Highlighting the ritual creates a healing attempt for a particular community and society on deeds that have been committed. Violence and community are intertwined consistently both in the plays as well as in the practices in Ancient Greece. The violence is never self-inflicted or – directed by a community but is typically towards another community. The *Iphigeneia in Tauris* concerns the Taureans outlook on to the Athenians.

Leitao (1999) noted that in some narratives it was another option to abandon violence outside a city limits for "the safer pattern of allowing…[the] eruption of youthful violence within the city…in which outsiders or tyrants are slain" during coming of age festivals (p. 268). Festivals eased no only intragroup and community tensions but also served a given community "like "smart bombs," designated at extracommunity targets…[and] affirmatively appropriate [violent ritual festivals] with a view to socially beneficial results" (p. 269).

Leitao further suggested, "that one of the functions which Greek festivals and feasts generally were designed to perform is indeed a deflection of violent instincts (perceived or real)" (p. 269). The "other" was the constant "victim" of violent acts of ritual for a community. Youth in these rites of passage learned "to make the right distinction between insider and outsider" (p. 269). Greek tragedies not only expose the existence of cultural practice but the value the actual practice had upon its population. Festivals reinforced community identity and traditions but also exposed their view on outside communities both beyond their borders of governance or outside their cultural identity characteristics, customs, and beliefs. It should also be noted that women were often found to be placed in the "other" category, less as murder victims but more so as sexual targets if they fell within another "kinship group" during many of these rites of passage festival "raids."

ROLE OF SPORT IN AN ARENA OF VIOLENCE

The ancient Panhellenic festivals of sport of the Greeks "paid homage to the gods but also pursued sports for more worldly ends [i.e.] physical excellence, entertainment and financial remuneration" (Rader, 1979, p. 314). According to Birrell's (1981) analysis "some historians feel the roots of many modern sports can be found in the ritualistic practices associated with fertility festivals and other religious ceremonies" (p. 354). Sport is specifically a tradition of ritual (Henderson, 1947). Although many of the overt religious connotations in sport are non-existent or apparent today there is still what some refer to as the "the ritual power of sport," as is suggested in Huizinga's (1955) *Homo Ludens*.

For Huizinga in sport and play the "feeling of being apart...of sharing something important, of mutually withdrawing from the rest of the world...retains its magic beyond the duration of the individual game" (p. 12). Sport strengthens a sense of community as much as it creates one. This continued connection of leisure related activities to nurture and maintain cultural identity makes the case of violence highly relevant.

ROME: THE SPECTACLE OF VIOLENCE

Kyle (1998) suggested that, "to reinforce the social order violence must be performed or proclaimed in public, and public violence tends to become ritualized into games, sports, and even spectacles of death" (p. 7). As the Roman Republic and later Empire expanded so did the level of the spectacle of violence. Although there was no separation between the secular and the state, festivals began to take military connotations denoting triumphs over foreign entities. Rome was extraordinary in the sheer scale of the spectacle of violent sports and the multitude of method and manner the sports were displayed. Whether it was the arenas, amphitheaters, open fields, and circuses the Romans engaged their gladiator games, hunts, public executions, and shows with vigor, ingenuity, and enthusiasm. As Kyle indicated, "there was simply no widespread opposition to the inhumanity of the games" (p. 4).

According to Kyle's research in AD 107 the emperor Trajan "held 23 days of games in which 11,000 animals were killed and 10,000 gladiators fought"

(p. 35). Before Trajan, the emperor Titus in AD 80, over one hundred days, held games some of which consisted of a naval battle with three thousand men. The games were gifts of appreciation to their community from their leaders. Tiered rows of thousands of Romans from all classes cheered as people were mangled to death by a wild beast or some weak inferior was fatally dominated by the skill and power of a trained combatant. Foucault (1977a) clearly indicated that punishment (often times public) is directly intended for improved social order. Interestingly as Kyle pointed out, "the decline of the Roman Empire brought the decline of the Roman spectacles, not vice versa" (p. 6).

Throughout the Roman eras of these sports spectacles it is with the utmost importance to note the enjoyment of the crowd rather than the enjoyment of the athlete, fighter, or gladiator. Crowds cheered for violence and had a partial control over the degree of violence that would occur. The crowds were socialized to look forward to these displays of violence and through them the lesson of citizenship was taught. What it meant to be Roman was clear and the proper behaviors that went along with that identity, for to not be Roman would mean running for your life on the floor of the arena from some wild animal or shimmering axe. As long as it was not their life, all Romans were relieved and reveled in the gore for as Kyle stated that, "Romans saw the turning of a man into a corpse as a satisfying spectacle" (p. 2).

VIOLENCE IN CONTEMPORARY SOCIETY

The spectacle of the Roman sporting event has strengthened the notions of community and the value of the "other" from Grecian festivals as leisure has evolved throughout the eons up to more contemporary times. The issue of violence stretches beyond the actual "combatants" engaged in competition. The crowds attend the game, the audiences that watch from the comfort of home, and the institutions (ownership, sports authority, and media) that endorse and sponsor the exhibition are 'players' in the bloodletting. Even the violence that happened around an event, and not just during, is just as much apart of the heightened presence of violence in leisure.

THE OLYMPICS: AN ARENA FOR THE THREAT OF VIOLENCE

From the onset of the revival of the Olympics in 1896 by Pierre de Coubertin, the larger community, the national, was the basis of pride and extreme prejudice (Lapchick, 1978). Although Coubertin's personal agenda was more for national unity in the Franco-Prussian War, this is a stark contrast from the statement that Coubertin made in 1894:

> *"The games of the Olympic Movement are to promote the development of those fine physical and moral qualities which are the basis of amateur sport and to bring together the athletes of the world in a great quadrennial festival of sports thereby creating international respect and goodwill and thus helping to construct a better and more peaceful world." (Berlioux, 1972, p. 1)*

On a global scale, the Olympics are a prime example of the presence of violence off the field but still associated with the games that are taking place on the field. At the expense of the "other," one nation will attempt to accumulate medals of athletic achievement while also leveraging attention to their causes and issues for "the development of national pride and chauvinism is one of the primary political returns that countries, powerful or chauvinism is one of the primary political returns that countries powerful or underdeveloped, expect from their Olympic investments" (Czula, 1978, p. 19). To gain attention for the suffering of thousands to build an Olympic setting and the funds expended by the government, "thousands of Mexican students marched..." only for "over 300 students" to eventually be shot and bayoneted to death for the 1968 Olympic games (p. 21). While the 1996 Atlanta Olympic games are momentary alarmed by a possible bomb threat.

Nothing compares tragically to the 1972 Munich Olympic games where armed Palestinians kidnapped and killed 11 Israeli athletes in protest to longstanding territorial disputes. As Czula (1978) noted, the Palestinians "seized the Olympic microphone by force" (p. 23). Unfortunately, as Czula also stated, "today, however, many competing Olympic countries may be killing, over a period of years, countless innocent victims to make their political statements," all in relationship to this major sporting event (p. 23).

THE HOOLIGAN

The spectators even take a new role as the hooligan when they act above and beyond simple cheer and support a team or player. Williams noted the "the football hooligan phenomenon embraces both ritual and violent forms" (p. 111). Although "hooliganism is very rarely characterized by the resort to physical violence," when it occurs it is profound (p. 106). According to Dunning (2000), the hooligan, a disorderly fan or crowd, "have historically

been a near universal addendum to…[the] global idiom of football" (p. 142).
Hand to hand fights between them are common but "confrontations can also
take the form of aerial bombardments using as ammunition missiles that
range from innocuous items such as peanuts, bits of orange peel [to] even
potentially lethal ones, such as darts, metals discs…broken seats, bricks,
slabs of concrete, ball bearings…[or] crude petrol bombs" such as the case
with Doc's Red Army, fans of Manchester United Fans in the 1970s
(Dunning et al., 1986, p. 223). However, whereas hooliganism is rooted
solidly in a lack of social order and control (Dunning, 1999), lynchings are
firmly grounded in social order and control.

LYNCHING VIOLENCE AS LEISURE

The history of lynching is an area of American history that resides outside
the experiences of many who live within the borders of the United States and
outside the knowledge of many who live beyond those borders, today. Based
strongly on the existence of newspaper clippings and picture postcards,
lynchings are far from a brief and isolated chapter of history.

Photographs are rich vestiges of history due to their capturing of human
behavior in the image, and with the photographer's choice of what to
photograph. As a result meanings are simultaneously displayed in the image
and their selection. According to Susan Sontag (1977), "a photograph is not
only an image… an interpretation of the real; it is also a trace, something
directly stenciled off the real, like a footprint or a death mask" (in Evans and
Hall, 2004, p. 80, 81). Through the medium of photography and the use of
visual methodologies this discussion is made possible.

Yet lynchings have a strange familiarity regardless of being outside many
experiences of the contemporary Black and White community. In looking at
the images many White and Black Americans feel a distant closeness to the
lynchings, primarily due to their racial representation in the images as the
audience of supporters and as the lynched, respectively. For other racial and
cultural groups, the discussion provides a violent backdrop to American
history. Positive and negative expressions of race are another ember that
flames the fires of racial tensions and continue the line of the "other" that
violence is often directed, at least between White and Black Americans.

Lynchings have occurred in a wide array of settings and times. Based on
the accumulation of newspaper clippings it has been estimated that from
1882 to 1927 close to 4000 lynchings of Black men and women occurred
(White, 1992). This number fails to encompass lynchings that occurred prior
to 1882 and during the time of enslavement in the United States

(White, 1992). For example, in the new 1992 introduction of White's 1929 book, *Rope and Faggot: A Biography of Judge Lynch*, Kenneth Robert Janken, associate professor of Afro-American studies at North Carolina University at Chapel Hill, wrote that a "1872 Congressional investigation found that during a span of a few weeks in 1868 more than 2,000 African Americans were murdered by mobs in Louisiana; an incomplete count in Texas revealed that 1,035 were lynched between the end of the Civil War and 1862" (White, 1992, p. xii).

Further, this estimate does not include the number of Black victims during any period of time that failed to make headlines. White (1992) cited the 1919 National Association for the Advancement of Colored People (NAACP) publication *Thirty Years of Lynching in the United States, 1889–1919*: "It is believed that more persons have been lynched than those whose names are given...only such cases have been included as were authenticated by such evidence as was given credence by a recognized newspaper or confirmed by a responsible investigator" (White, 1992, p. 229). The total number of lynching victims does not include the number of lynchings that still happen, case in point, the racially motivated murder/lynching of James Byrd, a black man who was chained to the back of a pick-up truck and dragged to death in Jasper, Texas in 1998 (King, 2002).

White's (1992) work serves as an example of a similar accounting of lynching that was documented by Ginzburg (1988) in *100 Hundred Years of Lynching*, that ties the statistics of lynching numbers to their actual newspaper reports and promotion. Cutler (1905) in *Lynch Law* provided an account of lynching numbers prior to other researchers and investigators. He also catalogs the recording of lynching numbers prior to 1889. The work of Ida Wells-Barnett will be detailed in the next section. Ida Wells-Barnett, famed journalist and founding member of both the Niagara Movement and the NAACP, researched, exposed, and campaigned staunchly against lynching activity. Besides the numbers of lynchings that she cataloged, her work took a different dimension raising political discussions intent on creating an anti-lynching legislation (Royster, 1997).

The body of the lynched reflects history. In regards to the characteristics of a lynching, what was unique about them? How did the lynchings racially differ in regards to the victim? What lays in the "spectacular" and spectacle-like nature of lynchings that calls into question this critique on society? The manifestations showcase the abusive expressions of power as well as expose the reversals of power that are an integral part of current discourses on lynching phenomenon and photography. According to Foucault (1977b), the "effective history" of lynching history and the lynched, that this history is engraved on, stands as a "...differential knowledge of...failings, heights and degenerations, poisons and antidotes. [For its] task is to become a curative science," for contemporary society and the present bodies of America (p. 156).

These rich, yet brutal images of lynching photography give way to an analysis of social behavior. The images document more than the remains of the victims, but also the manner in which those remains became a part of the ritual of victory over one race. In some cases photographs were taken as the progression of the event took place. In other cases the lens focused on the crowd and their participation and emotional involvement in the event. In other cases, the pictures served as a pictorial display that was accompanied with souvenirs from the event that were, at times, body parts of the victims.

White (1992) wrote,

"One morning shortly afterwards I walked along the road which led from the beautiful little town to the spot where five Negroes had been burned. Three shining-eyed, healthy, clearly children, headed for school, approached me…the eldest…asked if I was going to the place where 'the niggers' had been killed…Animatedly…she told me…of 'the fun we had burning the niggers.'" (p. 3)

The response of the child speaks to the normalcy of the lynching of the Black individual in American society, primarily in the Southern States. This effect on the social environment was widespread. White (1992) stated:

"Nearly a century of lynching and nearly five thousand mob murders within less than half a century have done an incalculable harm to American minds…Some of the effect can be seen in the frequency with which the phrase is heard often from the lips of normal law-abiding people even in the North and West – 'he ought to be strung up to a tree'" (p. 5).

Lynchings were of the culture. Not a separate world, but very grounded in the society at-large. Lynchings expanded in structure as society likewise expanded due to technology, the growth in economy and the sheer expansion in space. As rail systems were developed, they were then used to transport people to the sites. As the radio was introduced, they were brought in to the site in order to give others from far way an update on the progression of the torture and murder. But more importantly, the single technology of culture that played the most part in lynchings was that of the camera. With the camera, the creation of the ability to communicate across distance and time was equally established. Also, the camera made it possible for lynching "paraphernalia" to become a commodity. The camera captured the event and assisted the forging and strengthening of a White racial identity.

Kirk Fouss (1999) took this further and developed the notion of lynching performances. He noted that, "the New York Tribune published a cartoon entitled "The Theatrical Business is Looking Up In Kentucky" in reference to a lynching held in an "Open House" (Fouss, 1999, p. 2). Even a Paris newspaper published an artist's rendering of the event, giving suggestions of a sense of the scope and expanse of the communication and value of this theater of violence (Fouss, 1999, p. 2). Fouss (1999) posed that lynching should be viewed as "performance phenomenon." There were advertisements on flyers, posters and in newspapers to inform people to "be on hand" (Fouss, 1999, p. 6).

Other daily routines were suspended and "special round trip tickets" were offered to ensure a large audience. Although there were cases of lynchings happening indoors, most occurred outdoors to ensure that the greatest number of people could view the spectacle. The site of one lynching, for example, was described as, "a natural amphitheater...and about another lynching site...A better place could not have been selected for the convenience of the crowd..." (Fouss, 1999, p. 6).

Besides advertisements and the creation of a "stadium," the lynchings "followed a more or less structured order of activities," sometimes having a program on hand (Fouss, 1999, p. 9). Fouss (1999) went in-depth with theatrical concepts of performances discussing the artificial drama the crime hyped up, the seizure of the victim and the parade, and the procession to the lynching site through significant areas of a given locale. At the event, he raised the point that as technology advanced, on-site narrating or "play-by-play" was delivered to the crowd or listeners tuned into the radio.

As viewed through a perspective influenced by Foucault, this "[Black] body is the inscribed surface of events...imprinted by history" and as a result reflects back America, its history, traditions, and most importantly, its values (Rainbow, 1984, p. 83). Upon this Black body, one such form of historical "text" is encoded. To Foucault, history hosted an "endlessly repeated play of dominations..." and as result leads to the understanding that "...the domination of certain men over others leads to the differentiation of values" (Rainbow, 1984, p. 85). If in Foucault's discussion, class domination led to the idea of liberty, as in the case of the French Revolution, then the racial domination, expressed through lynchings could lead to the ideas of humanity, of raising the issue of being human. The degradation that was the French way of life outside of the monarchy nurtured the idea of analysis and change, to liberate, one's existence. Is it possible that the degradation that is in the racialized American way of life could lead to another type of analysis and change?

THEORIES/APPROACHES ON THE GROWTH OF VIOLENCE IN CULTURES

Although leisure research has embarked on discussions that further expand the scope of what leisure encompasses, as a field, leisure studies is still relatively insulated, rarely entering new areas in terms of topics and methods of analysis. The use of non-traditional methodologies and methods could offer research initiatives in leisure research with a wealth of detail and information, especially in regards to the search, discussion, and interpretation of meaning.

Henderson (1990) called for a cultural meaning of phenomena by way of Interpretive Science inquiry. For in research, social reality no longer needed explaining (because it couldn't be) but in the research the effort could at least "describe [social reality's] meaning as precisely as possible" (Henderson, 1990, p. 284). In researching violence, alternative methodologies, theories, methods, and approaches must be utilized to gain a grasp of violence's presence in leisure behavior, both historically and in contemporary times. There are three approaches with their respective theories and methodologies that could provide examples of ways to analyze violence in leisure. Those approaches are: Psychological, Social, and Critical.

A PSYCHOLOGICAL PERSPECTIVE ON VIOLENCE

As a general theory of psychology, Kerr (2004) suggested the Reversal Theory in examining violence. According the Kerr, "the theory considers human behavior to be inherently inconsistent and argues that reversals between paired metamotivational states form the basis of human personality, emotion and motivation" (p. 19).

Metamotivational states exist in groups of pairs, one state (the Telic) representing one side of a coin and the other state (the Paratelic) the other side. Furthermore, the telic and paratelic are also what comprises two other paired states, the negativistic and mastery states. People's experiences and motivations (both cognitive and emotional) are heavily influenced by structures and patterns but their responses to these are neither set nor consistent. People, however, can switch from one state to another state, thus representing the reversal process.

However, opponents of reversal theory argued that anger and aggression (what are thought of precepts of violence) are not linked and that both can occur without the other. Others argued that the theory does not take in to consideration any genetic or cultural influence that predisposes a behavior of violence. However, reversal theory does entertain that there could be "different types of aggressive and violent behavior...[and could be] multiple causes for aggressive and violent behavior" (p. 38). Violence, for some who extend the reversal theory, is composed of four areas anger, thrill, power, and play (Apter, 1982).

A SOCIOLOGICAL APPROACH TO VIOLENCE

A subculture approach to violence is a sociologically situated analysis of violence in society. Parker (1989) explained that approach is based on a "notion that there is exists a subculture in U.S. society in which the use of violence as a legitimate means of interaction and problem solving" (p. 984). Furthermore, within this subculture of violence "values are held which legitimate the use of violence in some social situations...origins may be situational...[or] transmitted intergenerationally" (p. 984). The situational occurrences and transmitted predispositions may also be linked to further determine a behavioral stance.

Drawbacks to the approach surround the overabundance of empirical investigation on southerners and Black Americans. Justification of this overabundance is due to the supposed historical evidence linking them to develop a subculture of violence. The Civil War and post-Civil War effects influence the southern behavior while slavery affects the behavior of Black Americans. The study also relies upon more rural populations in the case of southerners while urban explanations of homicides tend to tilt towards to Black Americans. Both southerners and Black Americans have a disproportionate number of individuals in poverty which most researchers following this approach have concluded is one of the main factors for homicide and other violence crime (Gastil, 1971).

Moving past the isolation of southerners and Black Americans in subjects and expanding subject pools to the stated intent of the approach, "values [that] are held which legitimates the use of violence in some situations" could be invaluable (p. 984). What explains subculture of violence that involves dog fighting rings, backyard wrestling, or other "fight club" circuits? What explains more excepted forms of violence in sporting arenas such as hockey, football, and boxing? What explains the subculture beyond the fighters or players but instead of the spectators? Looking into other situations beyond violent crime that violence is conducted the field of leisure studies could truly contribute to this approach's discussion.

CRITICAL THEORY APPROACH TO VIOLENCE

If we move with the view and understanding that, "how we see the world, helps us devise questions and strategies for exploring it," then our research will be better informed, more useful to our lived realities, and inclusive of all the complexities that diversity has to offer (Kincheloe and McLaren, 2000, p. 281). From having this view of the world then if we move in our research with the "belief that injustice and subjugation shape[d]...the lived world" then our call in research ought to be social justice (Kincheloe, and McLaren, 2000, p. 280).

Krieger (1985) stated, "we are not, in fact, ever capable of achieving the analytic 'distance' we have long been schooled to seek," for "we bring biases and more biases. We bring idiosyncratic patterns of recognition" (p. 309). This constitutes critical theory's main problematic area of consideration as an approach to researching violence in leisure. In addition, critical theory also tends to not provide suggestions that lead to the "alleviation of suffering and the overcoming of oppression" (Kincheloe, and McLaren, 2000, p. 303). Critical theory takes the stance the social arrangements and processes in the lived world are heavily based power interests, power plays, and other inter-actions based on gains and losses. Notions of privilege and victimization are also areas of analysis. Critical theory is also not bound by any particular methodology or method. How we see is directed by who we are and where we have been.

SUMMARY

Kelly (1983) connects leisure activities to the socialization process of a society, making it an essential element of it. As he stated, "leisure, then is a social space of the particular culture with its social structures and values, its socialization processes and elements of differentiation" (Kelly, 1983, p. 98). In continuation, "...since leisure is ethnic, of the culture, then the value-orientations of that culture permeate not only what is done but how it is chosen and valued" (Kelly, 1983, p. 113). If violence is a part of a leisure experience, if it is valued, if it is socialized process of behavior then what can be said of history's relevance to leisure, the interaction between one group to the "other," or the need for social justice directed research. A participant in a leisure setting forms "role identities that are given trial runs, refined and received validation in leisure settings [that] may become central to the actor's repertoire and brought into role after role" (Kelly, 1983, p. 113). These leisure identities become a part of a person's overall identity. These identities are modeled or acted upon in rituals or ceremonies (custom and behaviors) in life. Those rituals or ceremonies can also be either individual-based or collective, but they are standard part of a person(s) traditions and genealogical history.

HISTORY

Foucault stated in *Nietzsche, Genealogy, History* (1977),

> *"The domination of certain men over others leads to the differentiation of values…this relationship of domination is no more a "relationship" than the place where it occurs is place; and precisely for this reason, it is fixed, throughout its history, in rituals, in meticulous procedures that impose rights and obligations. It establishes marks of power and engraves memories on things and even bodies…the law is a calculated and relentless pleasure, delight in the promised blood, which permits the perpetual instigation of new dominations and the staging of meticulously repeated scenes of violence"* (p. 150).

According to Floyd (1998), "historical and contemporary racism and discrimination" have not been accounted for in the course of leisure research and as a result need to be delved into in order to give outcomes of current research in the rightful context that they ought to be placed (Floyd, 1998, p. 9). For example, many of those manifestations have been violent.

An example of the profound input that historical interpretation could have on the field of leisure studies is in McAvoy's article on "American Indians, Place Meanings and the Old/New West" (2002). American Indians (Native Americans, Indigenous Peoples) perceived the West as places of tradition, history and ritual. In the reading, this perception stood in opposition to what White Americans, conservationists and mountain climbers believed about the West (The Old West, in particular). Many of those same areas to be conserved, according to White Americans, were often places for their own leisure opportunities and had long histories of their own making.

McAvoy (2002) used an example from another article (Giago, 2001) where Mt. Rushmore is a symbol of oppression to Native peoples, while other Americans (including other racial groups beyond White and Native Americans) see it as an architectural marvel, as well as a historically and culturally sacred place (Giago, 2001). Almost all native and westward regions are up for racial contestation based on McAvoy's argument, since most of the lands are former territories of Red Nations or have images and histories that spark feelings of racial oppression. Places can foster racial identity affirmation, racial trauma or even racial conflict.

THE "OTHER"

As Barbara Fields (1982) contended, "one human being can be a simple extension of the will of another," in reference to slavery, all relationships henceforth are problematic (Fields, 1982, p. 161). This will forever affect the interaction and intention of a people. This will forever affect the feelings and interaction with locations. It is clear with by looking at violent leisure-based activity in history an odd paradox was erected. On one hand, leisure reinforced a sense of community and cultural identity while on the other hand reduced outsiders to a status undeserving of life. Research on violence would profit from exploring this paradoxical dilemma and the questions it challenges society with.

SOCIAL JUSTICE

In agreement with Allison (2000) that "issues of justice and injustice have only been tangentially addressed in the leisure literature," then adopting a social justice paradigm in research ought to be our position (p. 20). It has been recognized that "the role of violence in constricting leisure choices has yet to be thoroughly explored" (Allison, 2000, p. 4). We must take notice that a paradigm is needed that will expose and challenge "the ideological suppositions that underlie...scholarly endeavors," for we would be naïve to think that leisure "science and profession has [not] contributed to the unintended marginalization and exploitation of particular groups in...research...professional endeavors" (Allison, 2000, p. 5).

If leisure is a tool for the expression of our inner selves then what can be said of lynchings, of blood matches, or hooligan violence? If they are a leisure activity, then the people who conducted them, who watched them, as a result, are impacted along with those who were the relatives of victims of a lynching. What can be said of the essence of American society that is clearly stained by these occurrences?

The brutality of violence only extends the essence of power relationships and the institutions that it creates, especially within the socialization context of leisure. When one looks at the photographs, read the texts, examines the pottery, it is evident that something awful happened, something violent, something that was "fun," and in some cases, something very American.

REFERENCES

Allison, M., 2000. Leisure, diversity, and social justice. Journal of Leisure Research 32 (1), 2–6.

Angelou, M., 1993, January 1. On the pulse of morning. The Kansas City Star C5.

Apter, M.J., 1982. The Experience of Motivation. Academic Press, London.

Baldwin, J., 1972. No Name in the Street. Library of America, New York.

Bennett, G., 2008, October 28. Charles Barkley: Future governor of Alabama? Npr: News and Views, Retrieved from www.nor.com.

Berlioux, M. (Ed.), 1972. Olympism. International Olympic Committee, Lausanne.

Birrell, S., 1981. Sport as ritual: Interpretations from Durkheim to Goffman. Social Forces 60 (2), 354–376.

Cutler, J.E., 1905. Lynch-law: An investigation into the history of lynching in the United States. New York: Longmans, Green.

Czula, R., 1978. The Munich Olympics assassinations: a second look. Journal of Sport & Social Issues 2 (3), 19–23.

Driver, B., 1992. The benefits of leisure. Parks and Recreation 27 (11), 20–25.

Dunning, E., 2000. Towards a sociological understanding of football hooliganism. European Journal on Criminal Policy and Research 8 (2), 141–162.

Dunning, E., 1999. Sport Matters: Sociological Studies of Sport, Violence, and Civilization. Routledge Press, London.

Dunning, E., Murphy, P., Williams, J., 1986. Spectator violence at football matches: towards a sociological explanation. The British Journal of Sociology 37 (2), 221–244.

Evans, J., Hall, S., 2004. *Visual Culture: the Reader*. Sage Publications, London.

Fanon, F., 1967. Black Skin, White Masks. Grove/Atlantic, Inc, New York.

Fields, B., 1982. Ideology and race in American history. In: Morgan, J. (Ed.), Region, Race, and Reconstruction: Essays in Honor of C. Vann Woodward. Oxford University Press, London.

Floyd, M., 1998. Getting beyond marginality and ethnicity: the challenge for the race and ethnic studies in leisure research. Journal of Leisure Research 30 (1), 3–22.

Foucault, M., 1977a. Panopticism. Discipline and Punish. Penguin, London, UK.

Foucault, M., 1977b. Language, Counter-memory, Practice: Selected Essays and Interviews. Cornell University Press, New York.

Fouss, K., 1999. Lynching performance, theatres of violence. Text and Performance Quarterly 19 (1), 1–37.

Gastil, R.P., 1971. Homicide and a regional culture of violence. American Sociological Review 36, 412–427.

Giago, T., 2001, June 24. Passing the torch. St. Paul Pioneer Press, A9.

Ginzburg, R., 1988. 100 Years of Lynchings. Black Classic Press, Baltimore.

Goff, B., 1999. The violence of community: Rituals in the Iphigeneia in Tauris. In: Padilla, M.W. (Ed.), Rites of Passage in Ancient Greece: Literature, Religion, Society. Bucknell University Press.

Henderson, K., 1990. Leisure science, dominant paradigms, and philosophy: an introduction. Journal of Leisure Research 22 (4), 283–289.

Henderson, R., 1947. Ball, Bat and Bishop. Rockport, New York.

Hexter, J.H., 1971. *The History Primer*. New York: Basic Books.

Huizinga, J., 1955. Homo ludens: A Study of Play Element in Culture. Beacon Press, Boston.

Jackson, E., and Burton, T. Eds. Leisure Studies: Prospects for the Twenty-First Century. Venture Publishing, Inc., State College, PA.

Jamieson, L., 2007, October 25. Personal interview with Pan Zhiwei. Chinese Olympic Federation, Bloomington, Indiana.

Jantzen, G.M., 2004. Foundations of Violence. Routledge Press.

Kelly, J., 1983. Leisure Identities and Interactions. George Allen & Unwin, London.

Kerr, J.H., 2004. Rethinking Aggression and Violence in Sport. Routledge Press, London.

Kincheloe, J., McLaren, P., 2000. Rethinking critical theory and qualitative research. In: Denzin, N., Lincoln, Y. (Eds.), Handbook of Qualitative Research. Sage Publications, Thousand Oaks, CA.

King, J., 2002. Hate Crime: the Story of a Dragging in Jasper. Pantheon, Texas, New York. Press.

Krieger, S., 1985. Beyond "subjectivity": the use of the self in social science. Qualitative Sociology 8 (4), 309–323.

Kyle, D.G., 1998. Spectacles of Death in Ancient Rome. Routledge Press, London.

Lapchick, R.E., 1978. A political history of the modern Olympic games. Journal of Sport & Social Issues 2 (3), 1–12.

Leitao, D.D., 1999. Solon on the beach: some pragmatic functions of the Limen in initiatory myth and ritual. In: Padilla, M.W. (Ed.), Rites of passage in ancient Greece: Literature, religion, society. Bucknell University Press.

Martin, R., 1997. The essential difference between history and science. History and Theory 36 (1), 1–14.

Orr, T., 2009, February 6. Personal interview with Margie Brekken.

Parker, R.N., 1989. Poverty, subculture of violence, and type of homicide. Social Forces 67 (4), 983–1007.

Pohlandt-McCormick, H., 2000. 'I saw a nightmare…': violence and the construction of memory (Soweto, June 15, 1976). History and Theory 39 (4), 23–44.

Rader, B.G., 1979. Review: modern sports: in search of interpretations. Journal of Social History 13 (2), 307–321.

Rainbow, P., 1984. *The Foucault Reader*. Pantheon Books, New York.

Royster, J. (Ed.), 1997. Southern Horrors and other Writings: the Anti-lynching Campaign of Ida B. Wells, 1892–1900. Bedford, Boston.

Russell, R., 2002. Pastimes: the Context of Contemporary Leisure. Sagamore Publishing, Champaign, IL.

Schwandt, T., 2000. Three epistemological stances for qualitative inquiry: interpretivism, Hermaneutics, and social constructionism. In: Denzin, N., Lincoln, Y. (Eds.), Handbook of Qualitative Research. Sage Publications.

Sontag, S., 2004, May 23. The photographs are us. New York Times.

Sontag, S., 1977. On Photography. Dell, New York.

Stokowski, P., 2002. Languages of place and discourses of power: Constructing new senses of place. Journal of Leisure Research 34 (4), 368–382.

White, W., 1992. Rope and Faggot: a Biography of Judge Lynch. University of Notre Dame Press, Notre Dame, IN.

Williams, J., 1980. Football hooliganism: offences, arrests and violence: a critical note. British Journal of Law and Society 7 (1), 104–111.

Young, I., 1990. Justice and the Politics of Difference. Princeton University Press, Princeton, NJ.

FEEL GOOD STORY 2.1

From NBA to USA

Charles Barkley has met and exceeded his goals to be an accomplished basketball player (All-Star team 11 times, 20,000 points, 20,000 rebounds, and 4000 assists); however, something deeper is developing as an even more important goal – that of becoming government of Alabama. Retiring in 2000 after he played 16 seasons with the NBA and recently inducted into the Basketball Hall of Fame, Charles Barkley is concerned about poor people. Noting the need to use his skills for the public good, he said that by 2014, he is hoping to run for the state's top job because he wants to work to end the poverty he sees, the racism that is still there, and to give something of himself since he feels he has been so fortunate. He chose Alabama because he believes it would be a symbol of change to see a black governor in the Deep South. The judgment of people he talks to that mention the bad part of town because it is poor, is just about haves and have-nots, and he would like to end that problem. Demonstrating his goals to be a person who can give the poor a voice, he wishes to use his leadership to end the poverty of discrimination over economics.

Bennett, G. (2008)

FEEL GOOD STORY 2.2

You've Gotta Know the Territory

Zhiwei Pan was at the right place at the right time, a difficult effort for a native Chinese man; however, his ability to translate, and translate well, landed him the position to be chief translator for China in its bid to become the 2009 Olympics site. The job description required him to own the 300,000 word bid specifications, knowing many languages well enough to interpret the information in such a way as to help his country earn this impressive opportunity. His early interest in translation allowed him to be tapped to translate for many scholars who visited Beijing Sport University. In doing so, he met Dean Tony Mobley from the School of Health, Physical Education and Recreation at Indiana University. He came to the university and earned his Master of Science in Recreational Sports in 2002. His adviser, Dr. Lynn Jamieson, worked with him on his master's study of sport policy featuring over 80 countries. Pan's abilities allowed him to introduce the concept of recreational sports to the country of China and to also become a division chief for the Beijing Organizing Committee of the Games of the XXXIX Olympiad. His involvement includes overseeing all the logistics of the technical officials of the games. To accomplish this, he needed to understand the cultural orientation of almost 200 countries that came to Beijing. His early accomplishments as an athlete were to represent his province in the national Chinese table-tennis championships, an honor he still holds dear.

Jamieson, L. (2007)

SPORT STORY 2.1

I swore at the ref at a hockey game in Jamestown and then recognized how I was behaving and felt so ashamed. I remember thinking 'I'm as school counselor, I can't be acting like this.'

Margie Brekken, Mother-in-law of Tom Orr

CHAPTER 3

The Status of Sport and Violence

"The hardest job kids face today is learning good manners without seeing any."
(Fred Astaire)

There are many controversial issues in competitive and recreational sports that have become debatable in the media and in society that relate to deviance, aggression and violence. The term sports rage has been used in a growing number of academic and non-academic sports publications to describe the type of shockingly violent incidents that occur at sporting events world-wide. The death of a hockey dad in Massachusetts over a youth hockey game challenged the media to draw upon a term that could describe an event that seemed inconceivable when one father killed another over a dispute relating to their sons ice hockey participation (Providence Journal, 2002).

An incredible brawl between the NBA's Indiana Pacers, Detroit Pistons and Detroit fans gave national exposure to another shocking incident of extreme violence at a sporting event that highlighted the dynamic relationship between aggressive fans and players. Sports Illustrated printed their weekly edition of their color magazine with a picture of notorious Pacer forward Ron Artest rushing a fan with the bold all capitalized text blaring, "SPORTSRAGE", announcing the terms true arrival on the national spotlight (McCallum, 2004).

There appears to be no sign of a Sports Illustrated jinx reducing sports rage in 2004, or any upcoming season. In fact, the abundance of media coverage surrounding the 2006 Duke Lacrosse scandal followed up this scandal and once again shown how sports has become a common ground for America to

CONTENTS

communicate with one another. Many of the allegations and issues at the heart of this sports scandal appear to be a "mirror" of what is going on in society outside of sport. The trial of these athletes raised comparisons to the media circus surrounding the allegations of murder and subsequent defense of former USC and pro-football Hall of Fame running back, O.J. Simpson. The second major trial of O.J. again highlighted the issues surrounding athletes being convicted of crimes.

If sports rage is new to our language, it is new in name only. Nearly every Boston Red Sox game against the New York Yankee contains some elements of rage. The rivalry has a history not uncommon to other sport rivalries all over the world at every conceivable manner. Baseball has a history of violence within the stands as fans are consistently barraged with insults that often lead to fights. Yet with all that history of violence, Major League Baseball and the American media were still able to provide some shock, when they showed highlights of Red Sox Pitcher Pedro Martinez threw down aging and grey haired Yankee coach Don Zimmer in a heated dispute between the rival teams that left many questions about respect and character of all those involved.

Though sports violence generally encompasses some type of physical violence, some of the violence can be verbal or even emotional. The damage caused in hazing incidents has been well-documented, with reported cases rising fast since 1980. A thin line between what is good natured peer relations and what can become horrific incidents of physical violation and even rape have evolved from some of the best intentions. Some tales of hazing indicate that some of the embarrassing and hurtful actions of teammates are destroying the lives of young athletes all over the country.

Ice hockey is one particular sport that has been known to be somewhat supportive of hazing. When all time hockey legend Wayne Gretzky was in juniors, even his star power could not escape the distinction of being hazed. His former teammate, Brian Gualazzi, shared a story about the time that the "Great One" was stripped of his clothes and locked into a car. As a rookie on the St. Marie Greyhounds, he and six teammates sat in the car naked. The police, who were part of the "set up", arrived quickly and arrested the group for indecent exposure and took them to jail. Gualazzi said that Gretzky uncharacteristically tried to use his name to get out of the incident and was surprised that the police didn't care. "The team veterans later showed at the police station and let the rookies in on the orchestrated prank" (Farrey, 2000, p. 2). Ironically, the police, whom we would expect to stop hazing, not only approved, but actively participated in the hazing of hockey's greatest icon.

A goaltender who was cut from the University of Vermont as a freshman and quit school decided to file charges against the university, for an alleged hazing incident at Vermont. According to his lawyers, freshman was forced to dress like woman and wear sexy woman's underwear and come to a drinking party. The severe hazing was said to have involved the players dipping their genitalia into beer cups and have a nude parade throughout the house, in which the players moved in a line while gripping the genitalia of those in front of them similar to an "elephant walk". It was also said that naked female strippers propositioned the freshman with dances; however, the players were actually male strippers in drag, creating a homoerotic fear.

The public fall out from the event led to the intervention of former Presidential candidate and Governor of Vermont, and Vermont University board of trustee Howard Dean calling for action, while everyone in the state wondered who would take the blame. Before many allegations could be substantiated and the doubts about a goalie who was cut and looking for a 350,000 dollar settlement could be investigated, the president of the university ended the season on January 15 and canceled the remaining fifteen games as well as post season. The alleged victim of the hazing incident has claimed to have suffered severe emotional distress, depression, anxiety and sleeplessness as a result of the hazing. Those who were members of the team that were alleged to have done the hazing were also said to have similar problems as a result of the investigation and stigma they went through and senior players had their college careers cut short. The earlier remarks by the Vermont coach definitely rang true when he said, "Somebody's head's going to roll…. It's not pretty for anybody. People got hurt. Supporters, parents and friends got embarrassed. The whole country can learn a lesson from this" (Lapointe, 2000, p. 2).

College hockey players throughout the United States have similar stories of sexual forms of hazing that are often true, and sometimes perhaps stories. "I've seen kids quit because they were so scared of that happening", said one college hockey player in North Dakota who spoke to ESPN.com on the condition that he will not be identified. While playing junior hockey in Montana, British Columbia and Saskatchewan, he said he saw rookies stuffed naked into the bathroom at the back of team buses, and games of tug of war in which skate laces were tied around rookies' penises. He said he also saw players who had strings tied around their penises, which were then connected to a hanging bucket that other players threw pucks into. (Farrey, 2000, p. 2)

The player in this article left out perhaps the most interesting part of the story. Many people familiar with the Minnesota town in which the puck bucket initiation game was known to be played in call it by another name because of the role the coach can have in the game. When the bucket is full and the player is in pain, it appears that the coach comes to his rescue. The coach asks the player what sound the train makes. When the allegedly shocked player asks the coach what sound it makes, the coach gives the skate lace attached to his penis two quick tugs as he yells, "Choo, Choo".

Women are not immune to the "rage". One particular incident involving the Oklahoma University Women's soccer team included charges of extreme sexual abuse. "Kathleen Peay and two other freshmen were allegedly required to wear an adult diaper and were blinfolded. According to Peay, the coach, Bettina Fletcher, led an exercise in which a banana was forced into her mouth as a simulated act of oral sex." (Farrey, 2002)

Both men and women have exhibited extreme aggression, or at least have made very poor decisions in hazing rituals that have included shaving, forced drinking, touching of genitals, rape, and even death. The recent growth of women's contact sports such as ice hockey, rugby and soccer is finally allowing researchers to study the sport aggression levels of females. None-theless, a simple powder puff football game between the North Brook Illinois High School Senior and Junior girls resulted in five girls being sent to the hospital, one with a broken foot and another needing 16 stitches in her head. Reports and videotape showed girls being beaten with buckets, fists, kicks and even shot with paintball guns. Further humiliation was added by the exchange of urine, feces, toxic paint, fish guts, pig intestines and their own blood. Though some boys were involved most of the violent rage behavior occurred in a female versus female context.

Is this rage a new American tradition that could be spread to other parts of the world? The "new rage" has already been thriving outside of the United States as incidents of violence have also been quite common, especially at lively rugby and soccer matches. Graphic sports violence has occurred throughout the world. The combination of several factors including an unruly crowd led to the eventual collapse of the Hillsborough terraces that claimed the lives of 96 soccer fans in England (Scraton, 2004). Memories of this incident still lead to bad blood between communities in the area. This disaster was more accidental in terms of the intent and breadth of the killings; however, soccer has had numerous murders and deaths.

Columbian soccer defender Andres Escobar made a mistake of deflecting the winning goal into his own net in a 2–1 loss versus the United States in the 1994 World Cup. The Columbian team was under intense pressure to win from illegal drug cartels that were rumored to be connected to the team. Ten days later Escobar was shot 12 times by a gunman as he left a nightclub. Witnesses reported that after each bullet his assailant yelled, "Goal." As horrible as this sounds, former Columbian soccer stars Miguel Mosquera and Albeiro Usuriaga were killed nearly 10 years later in another unusual but similar style. Former Colby University soccer player, Jamie Lue, was killed in his native country of Jamaica in another similar shooting. Manuel Riacuteos, a 31-year old soccer fan and father of two, was killed when he attempted to save a 13-year old boy who was being beaten for wearing the rival team's soccer jersey to the match. Even though Riacuteos was a fan of the same team, they did not spare him any mercy and he was killed by a vicious kick that collapsed his liver and lungs.

Sport violence and rage against athletes can even be a national policy. Recent investigations into sport policy in Iraq have brought international attention to the torture of athletes by Uday Hussein, former National Olympic Committee President and eldest son of Saddam Hussein. Uday was known to routinely beat his athletes, shaved their hair, held knives to throats and would prod athletes with electric torture devices if they failed in his competitive goals. When asked about the torture practices of Uday Hussein, A senior official in the U.S. State Department told a Sports Illustrated reporter,

"Two stories about Uday leap to mind," the State Department official told SI. "The first is the caning of the feet – called falaka – of the soccer team. That form of torture is well-known to be used by Saddam's forces as well. They beat the soles of the feet, which breaks a lot of the smaller bones, causes massive swelling and leaves victims unable to walk for a while. There were also reports that after a loss Uday forced the volleyball team, which was made up of taller athletes, to remain in a room he had constructed with a five-foot-high ceiling. He built the room so small that not all of them could sit at the same time. The only way they could fit was by having half of them standing and leaning over while the other half were sitting with their knees in their chests. He considered this a motivational technique. There was always a psychological element to the kind of torture Uday employed. You are supposed to play like tall players, so feel what it is like to be small. For the soccer players, you are supposed to be fast and quick, so I am going to beat your feet and ruin your livelihood. That was his thinking." (Yaeger, 2003)

ELEMENTS AND TAXONOMY OF SPORT RAGE

Several sports psychologists have pointed out that aggression has always been a part of the social structure of mankind in nearly every aspect of life (Coakley, 1986; Brock-Utne, 1987; Fellman, 1998; Lance et al., 1998). Early sporting affairs centralized on bloody if not deadly competition between rivals. Violence in sports has mirrored the violence of the general society and has been a topic of many athletic reformers who wish to keep sports safe, fair and ethical (Parry, 1998; Lance and Ross, 2000). Uncontrolled, hostile aggression that goes beyond the rules of the sport has created a level of deviance similar to the aggressive behaviors observed plaguing society as a whole.

Sports rage refers to an uncontrollable outburst of aggression and violence by a sports participant. Aggression does not have a widely accepted definition that conceptualizes all of the elements and behaviors of aggression. Sports aggression therefore follows upon that model and has not found a consensus on a unified definition but instead draws its meaning from a general understanding of the role and relationships of the behavior to sport. "Violence in sport violates the norms and rules of the contest, threatens lives and property, and usually cannot be anticipated by the persons affected" (Smith, 1983, p. 6).

One comparison for the new field of inquiry that can be useful for studying sports rage is by looking at the past research that examined the predecessors of sports rage. Road rage is one of the more traditional rages that seems to have a lot of crossover and comparisons with sports rage. Understanding the process of aggression and how this behavior can emerge and develop into a form of rage is a complicated process that is influenced by many personal and social factors. The ability to quantify and explain sports rage may be comparable to the pursuits by psychologist who have attempted to learn more about road, air, mall and rink rage (Dalrymple, 2002).

The effects on participants who were a victim of sport rage would be in a similar situation as those who have psychiatric distress from road rage. Prolonged and short-term psychiatric effects of people who had been a part of road rage have already been examined (Smart et al., 2003). It is important to realize negative outcomes of rage in order to put the dangers into a position to be improved upon.

The personal and community effects of sports rage may be similar to those of road rage. Studying sports rage may require using similar instruments and theories that have guided the studies on more traditional rages. Measuring rage on roads has already been attempted by several studies (Lawton and Nutter, 2002; Deffenbacher et al., 2003). Bruce Sharkin (2004) identified risk factors, assessment techniques and intervention strategies that provided an in depth look at road rage. The various ideas of these authors raise several important issues that may provide excellent models for examining sports rage.

Road rage is also present in one form of sport in a literal form. Sport rage and road rage have evolved into a matrimony that has excited fans of sport racing in a variety of forms. Riots over ancient Roman chariot races have paved the way for more recent violent clashes in American NASCAR events. The chariot races at the Hippodrome in 532 AD were filled with supporters of both the green and blue chariot teams, including the emperor Justinian. Blue and green factions had become a focus for various social and political issues, which each team representing themselves as something similar to a political party, a street gang, and a hooligan group. They frequently tried to affect the policy of the Emperors by shouting political demands between the races. The Nika revolt occurred in race 22, when the greens and blues finally agreed that they should unite against the emperor. Only after a daring meeting between leaders of a mob and the emperor in which the emperor played on their even deeper hate of each other could the riot be suppressed. Hypatius, the man who was being named as his replacement was a Green, and when the blues where reminded of this they left the coronation of Hypatius, only to come back with additional armies to kill the rioters and their alleged leaders. An astonishing 30,000 people were killed by the time that order was resored (Barnard, 1958).

In a modern fit of sport and road rage, Kyle Busch made the headlines in 2006 by being fined 50,000 dollars for throwing a safety device at fellow driver, Casey Mear's passing car. Busch himself was no stranger to this rage, as he had already been in trouble for two separate incidents with NASCAR champion Tony Stewart. A contrite Busch defended his actions in a manner typical of someone who realized their extreme actions of road rage after the fact. Busch said, "I lost my composure and disrespected NASCAR, especially its officials, and put my own team in a difficult position," he said. "The bottom line is I made a mistake that's a poor reflection on everyone I care about and there isn't anything that justifies it." (ESPN, 2006, p. 1).

NASCAR drivers before and after Kyle Busch continue to make headlines for their instance of violence, rage and aggression. Though the drivers are often seen punching each other, it is seldom that the rage spills over to the crowd in the manner of the ancient Roman games. The thought of a conflict between fans that would result in armies of death seem improbable. As sport and national identity continue to become more competitive it may only be a matter of time between the right political cause finds the right platform within a sports event to create such a disaster. The power of the World Olympics or even the American Superbowl may not be the perfect place for a crowd riot, but the same visibility and connection to the cultural issues and ideas of a population can be a powerful way to shock a national conscious. The Munich shootings, bombings in Atlanta's summer games, and the constant threats at American sporting events have been sad reminders of the connection between sports, power and cultural rage.

ESTABLISHING THE NEED TO IDENTIFY AND CONTROL SPORT VIOLENCE

What about the studies of rage in sports? The relatively fewer cases of aggression in professional and collegiate sports have received the greater attention from researchers than aggression occurrences of rage in recreational and youth sports. The use of violence and controlled aggression was often used as a tool to achieve success in competition and enhance the "tough" image of the aggressive dominant athlete. Spectators themselves seem to aid in a social facilitation that rewards violent acts as entertainment and justifiable occurrences. Sports researchers have come to understand that the socialization experiences of athletes in many sports include the learning of violent tactics (Coakley, 1986).

At first aggression and controlled violence in sport was seen as a healthy component of sports. Aggressive and violent behavior was identified more as a benefit of their program, than a problem to be corrected. Aggressive and violent acts themselves were seen as positive by the "catharsis notion". It was thought that by letting off steam through aggressive sport, individuals would better be able to control their behavior. Freud and early psychologists believed that sports could be a mechanism to relieve aggression (Freud, 1933; Freud, 1950). Boxing and violent sports were idealized as a way for men to discharge their emotions and allow them to recreate and be healthy.

Psychoanalytic theorist felt that recreation activities could discharge aggressive impulses in a socially acceptable manner (Menninger, 1960; Gussen, 1967; O'Morrow, 1971). The benefits to the individual would easily outweigh the relatively lower injuries and costs of harm in a sports setting as opposed to in "real life". Sports administrators supported by catharsis research could make statements such as, "a broken leg in a basketball game from his cheap shot was worth not letting all the anger build up in him until the next day when he shot a machine gun on the subway and kills dozens".

In the 1970s several social psychologists began to question this belief. Quanty (1976) and later Berkowitz (1978) found that aggressive sports did not seem to drain aggression. Social learning theorists found that aggressive behavior led to increased aggressive behavior in several studies (Feldman, 1995; Baron and Byrne, 1994). Bandura (1986) was able to provide support that modeling and imitating of role models who acted aggressively encouraged other people to act aggressively. Many behavioral theories would have significant crossover into sport behavior, especially when sports teams themselves have so many cultural norms. Teaching aggressive or violent behavior in sports would have a negative harm according to most social learning theorists. However, within the field of sport authors recognized the widespread use of the cathartic notion in recreation programming, despite evidence of its negative value to sports (Austin, 1999).

Many high profile sporting events have featured athletes exhibiting over-aggressive behaviors that cause injuries or fear of potential harm to their opponents. Sometimes these players that show dominant and aggressive behavior are rewarded within the contest, as they seem to achieve greater athletic success against an opponent who apparently seems to have changed their own will to compete. Fights in hockey, batters hit by pitches, and near fatal matches of hand to hand combat are some examples of how sports incorporate and embrace violence. This intimidation and power game displayed and accepted on the field by these athletes can have severe consequences when they are replicated in the context of their normal every day lives.

The current status of violence and rage in sports has become a hot topic in professional and commercial sports. The media and popular opinion have created a social environment that shows aggressive athletes as models for other individuals to imitate, model and set their own level of aggression tolerance and utility. Descriptions of a great number of incidents of aggression in professional sports settings are often marginalized and sometimes even glorified. Broadcasting these images of the professional players' behavior could have some effect on younger players as well as adult recreational players viewing these games or highlights.

Findings supportive of the beliefs of Social Learning Theorists would indicate that viewing aggressive sports or actions by others can increase hostility in the person who viewed the aggression. In a classic study published in Social Psychology Quarterly, researchers were able to detect a mood change among spectators who viewed wrestling and ice hockey aggression, while no increase in aggression was felt by spectators who were instructed to watch a swimming competition (Arms et al., 1979).

The media has been able to promote a feeling that emotions and violence can fit into society as a natural emotion of the male entity that should be glorified. This idea has also been profitable, as sports and violence continue to sell to viewers and fans at an unprecedented rate. In one academic study, violent acts were found to be more entertaining to ice hockey fans than hockey games that were not as violent (Comisky et al., 1977). A study on American football viewers produced similar results, as fans of football also reported higher satisfaction with the more violent football games (Bryant et al., 1981). In a highly respected study of violence and game attendance of NHL teams, the authors concluded that, "violence sells" (Jones et al., 1996, p. 242). The marketing strategy of the NHL and many other sports reflects this idea, as the big hit, or violent act continues to be the main focus of many publications and materials.

Ironically, the vast amount of articles condemning the violence may be guilty of reinforcing this image. The more propaganda that discusses the problems and needs to curb violence, may be providing a strong and persuasive argument that violence should be a part of a sports program. After all, if professional teams are guilty of hazing, fighting and having renown cheap shot artists or "enforcers" on their team, then other organizations who look at their model will feel that their own team norms would also include hazing, fighting and the inclusion of dirty players and enforcers on their own team. When students learn that all the other colleges are having hazing problems, they may come to a belief that hazing is the normal thing to do and may not actually need the advice to avoid hazing and instead feel a need to engage in the act. Of course to ignore the issue will not suffice in helping this or other problems that seem to plague all levels of sport.

WHY SAFE AND PRODUCTIVE SPORT ENVIRONMENTS ARE IMPORTANT FOR YOUR COMMUNITY

These attitudes have facilitated a consistent amount of players that exhibit acts of violent behavior to trickle down from the professional ranks to college, high school, middle school, and grade school athletes as well as recreational sports participants of all ages. Imitation and modeling of professional athletes are common in youth and recreational leagues. The implications of basing a sporting philosophy designed for professionals and imposing those guidelines and standards into a recreational sport's social climate has created unique issues in sports and human development that scholars are just starting to understand.

Recreational sports share many similar concepts and roots with competitive sports. However, there are many key principles of recreational sports that create an autonomous and unique setting for sporting situations. The field continues to evolve into a field that examines the philosophical differences between sports that are played for leisure interests instead of a competitive sports model that has traditionally governed varsity, collegiate, professional and a growing number of private and public youth sports (Smith and Caron, 2000).

Recreational sport is a form of leisure that allows people to play sports of their choice for a recreation and diversion from work. Cooperation and positive social and personal development are stressed ahead of winning and competition. "The goal in recreational programming is to provide everyone with an opportunity to select form a variety of activities; then, to assist participants in gaining a positive experience as the outcome" (Mull et al., 1997, p. 4).

Therefore the ramification of these acts can differ depending on the level of organization that they occur in and the social setting of the sports environment. A justifiable action during a brawl in a professional hockey game would not receive the same type of reaction as a player who goes out of his way to pick fights in a Sunday night adult recreational bowling league. If one National Hockey League player cheap shots the other one and causes harm there are different consequences. The victim in the NHL act has a primary job of playing hockey. Because they were injured they will still be paid their normal salary because of the contract they were given. If a self-employed carpet cleaner gets his knee blown out by a cheap shot during his men's bowling league game he would be in a great deal of financial and personal peril.

Benefits which are more popular in commercial sports such as high salaries can influence peoples' willingness to continue participation in the sport. Despite the now highlighted risk of Ron Artest's documented history of sports rage it is safe to say that the Detroit Pistons players will not quit basketball out of fear of future injury from Ron Artest. The physical match-ups aside it would make little sense for them to quit, not from fear of harm or injury, but instead they are motivated by the additional money they receive by their own contractual obligation that allows them to be monetarily rewarded for their willingness to play. The benefit of more money and the culture of the players to not to fear an opponent balance the risk of injury.

Injury is often viewed as part of the sport and most athletes have accepted the risk without true consideration of what a similar injury would mean in terms of their life outside of sports. A victim's main source of income in regards to sports injuries create a natural split between recreational and professional athletes and is further complicated by the wide variety of personal and social factors presented in each incident.

Regardless of the skill level or sport, any victim of a sports injury caused by intentional aggression feels many inherent problems arise in response to their new physical and often emotional state of being. The victim's teams can also suffer without the player's skills and participation. At a more personal level family and co-workers also lose the services and efforts that person normally puts towards tasks with them.

Ironically those who work for recreational sports are often targets of aggression. On the field officials are often victims of extreme anger and rage directed towards them. In a statewide survey of softball and baseball umpires it was found that assaults on umpires are not rare (Rainey, 1994). The study also concluded, "These data also suggest that fairly dangerous attacks such as punching, choking, or hitting with bats and balls, make up a significant percentage of umpire assaults" (p. 156). Attacks on officials would certainly be a deterrent towards considering a career in officiating. This is very problematic, as the less demand there is to be an official, the chance of having qualified officials available to meet the needs of the organization. Along with a cyclical effect of worsening the quality of officiating, less officials in the hiring pool would also drive up the price that groups would have to pay for officials. With fewer choices and fewer qualified officials, organizations are stuck with the responsibility of paying top dollar for a limited amount of certified referees who are capable of working the sport.

Despite the fact that most people play sports on the amateur level, most academic interest in sports aggression and rage has been centered on professional or highly competitive programs. At a time when participants are becoming more aware of the potential for severe harm in sports, safety has become a key concern. The inherent harm in allowing dominant and aggressive behavior by some participants is well-known to most sports program administrators and eliminating this deviant behavior should be a goal of any sports organization. Participants should benefit from this policy by enjoying safe recreational programs. Steps to increase safety and control disruptive behavior should improve the overall image of an organization and give sport enthusiasts confidence in the safety and control level of that agency.

The need for programming inclusive activities with minimal constraints is widely supported by academic scholars (Crawford et al., 1991). It is important for recreation providers to identify barriers, or reasons that people do not choose to actively engage in recreational activities. In order for the most community benefits to occur, it is essential that the benefits be distributed to the most possible people. Recreational satisfaction can provide many positive benefits for all people when managed correctly (Kelley, 1990). Despite the growing and prosperity of many sports organizations, recreation and sport programs have come under attack from a variety of sources.

The public's perception of sports rage and other elements that portray sports as dangerous can effect the public's support of sports as well as their own individual perceptions of their own safety. Common people do not have the duty to entertain as much risk and tolerance for dangerous conditions as professional athletes, therefore it is imperative that extra steps are taken to guarantee the safety of all. The legal climate of the sports environment also dictates that unless a program can meet basic safety requirements they could be liable for serious compensation to injured participants (Young and Ross, 2000).

Risk is inherent in sports, and no amount of rules can prevent all types of risk. When violent acts occur in sports there can be a plethora of negative consequences. There must be justifiable rewards in order for people to accept the risks involved in athletics. The amount of risk tolerated depends on the rewards perceived for avoiding the risk. Certainly someone would be willing to risk more in a major league baseball game if they were paid millions of dollars a year, then someone who plays in an amateur adult slow pitch league. Thus, there is a greater burden on recreational sports programmers to control the perceptions of risk in their leagues, because they would have the least amount of risk tolerance by their participants.

The people and community that have stake in the program may be affected by individuals with violent and aggressive behavior that results in sports rage. Actual harm can be physical, verbal, or emotional (Buss, 1961). If aggressive behavior is not controlled by rules and policy sports will result in a survival of the strongest. When competition is a goal of the participants their adversarial behavior may lead them to use aggression to triumph over the lesser opponents and gain success by means other than sports skill and ethical play. Many studies have provided support for the notion that aggression by participants can help facilitate winning (Shields, 1999). Intimidation has been used as a competitive advantage in many sports. A different study found some data to refute this popular belief and concluded that NHL teams that committed lower numbers of aggressive penalties actually had higher chances of winning the Stanley cup (McCaw and Walker, 1999).

Fear is intertwined with anxiety. If certain individuals are scared for their personal safety at any point during their participation in a recreational sport it is very possible that they will not participate in the sport for a determined amount of time. The sporting environment of recreational softball can create perceived barriers to participants with low self esteems, or other psychological factors that relate to social interaction and the social comparisons associated with participation. The sporting demonstration is done with and in front of members of the person's peer group and thus can put further stress and fear on participants with social anxiety concerns (Norton et al., 2000). When skill and ability are threatened players can become less inclined to continue a program or rejoin in future seasons. If someone is threatened with an extreme fear of violence or a verbal assault they may be intimidated from future events.

In the case that an incident of sports rage causes actual harm or injury to people there can be exponential fallouts. Participants and spectators alike can be negatively affected by their exposure to the event. How the sports agency deals with the incident at the front line and administrative level can influence how people perceive the safety and credibility of the agency. Rumors and allegations of a "rough" program can be the sports equivalent of a disease, as the program is quickly identified by most as a defunct product.

If people in your program become victims or even perceive themselves as potential victims for sports rage they may not be willing to participate.

It appears as though some individuals will choose to participate in sports even if their safety is severely threatened by the danger level of the sport (Colburn, 1986). However, it is also fair to propose that some specific populations may not choose to participate in sports because of the danger level in a sport that may otherwise interest them for other reasons. People who are aggressive may also feel isolated from their other teammates. Increased relational aggression in athletes was linked to an increased likelihood of peer rejection (Storch et al., 2003). It would thus seem to be intuitive that teams with aggressive players may marginalize or isolate certain teammates, perhaps most often on those that are least aggressive themselves.

Sports should be open for participation by all individuals. If an individual or specific group of people are missing out on the benefits of sports because of a fear of sports violence, this constraint needs to be identified. If this fear is impeding participation rates, steps should be taken to help individuals negotiate this constraint and steps to minimize occurrences of sports violence. Taking measures to reassure participants that you are providing a safe environment can help the individual overcome intra-personal constraints they may have and give them an increase in perceived social support.

The competition level can effect the amount of violence in a game. In recreational sports there needs to be a balance between cooperation and competition (Berkowitz, 1978). Violence can be reduced by lowering competition levels felt by intramural participants (Lance et al., 1998). Competition is a necessary component of sports because it creates a framework in which the sport is defined. Cooperation by teammates can be most effective when achieving an outcome based goal. Because winning and losing are often defined in a zero sum manner where winning is all that matters, the competition can become intense. Maintaining the integrity of the game requires that administrators, coaches, players, supervisors and fans do everything they can to show outstanding sportsmanship and work to provide a sporting environment that has a balanced perspective on winning and losing.

The sport environment can often lead people to believe their actions are acceptable because it is part of the sport. Many studies have examined the unique cultures of aggressive team sports. Bandura (1973) and subsequent social learning theorists have seen aggression as something learned largely through reinforcements and modeling that is directed towards causing intentional harm. In addition to the individual's thought process and reasoning, there appears to be a social influence that is subjective to the specific setting. A person's environment and the specific context of the situation will influence their interpersonal rationale.

Ice hockey culture has often been found to support plays that are aggressive as long as they comply within the socially constructed boundaries associated with the traditions of the sport. Silva (1983) found that the more athletes were accustomed to contact the more violence and rule breaking were accepted. Studies such as by Kelly and McCarthy (1979), Smith (1979), Harrell (1981), Colburn (1986), Worrell and Harris (1986) and Engelhardt (1995) looked specifically at violence and the reinforcement players receive. These studies looked specifically at the rewards and approval players received for their aggressive actions.

Many theories on behavioral control attempt to explain how administrators can effectively control social situations. Criminal justice, business and sports researchers can all provide support for a variety of methods and practical applications for controlling crisis situations that arise in general society. Few of these theories have been applied to sporting situations. Heinzmann (2002) recognized the lack of research from the academic world to explain and test what was happening when people got angry at sporting events. He stated, "We can utilize the vast quantity of social science research that has been conducted on youth crime/school violence to enhance our understanding of how the media may be influencing public opinion about sports rage." (p. 3).

A myriad of individual factors can lead an individual to become enraged. Though it may be possible to predict tendencies in participants, it would never be wise to exclude someone on their potential to become a problem, unless their actual behavior dictated a need. Therefore it may be best for agencies to examine their own external control processes in regards to handling a rage incident. Policies, procedures, employee selection and training can all be refined in order to prepare an agency for these activities.

Effective practitioners are looking for ways to implement theories that can help their agencies predict and control over-aggressive behavior by their participants. Just as the "school yard bully" ruined the playground for many trying to have fun, bullying on sports teams and using excessive aggression towards a teammate or an opponent may have similar consequences. If an individual in a sports agency intends to control sports rage through their behaviors as an employee there are a few factors that would influence their ability according to the theory of planned behavior. The theory of planned behavior looks specifically at the intentions of individuals towards performing a behavior (Ajzen and Madden, 1986). Several non-motivational factors such as the availability of requisite opportunities and resources influence the actual control over the behavior.

Intentions themselves consist of attitudes, subjective norms, and perceived behavioral control. These collectively measure the motivational factors that impact a behavior. Attitudes would refer to the degree to which the person feels the observed behavior is problematic. A referee or administrator would have to want to control the unfavorable act of sports rage in order to be motivated to stop aggressive and violent acts. The social factor of subjective norms would then describe the degree to which the pressure of the agency culture would put on the official or administrator to control rage behavior. Support from immediate peers as well as society in general could influence the decision of a person to attempt to control a difficult situation.

The final component of intention, perceived behavioral control was added to the original theory of reasoned action proposed in earlier studies (Ajzen and Fishbein, 1980; Fishbein and Ajzen, 1975). This third antecedent of intention refers to the perceived ease or difficulty of performing a behavior. Past experience and anticipated impediments and obstacles are generally represented in this category (Ajzen and Madden, 1986). Examining these three components of the behavioral intentions of officials, directors and mid-level administrators in recreational sports is useful in itself. Understanding the resources and opportunities each decision maker thinks they possess can add further support the use of planned behavior theory in administrative policies and official training programs. Icek Ajzen himself points out several common factors that provide value in using his theory towards recreational studies (Ajzen, 1989).

Knowing the value of using this theory would enable a sports supervisor to persuade his supervisor into paying for extra training sessions for officials. Understanding how important each decision made by an official can be, it would be important to educate them in the prevention of sport rage situations. The costs of training and employing officials are justified by understanding the benefits received by having quality officials as part of your program instead of inadequate officiating. It is also plausible to require a supervisor or official at every event offered, simply on the grounds of risk management and control of potential problems created by aggressive participants in any sports setting.

Additionally, Heinzmann (2002) suggested that hiring competent officials and quality coaches may reduce instances of sports rage. Little empirical research has been done that tested quality of officials and the effect they have on participation or participant comfort level. However, having qualified leaders present and trained on proper procedure in times of crisis would certainly make sense. The headlines of the newspapers and many negative stories often attributed to many "bad coaches" or "bad officials" should be tested with more academic research.

SUMMARY

If participants and spectators are exposed to an incident of sports rage their own satisfaction with sport may have been influenced. Young children could be effected even greater, as seen by the images of the kids crying scared and hiding behind their parents as brawls rage on at a sporting event. Undoubtedly the adult players will be modeling the behavior to each fan who is watching the game. The story of what happened at an event has the potential to be spread through a multitude of media sources to people outside of the span of the original incident.

This information can be spread by word of mouth and by the personal accounts of those people that witnessed the incident. Generally, that person will also form an opinion on how the agency dealt with the issue and include that in their story of the incident. Image maintenance can be vital in restoring the public's confidence in your program. If the public is aware of the risks but are also aware of your program's reputation on handling the situation perhaps that will be enough to overcome some of the perception of fear that can be a barrier to further sports participation. If people in your program become victims or even perceive themselves as potential victims for sports rage they may not be willing to participate. Taking measures to reassure participants that you are providing a safe environment can help the individual overcome intra-personal constraints they may have and give them an increase in perceived social support. This can ultimately determine the success of your sports program.

REFERENCES

Ajzen, I., Fishbein, M., 1980. Understanding Attitudes and Predicting Social Behavior. Prentice Hall, Englewood-Cliffs, NJ.

Ajzen, I., Madden, T., 1986. Prediction of Goal Orientated Behavior: Attitudes, Intentions, and Perceived Behavioral Control. Journal of Experimental Social Psychology 22, 453–474.

Ajzen, I., 1989. Benefits of leisure: A Social Psychological Perspective. University of Massachusetts at Amherst (paper provided by Dr. Ajzen). 1–12.

Austin, D., 1999. Therapeutic Recreation Processes and Techniques, 4th edn. Sagamore, Champaign, IL.

Arms, R., Russell, G., Sandilands, M., 1979. Effects on the Hostility of Spectators of Viewing Aggressive Sports. Social Psychology Quarterly 42 (3), 275–279.

Barnard, Hodges, T., 1958. Readings in European History. Macmillan, New York.

Baron, R., Byrne, D., 1994. Social Psychology: Understanding Human Interactions, 7th edn. Allyn & Bacon, Boston.

Bandura, A., 1986. Social Foundations of Thought and Action: A Social Cogni-tiveTheory. Englewood Cliffs, New Jersey.

Berkowitz, L., 1978. Sports Competition and Aggression. In: Staub, W. (Ed.), An Analysis of Athlete Behavior. Movement Publications, Ithaca.

Brock-Utne, B., 1987. Sports, Masculinity and Education for Violence. Interna-tional Peace Research Institute, Oslo.

Bryant, J., Comisky, P., Zillmann, D., 1981. The Appeal of Rough and Tumble Play in Televised Professional Football. Communication Quarterly 29 (4), 256–262.

Buss, A., 1961. The Psychology of Aggression. Wiley, New York.

Coakley, J., 1986. Sport in Society; Issues & Controversies, 7th edn. McGraw-Hill, Boston.

Colburn, K., 1986. Deviance and Legitimacy in Ice Hockey: A Microstructural Theory of Violence. The Sociological Quarterly 27 (1), 63–74.

Comisky, P., Bryant, J., Zillmann, D., 1977. Commentary as a substitute for action. Journal of Communication 27, 150–153.

Crawford, D., Jackson, E., Godbey, G., 1991. A Hierarchical Model of Leisure Constraints. Leisure Sciences 13, 309–320.

Dalrymple, T., 2002. Rages of the Ages. National Review 54 (2), 22–25.

Deffenbacher, J., Petrilli, R., Lynch, R., Oetting, E., Swaim, R., 2003. The Driver's Angry Thoughts Questionnaire: A Measure of Angry Cognitions When Driving. Cognitive Therapy and Research 27 (4), 383–402.

Engelhardt, G.M., 1995. Fighting Behavior and Winning National Hockey League Games: A Paradox. Perceptual and Motor Skills 80, 416–418.

ESPN. (2006). Busch 'disrespected NASCAR' by losing his cool. Retrieved June 1, 2006, at the official ESPN website: http://sports.espn.go.com/espn/print?id=2465073&Type=story.

Farrey, T. (2000). Like fighting, part of game. Retrieved June 19, 2000, at the official ESPN website: http://assets.espn.go.com/otl/hazing/thursday.html.

Feldman, R., 1995. Social Psychology. Prentice Hall, Englewood Cliffs, NJ.

Fellman, G., 1998. Rambo and the Dalai Lama; The Compulsion to Win and Its Threat to Human Survival. State University of New York Press, Albany.

Fishbein, M., Ajzen, I., 1975. Belief, Attitude, Intention, and Behavior: An Introduction to Theory and Research. Addison-Wesley, Reading, MA.

Freud, S., 1933. Introductory Lectures on Psychoanalysis. W.W. Norton, New York.

Freud, S., 1950. Why War? Hogarth Press, London.

Gussen, J., 1967. The Psychodynamics of Leisure. In: Martin, P. (Ed.), Leisure and Mental Health: A Psychiatric Viewpoint. A.P.A, Washington.

Harrell, W., 1981. Verbal Aggressiveness in Spectators at Professional Hockey Games: The Effects of Tolerance of Violence and Amount of Exposure to Hockey. Human Relations 34 (8), 643–655.

Heinzmann, G., 2002. Facts, Myths and Videotape. Parks & Recreation 37 (3), 66–72.

Jones, H., Stewart, K., Sunderman, R., 1996. From the Arena Into the Streets: Hockey Violence, Economic Incentives and Public Policy. American Journal of Economics and Sociology 55 (2), 231–243.

Kelly, B., McCarthy, J., 1979. Personality Dimensions of Aggression: Its Relationship to Time and Place of Action in Ice Hockey. Human Relations 32 (3), 219–225.

Kelly, J., 1990. Leisure, 2nd edn. Prentice Hall, Englewood Cliffs, NJ.

Lance, L., Ross, C., Houck, T., 1998. Violence in Sports: Perceptions of Intramural Sport Participants. NIRSA Journal, Spring, 145–148.

Lapointe, J. (2000). A hard winter in Vermont. Retrieved March 21, 2000, at the official New York Times website:http://www.nytimes.com/library/sports/hockey/020300hko-burlington.html.

Lawton, R., Nutter, A., 2002. A Comparison of Reported Levels and Expression of Anger in Everyday and Driving Situations. British Journal of Psychology 93 (3), 407–427.

McCallum, J., 2004. The Ugliest Game; An NBA Brawl Exposes the Worst in Player and Fan Behavior and Serves as a Frightening Wake-up Call. Sports Illustrated 101 (21), 44–51.

McCaw, S.T., Walker, J.D., 1999. Winning the Stanley Cup Final Series is Related to Incurring Fewer Penalties for Violent Behavior. Texas Medicine 85, 66–69.

Menninger, W., 1960. Recreation & Mental Health. Recreation & Psychiatry. National Recreation Association, New York.

Mull, R., Bayless, K., Ross, C.M., Jamieson, L., 1997. Recreational Sport Management, 3rd edn. Human Kinetics, Champaign.

Norton, P., Burns, J., Hope, D., Bauer, B., 2000. Generalizations of Social Anxiety to Sporting and Athletic Situations: Gender, Sports Involvement, and Parental Pressure. Depression and Anxiety 12, 193–202.

Parry, J., 1998. Violence and Aggression in Contemporary Sport. In: Parry, J., McNamee, M. (Eds.), Ethics in Sport. E&FN Spon, London.

Providence Journal., 2002. Hockey Dad gets 6 Years in Jail, 1. January 25.

Quanty, M., 1976. Aggression Catharsis: Experimental Investigations and Implications. In: Green, R., O'Neil, E. (Eds.), Perspectives on Aggression. Academic Press, New York.

Rainey, D., 1994. Assaults on umpires: A statewide survey. Journal of Sport Behavior 17, 148–155.

Schaak, Brad, Orr, T.J., 2009. Interview with Brad Schaak. Current and Long time Youth Hockey Coach, February 1.

Scraton, P., 2004. Death on the Terraces: The Contexts and Injustices of the 1989 Hillsborough Disaster. Soccer and Society 5 (2), 183–200.

Silva, J., 1983. The Perceived Legitimacy of Rule-violating Behavior in Sport. Journal of Sport Psychology 5 (4), 438–448.

Smart, R., Ashbridge, M., Mann, R., Adlaf, E., 2003. Psychiatric Distress Among Road Rage Victims and Perpetrators. Canadian Journal of Psychiatry 48 (10), 681–688.

Smith, M., 1979. Hockey Violence: A test of the violent subculture hypothesis. Social Problems 27 (2), 235–247.

Smith, M., 1983. Violence and sport. Butterworths, Toronto.

Smith, M., 2003. What is Sports Violence? In: Boxill, J. (Ed.), Sports Ethics; An Anthology. Blackwell Publishing, Oxford.

Smith, S., Carron, M., 1990. Comparison of Competition and Cooperation in Intramural Sport. NIRSA Journal, Fall, 44–47.

Storch, E., Werner, N., Storch, J., 2003. Relational aggression and psychosocial adjustment in intercollegiate athletes. Journal of Sport Behavior 26 (2), 155–167.

Worrell, G., Harris, D., 1986. The Relationship of Perceived and Observed Aggression of Ice Hockey Players. International Journal of Sport Psychology 17 (1), 34–40.

Yaeger, D. (2003). Son of Saddam: As Iraq's Top Olympic Official, Uday Hussein is accused of the torture and Murder of Athletes Who Fail to Win. Retrieved May 22, 2006. *Sports Illustrated* Online. Path: http://sportsillustrated.cnn.com/si_online/news/2003/03/24/son_of_saddam/.

Young, S., Ross, C.M., 2000. Recreational Sports Trends for the 21st Century: Results of a Delphi Study. NIRSA Journal 24 (2), 24–37.

Case Study 3.1

Many people have recounted the story of one of the most famous of all coaches and his separation from a major Midwestern university. The factors that lead into this separation have divided millions of people into two polarized sides of an all-too frequent argument – what do you do when behaviors of a successful coach are a cause for concern. In sorting the results of the separation of Coach Bob Knight from Indiana University, one matter is clear – then-President Myles Brand made one of the most difficult decisions in his life. While many know the end result of that decision, most are not aware of the preceding events that occurred that wound up setting important precedents for the control of violent behavior and establishment of a code of conduct.

It was also these events that developed the concept of zero tolerance.

In a letter from President Brand to the campus community, the following is stated:

"As most of you know, IU men's basketball Coach Bob Knight was the subject of a critical reports by the CNN/SI cable network shortly before the Hoosiers were to play in the NCAA tournament. The most explosive charge was the Coach Knight had choked one of his players, Neil Reed, during a 1997 practice. Shortly after the report was released, we appointed two members of our board of trustees to do a complete review of the CNN/SI allegations. The trustees also had the flexibility to pursue any other matters that came up in the course of their review.

As the review drew to a close, there was strong sentiment among many members of the board of trustees that, as a result of the findings, Bob Knight should be dismissed as IU's basketball coach. But Coach Knight showed a sincere willingness to change. He agreed to abide by the most stringent code of conduct applied to any coach in the nation. IU will enforce a policy of "zero tolerance" toward any further cases of uncivil or abusive behavior toward players, fellow employees, or members of the media by Coach Knight. Violation of this code of conduct will lead to his dismissal."

In sorting out some of the facts presented in this case, what would you do differently or similarly? What are the difficulties in imposing a new code on older habits?

SPORT STORIES 3.1

We were playing Fargo Shanley our big rival back in the late 1970s in the Fargo Coliseum in 1978. The first period saw two players drop the gloves 5 min into the game and both were ejected. The game was a tight checking low scoring affair from that point on. A player out of the Blue Jays did something that he is not proud of to this day. He and another player were going at it pretty good during the game and with 6 s to go in the game he swung his stick striking the other player in the back and broke his stick, one half of which went flying into the stands. Next thing ya know fans are on the ice and both benches cleared. First person on the ice from the stands was a priest from Shanley which is a Catholic school. Cops has to come in and get things in order. It was a scene straight out of Slaphot and I will never forget it. BTW we won the game 2-1 and had to be escorted out of the rink which wasn't the first time that has happened with the team.

Brad Schaak, 2009.

CHAPTER 4

Exploration
of Societal Factors

"My oldest son still remembers the shaming by a junior high soccer coach who called the boys 'sissies' if they didn't win and made them run laps until they collapsed. One father 'accidentally' broke his son's arm because he didn't attend the goal well enough. I saw a mother slap her son in the face because he didn't hit the ball in a little league game."

(Moz, 1999)

Author and community interventionist, Jane Middleton-Moz wrote an excellent book that highlights many ramifications of a society that promotes aggression and anger. Her book was not supposed to be about sports; however, the stories of athletic aggression fill many of the pages, linking sport violence and its spillover effects on our communities. The obvious need for society to curb aggressive actions in youth often centered on the cultural learning they received from youth sports experiences. In place of sportsmanship and aggression control, the main focus of athletics for youth has primarily been one of winning at all costs and developing talent in hopes of future rewards for the young athlete.

Organized sports for youth began to evolve in the early twentieth century in the United States. The need for masculine and physically fit boys was seen as a community need for a country that was militarily threatened by the mindset of the war prone world they lived in. Programs in the US emphasized competition as preparation for future occupational success in the military or civilian life. These programs were often run with discipline and military professionalism at the backbone of the program.

CONTENTS

Sport and Violence

Girls' needs were often ignored because they were not regarded in the same way as men when it came to professional and military attributes. These roots are hard to escape, as the current situation maintains a masculine image. "The environment we create for our children is the result of a complex interplay of numerous social contexts and interactions. The print and electronic media, major sporting events and, in general, the cultural institution of sport, play a major role in the fabric of the lives of American youth. Any cultural institution that invites or celebrates male aggression and violence contributes to the problem. Sport in our society does that. Male violent behavior is not only often unquestioned, it is often celebrated in sport (as it is in war) as heroic and exciting." (Women's Sport Foundation, 2009).

The warrior athlete represents the ideals of our culture. Athletes are encouraged to embrace violence and aggression as a tool of the trade. Athletes and spectators are groomed to celebrate big hits, dangerous plays and fights between players as a necessary part of the game. Hitting opponents and having large scale fights on the field is often accepted, while these same acts when repeated away from the playing field are measured by a different moral standard.

Those people who do not wish to participate or watch sports can feel isolated and different from those who identify themselves as athletes or sport fans. The aggressive behavior and language of athletes can appear alarming to those who are unfamiliar with a certain sport culture. Preferential treatment of athletes by schools, adults and peers can add additional pressure to split people between sports fans and those who do not like sports. Successful athletes receive attention and praise from the community that they are in, while those who are not athletically inclined are driven out. If this marginalization of some students by elite sport is coupled with other perceived problems in the social structure it is not surprising that individual resentment against sport organizations, coaches and athletes occurs.

In the case of Columbine High School in Littleton, Colorado, sport may have been a focus of the shooters. Both shooters were alleged to have had sport backgrounds that included dropping out of sport and being on the outside of most social circles in high school. Aggressive acts and bullying by athletes are sanctioned or even just passively accepted in many schools in the United States and reports have indicated that the shooters may have deliberately targeted athletes. Most media covering the incident reported that the two Columbine High School gunmen were specifically after athletes who had engaged in ongoing harassment and accusations of homosexuality against them. The national debate that followed allowed for a critical and deep look at the many issues surrounding sports, bullying, and social circles that have been embraced and chastised for their positive and negative elements. The win at all cost mentality and moral quandaries of elite sport were observed in a terrible tragedy that influenced a generation and their perspective on social belonging.

Despite the shortcomings of the system, many individuals developed into great athletes and great people. The sometimes harsh and stern authoritative leaders of this era gave way to a more participant friendly system. In some cases, the systems have become so participant friendly that they no longer contain many of the character development aspects and control mechanisms that had been an often implicit part of these programs. Legal liability and a fear of being sued or brought to court have scared many would be mentors into avoiding personal issues, morality and have stuck to teaching safe subjects only and treading lightly elsewhere.

If students are not learning how to control aggression in their extracurricular activities it places a higher priority on learning these skills in a school setting. Though classes on Sport and Violence are gaining popularity on college campuses, I would place this subject into a "null curriculum" category in most elementary or high schools. Sports themselves are taught in physical education classes; however, many simply teach sport skill or keep children occupied without setting goals for the classes. When sportsmanship and other controversial issues are not taught by schools how much is lost in educational values that would lead to better sportsmanship and ultimately, better citizenship? Additionally, these classes have been under constant attack like other extracurricular sport activities when it comes to funding and staff support.

A qualified staff member who shares an interest in sport with this student could cultivate their experiences and create more meaning and connections to assist the personal development of the student with problems such as controlling their tempers when reacting to a mistake on the playing field. Teaching proper self control at a young age may pay dividends in the future as the student may deal with a domestic issue that bothers them. For the price of a few dollars now, society may not need to send this person to jail for future spousal abuse. As more and more students attend private specialized sports programs and no longer have supervised recess or gym time, I feel that the misunderstandings can only grow worse and the results may continue to add more of our society to the ranks of those who are incarcerated at a rate of approximately $35,000 a year. This of course is far different future for the child whose parent hopes to be the next celebrity parent who can bask in the glory of their offspring they pushed to success.

DYING TO WIN: THE PRESSURES OF SPORT

The pressure society places on an athlete to reach a high level of success is often compared to the pressures that the average individual may impose on themselves as they also seek a desirable identity within society. Proponents who argue for the many benefits of youth sports are quick to point out the value in allowing children to face challenges and strive for success in an adult controlled environment. Learning how to compete and win is often the subject and method of coaching implemented by many youth coaches. Often times the line between what is "good healthy competition" and what is a dangerous and even deadly competition becomes marred.

Though the vast majority of people who play sports do not do so professionally, most of their training on sports has been done so on a model predicated upon winning and other principles of professional or competitive sports. It is no wonder that the basis of what is taught has been expressed often in terms of improving players' sport specific skill in order to win now. As coaches work to meet the pressures of winning it is not surprising that often the results of focusing on improving the athletic success of the team on the field naturally create less focus on sportsmanship, personal development, effective discipline, or any other off the field matters that may not have obvious short term ramifications for a team.

Sport itself needs an element of unknown, and the inherent conflict between two individuals with competing goals is often at the essence of the sport. The lessons learned on the playing field is often the first introduction to handling adversary. The values and ethics implemented in these situations often translate into how the athlete will handle similar situations when they interact in their everyday lives. Parents, family members, coaches, teammates, officials, administrators, and even the concession workers are potential role models for young participants in the program. Sportsmanship and citizenry behaviors critical to the future success of the participant are being influenced and formed as a direct result of their involvement in a sport organization.

One significant factor in learned aggression is the role that adult approval has in curbing or reinforcing violent behavior that is learned or reified in sport. Primacy is an interesting factor to consider in the context of your first coaches and sport role models. The role some of your first coaches have could be one of the most important role modeling interactions that could shape how you view sports as well as the world in general. Our learning and acceptance of violent tactics as well as our tolerance for violence by others is something that is shaped early on and should be programmed with the young participants' best interest in mind.

A leader has a wide arsenal of behavioral control techniques and a well-trained coach can use them to their advantage. A coach should state rules and desired behavior as well as the expected benefits and rewards to the team. The leader should reinforce good behavior and can tolerate some bad behavior if it is not a significant problem. Activities can be re-directed and modified for behavioral goals by using verbal and non-verbal cues. Listening, being honest and consistent while showing respect for athletes in the form of positive discipline is good approach for an assertive leader.

Controlling the environment is another important tool to consider. A coach can set the mood in even more peculiar ways, such as when Hayden Fry used his knowledge of psychology and sociology to paint the visiting locker room pink. Fry felt it had a calming and passing effect on people and that it would give his team a psychological edge. Many critics felt that his use of pink was a way to demean women and perpetuates offensive stereotypes about women and homosexuality.

Opposing teams recognized his ploy and sometimes would be clever in combating the situation. University of Illinois assistants all wore pink hats on the sideline at Iowa during a game in which they won 39-7. In 1996 Northwestern coach Gary Barnett had the wildcats home lockers painted pink the week before the Iowa game to prepare his team for the experience; lifting Northwestern to the victory in the game. Former Michigan coach Bo Schembechler, had his assistants paper the pink walls before the players entered so that they would not feel the effects.

The pink walls are controversial because of the social implications of pink being a soft or female color. Other colors such as red have been known to cause violence, such as the color of blood, or the cloth that is waived to infuriate the bull. Orange is a color of focus, and a team's logo and uniform can also be more or less aggressive. Music that is played can affect the mood the coach wants to establish as well as their choice of what signs and posters will be displayed for their team. These messages can influence the social development of the youth they are modeling for.

Coaches are of course just one social influence a young person is influenced by. The early years consist of learning values and sport skills from the child's family. Sport involvement in the community is often chosen by the child or parents according to interests and the amount can vary greatly from child to child. Schools provide physical education and attempt to teach a wide range of athletic games and life skills. Continuous involvement in other leisure activities as well as competitive youth sports are supplements to the education that should be instilling the participant with socialization skills and citizenship virtues through sportsmanship. Moral reasoning, social esteem, and conduct standards may be set according to views of parents, teachers, recreation workers, coaches, librarians, policeman, peers, siblings that we come into contact with throughout our lives.

Impacts from the family environment can influence the socialization and learning of the individual who will be an athlete and usually a fan. Tendencies for the individuals to become involved and stay involved with activities may be learned from those around them. Being part of an organization and adhering to their norms, rules and codes are a part of socialization. A winning ethic may be supported or damaged early on by the social group the person is surrounded by. The amount of adult control in activities will also vary, and some activities are more competitive than others. Each of these social factors make it very hard to pin point one specific reason or set of reasons that would explain the myriad of reasons for people to commit and act of sport violence at some point of their lives.

The many psychological reasons an individual may have for performing an act, must be taken into account along with the socialization of athletes and how they learn to view aggression. "Concerning human aggression, no one seems to deny that learning is critically involved in the acquisition and maintenance of hostile and aggressive modes of behavior" (van der Dennen, 2000, p. 1). The social learning theory is widely supported, but does not necessarily compete with the psychological theories for a zero sum winner, but instead works in a disorderly congruence with each other towards an agreeable action that seems to satisfy some but not all of each theory.

> "The main problem with culture pattern models is obvious. In explaining human aggression as essentially learned behavior, they cannot have anything interesting to say about current physiological research on aggression which is providing us with important new data on biophysiological links to aggression. A third, conciliatory path to explaining human aggression has been forged by those who posit that aggression is a disposition that can be inflamed or held in check through learning. Within the last forty years, it has become increasingly apparent that models that overwhelmingly favor either biological predestination or cultural and environmental factors in explaining aggression are flawed. Researchers are now coming to see that the two factors are inseparably conjoined. Biological factors predispose individuals to react to particular circumstances in certain ways, but upbringing and other environmental factors have an impact on aggression and even affect physiological structure itself".
> (Holowchak, 2003, p. 389)

The effect of the situation on the individual is apparent in the context of the violent action and the motivation involved in the decision. Motivated acts by human beings are almost always performed in a social environment. Other people and the social situation will have an influence on the interpersonal decision making of individuals when they are considering the merit of performing a motivated act of aggression. Leaders should strive to understand these sociological factors to that they can improve the quality of life for those they work with by educating people on good sportsmanship and proper behavior.

If aggression is at least partially learned, then it can be influenced by positive sport programming to develop an acceptable level of aggression through a well-designed activity. In areas of high crime rates where people have a high chance of getting into trouble a priority should be made for making connections with sport that will help foster better individuals that can improve the community. Despite the intuitive sense of helping those who need help the most, countries like the United States are still unable to offer programs to the poorest neighborhoods, while some communities have a surplus of resources and opportunities.

THE ECONOMY AND SPORTS: HAVES AND HAVE NOTS

In the United States the value of equality is cherished. The term is used in the Declaration of Independence, on the Walls of the U.S. Supreme Court, in the text of Title IV, in the legal summation of Brown versus Board of education and in the context of nearly every speech about what makes America great. Allowing equal opportunities for sport participation makes logical sense and should be a goal of everyone associated with sport. Though not everyone can be allowed to play for the New York Yankees, a more moderate goal of still choosing by free will to participate once a week in a co-recreational adult kick ball league can and should be a viable option. At a larger scale, when any well-numbered minority group formally approaches a community sport organization with a demand for service, a good professional should assist the person to meet their goals within the framework of their agency, or if the request is not feasible, at least provide references to others that may have the proper resources to help.

Generally speaking, those with more economic and social resources will enjoy more sporting opportunities. Social classes are one way in which clusters of people can be compared. A social class is a category of people who share a similar economic position in society based on a combination of their income, wealth, education, occupation and social connections. Each of these attributes has natural and inherent advantages when thought about in terms of athletic opportunities, and the stratification of social classes in everyday life has many implications in the sporting world.

With money and economic capital comes the ability to make sport happen. The facility, coach, equipment, clothing, and training supplies all carry a specific and constant cost. Technology that gives competitive advantages will cost more money, with inferior products often being priced the lowest. Thus athletes with more resources can enjoy lighter footwear with better traction, safer helmets, or synthetic golf drivers instead of the older wood or metal drivers that are now well within the price range of the lowest social classes.

Equality is a great and noble goal; however, the reality of the inequities in sport is exhaustive. The higher income class will enjoy more opportunities to play sports, more attendance at sporting events, and greater access to sports on television. Meanwhile, working class sport participation usually includes sports free by tradition or open to public. Recent efforts to cut funding or privatize many public sport agencies directly affect those social classes that are most in need of assistance. Leisure programs such as midnight basketball have faced skepticism in government's budgets when people are looking at trimming expenses. The long term effects of having programs available to kids do not seem as tangible, yet when thought in terms of the multitude of individual and community benefits that can be accrued, the investment makes sense. Helping share recreational resources to those who are marginalized by society may reduce violence in the community (Smith, 1998, p. 6).

If programs that enable low income classes to enjoy after school sport programs are disproportionately cut, there would be considerably less positive alternatives for the participants from low income homes. Without positive alternatives for approved leisure time much can be imagined on the potential deviant activities that would await any unsupervised juvenile with nothing to do. The necessity to continue these programs should be paramount when considering the high cost of crime and delinquency that can be caused now and in the future if the juvenile has still failed to learn basic civic values as an adult. The void that may have unintentionally been taken from current generations had been instilled in past generations through the recently endangered extracurricular activities.

Unfortunately, in the United States, government budgets are being consumed by incredibly high amounts of public dollars going towards prisons and correctional solutions to crime. The expenses of incarcerating inmates coupled with the need to be a high amount of labor costs to current and former correctional workers continue to plague local and state governments. Unfortunately, when budget increases go towards these uses, the other public entities have fewer resources available for them. Short term gains in cutting education and sports programs for youth, may create greater problems in the future. With less public support for professional leadership being available, the moral and overall development of the next generation is being compromised. If a new marginalized youth group is reaching an age of criminal activity and does not have access to appropriate guidance, the amount of crime will go up, and even more prison cells would be needed.

Often sport is viewed upon as an opportunity to move up the social ladder. The increased chance of attaining a boost in social class based on athletic success and professional pay increases the competition felt by those who aspire to reach the pinnacle of their own potential. Sport can provide a great benefit by giving hope to individuals who dream of a better future for themselves. A person may desire to fit in and conform to the team they are on or a team they wish to be on.

STEROIDS AND OTHER PERFORMANCE ENHANCING PRODUCTS

Success for athletes can be attributed to many individual factors. Each athlete will manipulate their training regiment in order to maximize their performance. Eating healthy, solid sleep and drinking lots of fluid have been a natural way for athletes to prepare for their event. Technology has since provided many forms of competitive advantage, especially for those willing to pay for the technology. Innovations such as Gatorade brand sports drink gave athletes a supposed hydration advantage over water, specifically engineered food can be purchased at sport training stores, and hyperbolic chambers can increase your quality of sleep. The national hockey league spent three years working with the athletic apparel company Reebok for developing uniforms that will reduce air drag and water retention in such a significant manner that all 30 teams who use them next season have been promised a "faster game" (NHL, 2007). Nearly every component of sport has evolved and been mined for training potential.

Despite the myriad of legal and socially acceptable training practices available to athletes, some seek for even greater advantages. The BALCO investigation into performance enhancing drugs has shed national light on this issue at a professional level, and the tip below this iceberg appears to be the great number of non-professional athletes who may have also used some type of performance enhancing substance that is no longer considered safe. The athletes most likely at risk for taking these substances are those who are eager to fit into the team and will over-conform to belong. The athletes most likely at risk for taking these substances are those who are eager to fit into the team and will over-conform to belong. This type of person would be inclined to side in favor of short term athletic success and team acceptance by cheating in the sport, then the long term effects the cheating may have on them if they were to be caught. The potential long term side effects a performance enhancing drug may give them may not be investigated or taken as a necessary risk and ignored.

Stories of steroids and death had been prevalent before the current generation of athletes' would have been at an age they could begin taking steroids, yet many of these athletes have ignored the warnings of those that went before them. The sporting ethic has created this need for over-conforming, and may not simply be an act of deviance through a rejection of norms, as many functionalist and conflict theorist have stated. Sport participants have a set of norms that they have accepted as part of being an athlete, and each athlete uses their perceived norms to shape their own identity and reach the criteria of being the type of athlete that they are striving for. Often times these norms teach the athlete to make sacrifices for their teammates and their team goals. Taking risks, playing through pain, and striving for personal distinction along with team goals are beliefs that most people hold about a normal athlete. In many cases the over-conformity reaches the point of an uncritical acceptance of team norms, on and off the field, so that the athletes can successfully claim their desired identity (Fig. 4.1).

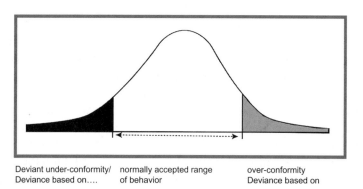

Deviant under-conformity/   normally accepted range   over-conformity
Deviance based on....   of behavior   Deviance based on

FIGURE 4.1 *Deviant under-conformity/*normally accepted range of behavior/*deviant over-conformity; deviance based on ignoring or rejecting norms, deviance based on unquestioned acceptance of norms*

The team and their mutual success is then viewed upon as the primary way the individual attains their own social needs while assessing themselves according to that criteria. The incredible pressures to win may cause individuals to seek any advantage possible to achieve their goals, no matter how unrealistic. So many competitive and recreational sports are winning oriented. A win at all cost mentality is a norm for many sport teams and the individual athletes conform to this ethos. Participants in sports are visible and are evaluated in terms of personal and team goals by real people and by perceived actions of people around them.

Researchers in social anxiety point out that in non-win-loss situations, evaluations can still be felt (Norton, 2000, p. 194). Even informal sports such as weight lifting, yoga or aerobics can put great social anxiety on participants who realize that despite numerous variations in personal goals, they may be being evaluated negatively based on someone else's grading criteria. Motivation to attain non-tangible rewards such as upward social mobility make it hard for the individual to deal with failure, especially when these decisions are not always based on factors that are apparent.

The excitement and thrills of sport become so great that many athletes find it very hard to give up playing. When these athletes attribute their own well-being to their achievements in sport, it becomes even more critical for them to do whatever it takes to continue to play a sport. When athletes are over-conforming and aligning themselves with the team culture they are likely to receive playing time and recognition for their attitude. The athlete who has low self esteem and judges their worth by their level of play and their expectations of what their peers, parents and coaches want, is at a great risk of considering performance enhancing drugs.

The use of performance enhancing substances is common in all types of sport, and will continue to be so as long as athletes believe that the substances will actually enhance their performance. The monetary rewards available to athletes and those around them have fueled a boom in the development of both legal and illegal performance enhancing substances. There seems to be a cultural fascination with technology and scientific training that can push humans to the limits of their body. Fans, coaches, sponsors, administrator and fans clearly encourage the majority of deviant over-conformity. The superiority of the athletic performance by an athlete on steroids has been appreciated unknowingly by many fans, and perhaps even by those that know of the tarnished performance. There is still cultural appreciation for the beauty of Ben Johnson sprinting at such speeds and moving so fluidly, though it is often a bitter reminder of cheating when thought of in its proper context as a steroid influenced performance.

The cultural appreciation for each sporting event being fair has dictated that many sports have decided to develop systems for scanning and detecting substances that they feel give an unfair advantage to players or must be regulated for some specific reason. In order to be meaningful and for records to have credibility, sport performances should be measuring natural abilities. It is imperative that testing be considered mandatory when a cohort of athletes is suspected of using performance enhancing drugs that threaten their health and well-being.

Many sports have resisted the call for testing their athletes, while some have slowly given into change. The thought of mandatory testing without cause is a loaded idea. The protection of personal rights and privacy of the athletes is important, and must be balanced with the need for a fair playing field that does not encourage the consumption of risky substances. The death and poor health of players in many sports who have been linked to performance enhancing substances have dictated a need to refine these ideas either through suggestions or law suits. The case of the widow of an NFL lineman, Korey Stringer against the NFL, brought about the review of the overall conditions of training camp and medical programs through a messy and long legal battle for all sides.

The National Basketball Association tested for performance enhancing substances well before they were able to get an agreement with the players that allowed the testing of athletes for drugs that were used for recreation, such as cocaine and marijuana. When viewing the right to play a sport as an inalienable right, it would be wrong to exclude those who cheat or do drugs as a past time. Only in the context of viewing professional sport as a distinguished position, with requirements for meeting league wide standards for behavior and morality were the changes made that would allow testing of blood and tissue without cause.

Many performance enhancing substances that are legal in some sports are illegal in others and many organizations have a hard time identifying what is ok for their sport and what is not safe or fair. The NFL set up a hotline to help their athletes determine what was legal and take the label reading and guess work away from the individual players. Confused athletes in the NFL such as Will Smith, Kevin Williams, Pat Williams and Jared Allen have claimed that the hotline is not effective and has been known to give late or bad advice if any at all. In one particular incident several NFL players were found to be taking water pills that were banned by the league. The players claimed to have called the league hotline and reported that they received bad advice. Even when accountability appears to be minimized, there still seems to be a hard time determining intention.

Drug use in sport itself is immoral and against the rules, so it is apparent that players who use illegal drugs will sometimes choose to intentionally deceive detection. Testing cannot determine or detect all substances available for athletes to use. Athletes and substance manufacturers are always doing their best to stay one step ahead of the testers. Companies are even in the business of developing masking chemicals and other devices to beat tests. Sports organizations are left in a tough paradox. If they test more, they will catch more cheaters; however, the quality of play may go down if some of the top athletes quit taking the substance. The increased testing will reveal more cheaters and the league will be associated with the substance they have determined they do not want to be part of their organization.

If a league does not test, they will not be known for having athletes fail tests, and will have athletes performing at some desired level. The long term consequences for the players' health and the likelihood of the media uncovering what the drug testing missed has been applied to many high profile sports. A photograph that exposed U.S. Swimming hero, Michael Phelps holding a marijuana smoking device was an embarrassing situation for him that hurt his standing with sponsors. Despite this being another prime example of the media loving to cover the fall of another golden athlete, the drug linkage was not something that was an issue during his winning of the medals and in no way gave him any foreseen advantages over his competitors.

The amount of tarnish from drug use on steroid-laden sports events is yet to be determined. Sports like women's gymnastics, men's cycling, professional wrestling, and the National Football League are constantly defending accusations of steroid use by their players. The rash of Major League Baseball players who apparently avoided detection for many years despite recent admissions of guilt and perhaps intentional flaws in the detection process used by Major League Baseball have created a tough situation for their sport. The return of the homeruns and excitement of superhuman players have been cited for bringing baseball back to glory in the US, however, much of the excitement has been curbed by the constant flow of evidence pointing towards wide spread drug use.

IS SPORT A CULTURE THAT ENCOURAGES EXCESSIVE AND CRIMINAL BEHAVIOR OUTSIDE THE FIELD OF PLAY?

Drug use was America's first clue that Michael Vick may have been less than a model citizen. After a narrow escape from allegations of a marijuana smell coming from a water bottle during a flight, Vick became America's new found fallen hero for an even greater crime. Vick was tried and convicted for breeding dogs, gambling on dogs, as well as promoting and hosting dog fighting events. He went from being a millionaire celebrity athlete to being a convicted felon with huge financial problems in a little less than one year for his crime.

Proponents of dog fighting argue that the violent sport is tradition-rich and allows the animals to do what nature intended them to do. After all nothing is more natural than a dog fighting a cat? Most animals fight in nature whether they live on land, sea or even fly in air. Dogs themselves have low IQs and would not understand the consequences of their action, but would only be driven by their own instinct to survive.

The specialized training of dogs have made them bigger, faster and stronger, mirroring what is going on in human sport. The dogs are taught rage and are even allowed to attack and kill the training dogs. It should be noted that there are no refs to break up dog fights that get too violent, or owners that throw the towel in. On the other side of the analogy, it is not common for human fighters to be shot, or electrocuted and buried as a result of a poor fight.

Many people have pit bulls and raise them with their children and report that they are wonderful animals, as loving as other dogs. The belief that what they do in these violent matches where the loosing dog is destroyed after the fight is natural and normal makes little sense. The dogs do not have any choice but to fight and are not allowed to flee, avoid the fight, or make peace as would be options in a normal environment. The justice system has agreed with these sentiments as evidenced by the sentencing of Michael Vick and several other known dog fighters in America.

The public was amazed at Vick's arrogance when the trial began and many wondered if he would be the next celebrity to be let off completely or with minimal punishment. People wanted to know why Vick would commit an illegal act and then show such little remorse. Examining the social process of elite power and performance sport in the context of celebrity athletes reveals the bond athletes feel as they conform to what they feel is the normal sport ethic. Athletes are separated from the rest of the community as they over-conform to their subcultures. This sense of arrogance and superiority impresses and inspires people who adorn them with admiration. The ability of the athlete to inspire this awe amongst the community leads athletes to develop even more separation, and problems between them and the community.

The social bonds athletes have can normalize risk taking as it did in the case of Michael Vick, who claimed that it was how he was raised and that his boyhood friends were all into it. His extreme degree of hubris grew as he displayed risky behavior on and off the playing field. People in the community saw him as special because he could overcome such dangers and perform amazing acts of physical ability. His attitude towards the community, and the communities attitude toward him seemed destined for the predictable clash that occurred when the truth of his human flaws were exposed to his fans as well as his boss and biggest fan, Atlanta Falcons owner Arthur Blank.

Hubris and group empowerment is a dangerous mix when sexual aggression is involved. The team a person is in can have significant influences on an individual's likelihood of committing or approving an act of sexual aggression. Teammates are a special set of peers that can wield an exponential amount of pressure. Some teams have a moral climate that allows sexually aggressive norms amongst their players, and other teams seem to have a moral climate that teaches other values.

If a leader's or peer group's approval of sexual actions is favorable, it tends to permeate that belief throughout the team that actions of a sexually aggressive manner would in turn, be approved by the leaders and peers. According to one study, people who were in teams where being aggressive with the opposite sex is not an approved behavior; players do not feel the reinforcement to act in an aggressive manner towards others. The study shows that men who hold rape-supportive beliefs and are more hostile towards women are more likely to commit rape (Smith and Stewart, 2003). Considering the sexual nature of the legal cases of boxer Mike Tyson, football player O.J. Simpson, basketball player Kobe Bryant, and even a non-contact sport athlete, golfer John Daly's hubris and sexual aggression have strong anchor in sport violence.

Controlling hubris and precursors to aggression should be a concern of those engaged in offering sports to youth populations. Professionals should be able to identify the forms and dynamics of over-conformity among athletes. Team norms should be established that discourage over-conformity to the sport ethic, while raising questions about the meaning, organization and purpose of sport. Athletes should be encouraged to strike a balance between accepting and questioning the norms of their sport and team. Finally, the organization should work to instill a sense of the well-rounded individual within the persona of each athlete so that they can experience success outside their chosen sport.

Controlling hubris is just one way that a concerned leader can help establish a positive environment for sports to occur. Sport programming is designing leisure opportunities by intervening in social interaction. Authorities are manipulating and creating environments in a manner that maximizes the probability that those who enter them will have the leisure experience they are seeking as well as one that meets the goals and objectives of the program. Managing participant behavior is more effective when programming for the societal factors that will influence the situation while educating participants continuously on proper behavior. If participants are over-aggressive, cooperation should be praised, while competition is de-emphasized.

SUMMARY

Human kind continues to evolve both physically and mentally as athletes and as people in a more complex society. Technology and human performance enhancement have created an intense environment for people to constantly improve in order to maintain their athletic and social status. Winning and reaching goals are emphasized at an early age and repeated on a consistent basis in most sport organizations. When people strive to be the best, there is strong emotion present as they are trying to win for themselves and their team. The intense competition and high emotion involved at the individual level, can be enhanced by the intense pressure put on the athlete by coaches, teammates, and fans in the crowd to succeed for not only their own personal reasons, but also for other peoples' expectations and goals for the team and the players.

When teams and organizations value winning and domination, it creates a zero sum game, where loosing is not a viable option for those who wish to maintain their esteem within the team. Success should be defined in ways that allow elite athletes to continue to develop their talents, while athletes who are further behind them in talent or the learning curve are able to still have fun and fill as though they have a value to their team, and to themselves even if they are not the winner or the best at something.

Peoples' abilities and interests will peek and valley at points of their lives. How they handle these social interactions can be a major factor in their own personal health as well as the well-being of entire communities. The choices people make in a sporting environment are reflections of how they will handle their moral and ethical choices when they confront them in situations outside of sports. Using each moment as a teaching moment and finding the positives and gleaning these incidents for better practices to be used in the future, is an important concept to have within an organization. Successful sporting interactions should mirror successful social interactions in the real world. Each sport organization is an important part of a communities' overall culture and supports the prestige and social esteem of the people at a group and individual level.

REFERENCES

Holowchak, M., 2003. Aggression, gender, and sport: reflections on sport as a means of moral education. Journal of Social Philosophy 34 (3), 387–399.

Keown, T., 2001. If at first.... *ESPN*, 4(11), 82–87.

Moz, Jane-Middelton., 1999. Boiling Point: the High Cost of Unhealthy Anger to Individuals and Society. Heath Communications, Florida.

NHL, 2007. Making sense of the NHL's new uniforms, what's changed, what's the same. Retrieved January 21, 2007, at the official NHL website: http://www.nhl.com/nhl/app/?service=page&page=NewsPage&articleid=287803.

Smith, D., 1998. Recreation as a strategy to prevent juvenile delinquency: a case study examination of the role of recreation in facilitating primary and secondary social institutions. Unpublished doctoral dissertation. Indiana University Libraries, Bloomington.

Smith, D., Stewart, S., 2003. Sexual aggression and sports participation. Journal of Sport Behavior 26 (4), 384–395.

Therber, F., 2009. A Hawkeye turned Hoosier, Goldman has built IU's wrestling program. *Herald Times*, February 3, B1.

van der Dennen, Johan M.G., 2000. Problems in the concepts and definitions of aggression, violence, and some related terms. Retrieved January 21, 2009, at Wiley website: http://rint.rechten.tug.nl/rth/dennen/problem1.htmlÒ.

Women's Sport Foundation (2009) Sports culture, sports business, and Columbine High School. Retrieved, February 1, 2009, at the official WSF website: http://wsf-staging.mediapolis.com/cgi-bin/iowa/issues/business/article.html?record=138.

FEEL GOOD STORY 4.1

Dwayne Goldman – Wrestling Coach Extraordinaire

Every now and then, there are reasons to be proud of a sports program. This particular time, the career of a Big Ten wrestling coach, Dwayne Goldman, is a positive reflection on his attainment of 200+ career victories. Recently touted as an excellent coach in the local campus newspaper, Goldman's coaching philosophy and demeanor is a role model to all who come in contact with him. Not only is he successful, but he also has the kind of philosophy that leads his wrestlers beyond their sport. He has achieved 200+ wins, had 14 All-Americans, three national champions, one team Top Ten finish nationally, one repeat national champ and two top 10 recruiting classes. In addition to the impressive record, his team has gained prominence among other schools, and his university has been elevated in fame as a result of his success. His players note his motivational expertise and ability to read athletes. He is considered to the point and honest. His peers consider that Goldman is successful due to those qualities that are difficult to measure.

(Therber, 2009)

FEEL GOOD STORY 4.2

How Mientkiewicz Got Demoted to the Minors and Found Fun in Baseball

Somehow, Doug Mientkiewicz never learned how to have fun with his talent for baseball. Early influences from his family, particularly his father, led him to believe that this sport was just hard work and never-ending analysis, supplied by his dad who remained wired to him through phone and e-mails. Every time something did not go right, he felt he was disappointing his family – as he progressed, he, too, became obsessed with analysis of his athletic issues, to the point that the pressure was extreme and he never had fun. The, oddly enough, while playing for the Twins, that he was demoted to the minors and it was there that he found the fun of baseball. With no one to please but himself, he learned to enjoy the sport now that the pressure was off – and when he came up again from the minors, he has learned his lesson. The extra attention of his parents all through his career was excessive, and now he has learned not to give his own son advice unless asked for, and to continue to have fun, because, isn't that what it is all about?

(Keown, 2001)

SPORT STORIES 4.1

I have had many experiences with sports violence growing up in the inner-city. The best example of violence that I experience in sports was when I played for a youth football team in my community. My father was the coach of the team. It was the last game of the season and I think that it was the championship. One of my teammates father was drunk at a game. The man started to yell and curse at my father who was the coach. Although we were winning the game he felt that his son was not getting the right amount of playing time. The coach ignored the out of control father and kept coaching as usual. After the game the whole team huddled up to talk about the game and tell everyone that they had a good season. While in the huddle the drunken man ran up and jumped on the back of my father. He tried to choke my father. The other parents pulled him off and everything went on as normal. The police were not called and there were no other attempts of violence directed toward my father or anyone else at the football field. The drunken parent apologized to my father later that week. I believe the level of violence all depends on the environment where it occurs. If the parents are truly in it for the children, then there would not be so much violence.

Christopher Phillips, Former Sport violence student and Indiana Hoosier Football Team Captain

Change happens in one person at a time with one small act at a time. Which of the following can you do?

1. Establish an annual program or workshop for athletes and coaches that addresses the issues of diversity, hate and violence.

2. Embrace diversity training in the workplace.

3. Use the advertising page in the athletic event program that is part of your sponsorship to educate spectators about sportsmanship.

4. Refuse to buy, advertise in or produce print or electronic media that celebrates violence, objectifies any class or group or salutes any team or individual who does not demonstrate respect for the person of others.

5. Proactively address the distinctions between acceptable and unacceptable physical contact and aggression in advertisements and articles.

6. Convince the youth league in which you coach or have a child participating to require coach training in handling these issues.

7. Question the cultural desirability of our elitist sport emphasis. Figure out how your company can support mass participation sport – a sport for every child and a child for every sport. We and they are very hard distinctions when everyone is on a team. How can we make sure that sport is inclusive rather than exclusive? How can we make sure that athletes do not abuse their elitist status at the expense of those who may not be as physically gifted?

8. Teach your children how to object to violent or insulting language on the part of any coach, teammate or opponent, including slurs against women or homosexuals. Teach your children and your employees the importance of speaking out against wrongs.

9. Support stiff penalties and removal from play for any player who attempts to intentionally injure another.

Source: Women's Sport Foundation. Women's Sport Foundation. (2009) Sports culture, sports business, and Columbine High School. Retrieved, February 1, 2009, at the official WSF website: http://wsf-staging.mediapolis.com/cgi-bin/iowa/issues/business/article.html?record=138

CHAPTER 5

Causes of Sport Violence

"It is difficult for young players to learn – because of global emphasis on records-but, ideally, the joy and frustration of sport should come from performance itself, not the score"

(Gilbert, 1988, p. 50)

As with any social problem, sport violence has many causes; however, what is most important is to discover root cause that can be a starting point for identifying potentially violent outcomes of sport experiences. In this chapter, we will explore what appear to be notably both root causes and potential causes of violence in the sport arena. Of course, violent acts are a part of society and in many instances have similar causes; however, sport violence seems to extend beyond any one group or social problem and is not merely concentrated on a particular social group, is not based on any economic tier, or on any specific sport or region. What sport violence is not is exclusive! It occurs in every area within almost any sport, and it has the potential of destroying programs when it occurs. We will discuss major reasons why we see violence in sport: cultural factors, sport structure, anger/aggression scenario, child development, management, media, pressure, sport experience, sport structure and investment.

What are the causes of the eruption of violent acts that are associated with sport? According to Miller (1997), it is difficult to identify the role of violence in society as it is noted as a "Glue, seed, state, or psyche?" Each of these descriptors is explored to determine the ultimate role of violence in sport; however, its role is difficult to determine in society, let alone trying to depict

CONTENTS

how violence permeates sport. Suffice it to note that sport violence causal factors are noted in much of the research, media, and anecdotal literature. Obviously, it is difficult to determine root causes for all acts of violence and deviance, but upon analysis and review of all the incidents, there are recurrent themes that can be presented and analyzed. Through this analysis, solutions may be crafted to mitigate the initial starting points to the incipient problems that occur in the sport environment. The major categories, or themes associated with the causal factors of sport and violence are explained through availability of research and documentation and observation.

SOCIETAL FACTORS

Earlier in this text, reference was made to the role of sport within a national and international society. Sport as a mirror of society, a marker of national achievement, and a way to measure excellence, tradition, and contribution to global society reflected many social constructions that gave way to a national personality. The original thought of international peace through the Olympic movement, ways to improve economical strength, prominence, and a place in the world theatre. According to Semyonov and Farbstein (1989) sport violence is seen as characteristic of many social systems and parallel to other social constructions in society, such as urban life, cultural norms, and political systems. Sport involvement may be viewed as a key to social interaction, a country bid for excellence, a way to improve social conditions, or as a key to leverage other improvements. From a societal standpoint, sport may be viewed as necessary for health and welfare, a result of hard work and reward, a utilization factor to leverage power among nations, a means of securing money and power, and a combination of part or all of these factors. Sport is also seen as a bridge to improve society, such as the removal of apartheid in South Africa, a means to improve equity among those who are disenfranchised such as programs for aboriginal peoples of Australia, women and men, those with money and those without, accessibility for those with disabilities, and many other factors that are identified or targeted for change. This will be covered more comprehensively in the chapter concerning the role and effect of exclusion in sport. Generally, it can be said that society and its systems may be organized to yield great opportunity or great disparity depending on who is in power and who benefits from access to sport. Some countries have approached societal aspects of sport equitably whereas others have not yet succeeded in making sport opportunity availability regardless of ability to pay.

Opportunities in sport are also seen as made available in an uneven way depending upon how society views its residents. Most notable is the exclusion of sport from those who believe women should not have any sport opportunities, or those who do not believe that those with disabilities should be accommodated so that they can also participate. In discussing sport structure issues that may prove to be causal factors in violence, the opportunity and access issues will be developed more fully.

Media

Print and broadcast media portray sport in entertaining ways to secure ratings approval and readership. When one reads or sees a portrayal of a sport experience in the media, one receives a skewed depiction of the actual experience; therefore, this experience requires mature processing of intellect and information in order to prevent being unduly influenced by what one sees and reads. This, of course, is higher order reasoning secured through many educational and practical experiences throughout life. If an individual is limited in the ability to rationally process the information due to lack of education, awareness, age or other factor, then one may be influenced to believe the message and follow it without restraint. In youth sport, we see how adults behave when coaching, cheering, and interacting. Much of what is viewed is a copy of what has been seen in media depictions of interscholastic and professional competition such as certain cheers, clothing, language, and other factors. The uniqueness of a child learning from a mistake, enjoying the new activity, or succeeding in accomplishing a skill seems to be of lower priority than creating a replica of what is seen or reported. There are special ways the media creates this scenario with respect to sport through language, promotion, trivialization of violence, and pressure.

USE OF LANGUAGE GENERATED BY SPORTS JOURNALISTS AND BROADCASTERS

Segave (1997) notes that language regarding sport intones words that has to do with the themes of violence, life and death. By using the terms such as destroy, slaughter, bury, and other words, one is affected by the thought that the end result of winning or losing is equated with life and death. Other terms such as connected with the loss of a game are depicted as "the team fell", "hopes died", "season ended", conjure up loss and injury of both physical and psychological natures. These terms have evoked mostly in football as a frequent way in which the sport is reported; however, these and many other phrases have been used when reporting game accomplishments and consequences such as "tanked", "the fallen", "bit the dust" and other words.

It was also noted that reference to sexually-laden terms are replete in many reporting sequences such as the use of drive, penetration, creamed, and even scored. This reference to predominately male functions refers to power infused terminology depicting a power structure of gender favoritism. Words also conjure up machinery or a non-human quality beyond the scope of the limits of human power such as "rev up", "burn up the track", "well-oiled", "speed-demon", "roared by", and similar description. Additionally, war terminology creates drama by using the terms "victory", "concede", "surrender", "defeated" and "takes no prisoners". These descriptors, used by volunteer coaches and parents during a child's initial exposure to sport experience are strong influence as to what the expectations are from an external standpoint; and, as the child proceeds with his or her own reading, this influence of media is reinforced in all experiences as a powerful mantra.

USE OF SEXUALITY AND VIOLENCE FOR PROMOTION, ADVERTISEMENT, AND MARKETING

In the study of sport from a marketing standpoint, it is interesting to note the salacious use of sexually-laced and violent phrasing within commercials, sponsorships, and other promotional materials. Professional sport broadcasts feature scantily-clad females as cheerleaders, references to violence, and expanded use of terms featured in media reports of contests. The use of fireworks, the references made to the privilege of players, and other factors also send a message that is absorbed. Jackson and Deiser (2008) documented the effects of violent images and video within recreation by conducting a meta-analysis of 215 scientific studies, noting that this type of entertainment was shown to depict "different types of aggressive behaviors" (pp. 22–23).

Supporting this thesis were two studies that explored the use of video games and that connection to aggression that continued into other settings. Anderson (2001) conducted a laboratory study with 227 male and female university students. By placing these students in a laboratory with two sessions of violent video games, Anderson found carryover aggression tendencies that played out in and out of the laboratory. Those who viewed non-violent video games had a lower rating according to the aggression scale and self-reports than those who were engaged in violent gaming. The other study involved 607 eighth and ninth graders in a school (Lynch et al., 2001) found a positive correlation with hostile attribution bias, arguments with teachers and fighting, and hostility.

Mimicry

The viewing of media that depicts violent images is a source of information that results in mimicry of events that are viewed. Most noteworthy is how youth respond to the player role models they view within a game. There is a tendency to replicate the "star quality" of professional athletes as they are depicted in the very visible game situations and in the altercations that take place. The players who have attained the top honors are imitated for their positive and negative images. Coach behaviors are also imitated by those who aspire to be considered a top-notch coach. This was most noted during the Bobby Knight era at Indiana University. Noted internationally as one of the world's most successful basketball coaches of all time, Coach Knight was controversial in reacting to issues and problems with intimidation, anger, and a personality style that many admired and imitated. Some of the more publicized incidents, such as throwing the chair across the court, were depicted with comedians, amateur coaches, and many others.

When these behaviors escalated and Coach Knight was forced to resign, there was a very controversial action that continues to be discussed and debated to this day. Suffice it to say that it is difficult to ascertain when a series of behaviors as viewed through media become a problem in the cycle of violence that permeates throughout contact sports.

The mimicry of high profile acts of players against fans, women, and others can provide a potential for off the field violence. Widely reported media events such as domestic violence, generalized violence against women, and other forms of acting out among professional sport players may be the cause of some to imitate these behaviors or feel justified to engage in similar behaviors. While the linkage of watching or reading reports of high profile athlete violence has not been proven, the reaction to these reports may develop the feeling of tacit approval in those who already have a tendency toward domestic violence. In that regard, it could be one of many instigating variables that set off an already classic abuser on yet another cycle of violence. In understanding the etiology of an abuser, these tipping points have been described as many and varied; therefore, there is no support of a direct relationship inasmuch as a classic abuser needs little excuse to be violent.

THE TRIVIALIZATION OF VIOLENCE IN SPORTS

The media also tends to play up the athletic contest or conquest and minimizes the violence seen or read. If a player receives an injury and leaves the field in a back brace, that individual seems to disappear with subsequent medical reports being minimal and scores more important. There is no message about the issue of professional or athletic sport injury, and therefore, parents and players may assume that less caution is de rigueur for the activity engaged in. The laissez-faire attitude is depicted in phrases used in practices with admonitions such as "play through pain", "no pain, no gain", "don't be a baby", and other pressures to continue playing. Further, doctors are reporting a growing incidence of sport injury among a younger group of recreational sport athletes, with a percentage of these injuries being considered "career-ending".

Media trivialization of athlete roles in off the field fights and other issues may also lead viewers and fans to believe that these individuals can get away with anything. The highly viewed and continuous criminal acts of O. J. Simpson provide an interesting example of a sport hero and a mighty fall that occurred as a result of the continuous efforts of victims' relatives to get justice. The lack of early conviction of this individual for the death of his wife and her friend led to a cynicism toward many athletes. Crosset (1999) noted the difficulties studying violence against women as too broad to relate to athletes and their lives. Further parsing of variables that are more measurable could tease our issues unique to the athlete; however, more study is needed of the broad societal issue that predicts violence to loved ones.

Pressure

The adult role modeling that most often affect children engaged in sport activity is the parent or guardian and the coach or leader. Added to this mix are many internal pressures felt by not only an aspiring athlete but also one who is enjoying a sport for recreational participation, thus leading to a "Perfect Storm" of undue or unwanted pressure. Stanczykiewicz (2008) noted the effect of this on affluent youth where "parents of middle and upper income families are prone to put too much pressure on kids to perform or excel" (A8).

Time Magazine noted in its article (Ferguson, 1999) on sport-crazed kids, that American children are involved in a schedule to achieve high levels of sport excellence that include getting up at 4:00 AM, going to practices, going to school, attending other sessions, going to more practices, coming home at 10 to do homework, going to sleep at 11 and getting up at 4:00 again to repeat the same schedule for 5–6 days a week not counting competitions. In addition, when that season is over, another sport takes over. Parents often are saddled with the driver and meal preparation responsibility, along with their work schedules, the costs of the sport involvement, and the impact on other family members. When a child in a family experiences success, the rest of the family is often held hostage to those schedules. When there are more than one in a family, cost, time, and schedule factors pile up and add stress to the family structure. Often, families have moved to be closer to better coaching and opportunities. The all-time pursuit of that elusive scholarship, success, and improved status and reputation seems to be overwhelming and all-encompassing.

Not all societies are affected by this craze, but the United States is viewed as a successful role model for sport. What is less known is the ultimate effect of this kind of lifestyle on the average family, and whether this type of investment is really the best way to raise a family and keep the family cohesive.

Siegenthaler and Gonzelez (1997) explain this as a rise in what is known as serious leisure where some of the same elements that develop hubris in accomplished high school and postsecondary athletes; however, this is developed with young recreational participants during elementary school and earlier. They describe serious leisure as requiring significant personal effort to attain athletic prowess, playing through pain and injury, looking toward sport involvement as a line to greatness, having a strong identity related to the sport, the development and participation in a sport subculture with related values, and long lasting benefits accrued to participation.

Serious leisure developed as a result of fear due to perceived lack of safety and security in communities and a belief that children need to be under continuous supervision for their safety. While providing an important venue for children's activity, the unintended consequences of this change resulted in additional pressures to perform instead of helping children to participate in an activity they enjoyed.

Sport development

How a child develops into an athlete should follow sound developmental practices that are parallel to how one is expected to learn in an academic setting, and how one develops physically, socially, and psychologically. The following listing shows typical maturational aspects of young children up through adult development that should be taken into consideration when planning any learning experience whether it is physical, social, intellectual, psychological, and spiritual.

- Age 0–5: Early Childhood Development

- Age 6–12: Youth 6–12

- Age 13–19: Adolescence

- Age 20–39: Early Adulthood

■ Age 40–65: Middle Adulthood

■ Age 66 and older (adapted from Mull et al., 2005, p. 41)

In Table 5.1, the primary characteristics are shown for ages 6 to beyond 66; however, there is nothing shown for under six. For that category, the table from Mull et al. (2005) shows developmental characteristics that reach beyond the scope of what is recommended for most organized sport programs. Their skills are purportedly within the range of the parent to

Table 5.1	Developmental Characteristics from Early Childhood to Late Adulthood
Age Group	**Characteristics Pertaining to Sport Involvement**
0–5 Years	Important years for early childhood development. Role of parental care is most important. Movement exposure should involve individual skill development, the beginning of social involvement with others, speech, hand–eye coordination, reinforcement of care and security, and the beginning of independence through the attendance at school, either through pre-school or the beginning of K-12 educational experience. Minimal to no involvement with team oriented sports due to lack of ability to interact socially and physically during this developmental stage.
6–12 Years	Can play sports and develop skills, with team sports occurring at around the midpoint of this age period. Growth inconsistencies important to note within and among age groupings for talent diversification. Intellectual development allows for learning the rules and emotional independence with adult guidance important. Likes working and playing with others. Can start to see differences between parent and self-developing value systems.
13–19 Years	Varying growth spurts and development of sexual characteristics. Cognitive development spurts along with identity with significant others. Develops independence that should allow for decision making on matters important to daily life and use of time with continued adult awareness. Conflicts with parents heighten. Close friendships become established. Career opportunities become of concern during higher education or in establishing employment at any point.
20–39 Years	Making most if not all decisions. Body continues to benefit from higher levels of activity. As independence grows, so do life choices for career, family, commitments. Often roles change and changes occur in amount of leisure time available for exercise and healthy living, making these activities highly important. Evidence of great ability for all levels of activity including higher levels of competition throughout adulthood.
40–65 Years	Some development of aging issues; however, many can continue to establish highly satisfying active living experiences, competition in masters programs, and continued vitality to delay the aging process. Intellectual maturity and discipline can be oriented to have fun and work hard. Many options open for sport development; however, services may not be available for all levels at all interests.
65 Years and up	Higher risks of heart disease and other illnesses coupled with other health issues if individual is sedentary. Exercise should proceed as usual with care for safety and following appropriate guidelines. Individuals are very independent and fully benefit from social interaction along with active living; however, adherence is difficult if they live alone.

develop; however, we see many children start highly organized sports within this age group, and this produces a conflict developmentally with what children are prepared to do at this age.

In working with these characteristics, it is necessary to recognize that these are guidelines for development and are not identically applicable to all people; therefore, the sport system must be flexible enough to allow for varying developmental advances.

In today's highly organized and somewhat rigid talent identification system, many aspiring athletes are lost in the process of participation, cuts, and other mechanisms. This issue was all too noteworthy when accomplished athletes like Michael Jordan were not fully developed until after high school. In fact, post-secondary athletic development is not often factored into the opportunities extended to children, since most of the sport involvement progression is manifested in high school and only a few go on to college as athletes.

INITIATION INTO THE SPORT EXPERIENCE

The age that a child commences an activity should be subject to scrutiny that factors in readiness to engage in a particular sport from the aspect of childhood physical development. By the same token, the age of cessation of particular sport activities should also be considered there are physiological issues associated with contact sports that may preclude involvement as one ages, particularly if an individual has not been preparing for involvement by becoming fit. Of particular concern is the start of contact sports before a child is ready – the physiological concerns stem from maturation of the bone structure, strength that is apportioned to the level of contact in a sport, size, and fitness level. While experts in physical education have written many textbooks about childhood physical development suggesting onset of contact sports at around 3–4th grade, the age of a child starting such activities has been declining to preschool.

SPORT SPECIALIZATION

In addition to concerns about the onset of initiation of contact sport, the pressure to begin specializing in a sport is also causing children to restrict sport involvement to one or two per year. This comes at the request of coaches who are not trained in child development or a particular sport. Such advice comes prior to any qualified role model, such as a high school football coach, and children wind up getting the conditioning only inherent in the particular sport that they specialize in. Sport specialization is enhanced further by off season training and development schemes that preclude getting involved in other sports. Or, even more intense is the continuance of a sport year around in indoor facilities and, weather permitting, outdoors all year. Participation in sport specialization can cause burnout, a condition that is very difficult to reverse, in which a player loses all motivation to play. A burned-out athlete usually becomes frustrated with the sport and becomes careless about commitment to the sport, resulting in shoddy play, anger, and a potential violent continuum. This ultimately results in quitting. During the process of burnout, if recognized early enough, a player can take rest and hopefully return; however, it has been found that this rarely occurs.

ANGER–AGGRESSION CONTINUUM

It is important to create a purposive linkage to generally accepted work on aggression modeling in order to provide a causal explanation for what occurs in the sport environment. Anderson et al., developed a diagram of concepts normally associated with aggression and retaliation (1998). In this diagram, the basic concepts of hurt, harm, kill, shoot, and gun were linked to the retaliation concepts of pain, intentional, ridicule, anger, retaliate, and using gun. This network linkage appeared in the text titled Social Psychology of Good and Evil (Miller, 2004). The contribution of the network linkage to an eventual model that explains a number of proximal and distal factors causing violence is as follows (Fig. 5.1).

Thus, it can be seen that many factors may lead to violence – but that the relationship of many of these variables may create a destabilization of the sport environment to induce a violent act, whether it is within the playing scenario or outside of it.

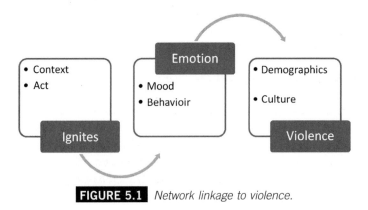

FIGURE 5.1 *Network linkage to violence.*

It should be noted that in no case does an explanation of anger and aggression reduce responsibility of those who perpetrate violent acts; further, the exacerbation of sport violence points to potential perpetrators who may be able to be dealt with earlier in the cycle of anger, aggression, and violence. For example, if it can be determined that certain distal factors exist in a sport environment such a maladaptive families, such a factor may be recognized and mitigated well before something occurs that is of danger or fear. Also, situational factors may be controlled such as use of weapons, noise factors, or other items that can contribute to escalating conditions in the sport environment. Lastly, proximate factors, particularly those that are harder to detect, may be examined in light of occurrence and addressed earlier in a sport process instead of later when something happens.

Studies regarding sport and several variables have shown linkages between anger, aggression, sexual aggression, hostility, morality, insult, performance, cheating and other factors (Bushman and Anderson, 2001; Cohen et al., 1996; Stephens, 2004; Reeder et al., 2002; Smith and Stewart, 2003; McCarthy and Kelly, 1978; Shields et al., 1995).

In these studies, various factors were attributed to the linkage including age and experience in sport, contact sport involvement, perceived motives, team norms, subculture characteristics, hostility and instrumentality. It was found that the perceived linkage to hostility and aggression in contact sports is not necessarily attributable to those who play; whereas, the relationship with the team and identification with team norms may play a more important factor in developing of anger and aggression in any sport.

One factor that has been regularly researched is the relationship of viewing.

Shields (1999) conducted a survey of intimidation and violence among high school male athletes and found that violence manifested itself with precursors that included physical intimidation, verbal intimidation, and physical contact leading to violence. These acts occurred primarily in heavy contact sports, and while the survey respondents were not comfortable with the level of this behavior, they had come to accept it as a part of the sport experience. Another study by Nixon II (1997) noted that male university athletes demonstrated exhibited aggression also outside of the sport environment while women athletes showed signs of aggression in the game situation only and specifically with contact sports.

Finally, the concept of team norms contributing to violence along the anger, aggression, violence continuum was noted in several studies (McCarthy and Kelley, 1978; Bushman and Anderson, 2001; Wann and Pierce, 2003; Wann and Pierce 2005; Wann et al., 2003; Shields et al., 1995). Within sport aggression was shown in a study of ice hockey where those who were higher in shots were more aggressive; therefore, the conclusions of the study pointed toward a distinct relationship to performance variables and aggression leading to success in scoring (McCarthy and Kelly, 1978). Wann and Pierce (2003, 2005) explored team identification noting social well-being was also noted as a factor in sport, as well as the effect of this identification on willingness to become aggressive within and outside of a contest. An entire chapter has been devoted to the role of the spectator, ergo fan on violence, and this factor is explored further to create a better understanding of the fan's role in the dynamic process.

In an attempt to further understand the role of spectators in a game situation, Russell (1995) sought to further understand if there is a particular personality type that would tend to cause a disturbance. It was conjectured that individuals who reported an attraction to fighting led an individual to believe that there were others who were there for the same reason. Russell notes that "those who enjoy watching fights and who estimate greater numbers of like-minded spectators to be in attendance may as a consequence assume there is general support for aggression" (p. 98). This assumption was posed as a false consensus that could lead to instigation of aggression and violence.

The variables of impulsivity, fight history, and camaraderie were added in an Arms and Russell (1997) study willingness to escalate a disturbance. It was found that men were attracted to the potential of player violence and these variables supported the propensity to escalate a disturbance. This study has been important in that it is potentially possible to begin to identify those who may disturb an event by preliminarily profiling potential violators.

PARENT AGGRESSION TOWARD KIDS, COACHES, REFEREES

News accounts of many forms of parental aggression and violence toward all aspects of the sport experience abound. Each and every day, a reader finds accounts of parental actions toward their children, other children, coaches (who also act as coach and parent), other parents and adults in the sport environment, referees, sport administrators, and many entities that affect the sport experience. In order to understand the parent, the anger-aggression theoretical framework and individual psychological histories are helpful; however, parent behaviors are so commonly disruptive, that there must be some common explanation as well. An example of parents gone wild is a report in Reader's Digest (Crowley, 2007) that reported an altercation during a community league basketball game for girls ages 10 and 11. One angry father allegedly kicked the wife of the winning team's coach.

This woman was taunting players of the other team. It was reported that the players watched as their parents acted like juvenile delinquents. This type of behavior was further displayed in the cartoon sitcom South Park that showed players upset at angry parents who fought at each game. The team's celebration that the season was over and summer was nigh was squelched by their coach's announcement that they had qualified for the post season tournament season. Even in plotting to lose, they were met with parental anger and pressure.

While some of the explanation for these and other behaviors is covered in other sections of this chapter and throughout the text, the authors' experiences and observations have shed light on yet another source of pressure that may prompt many parents to lose sight of the role of sport in their children's lives and move more aggressively toward retaliation as a form of resolution to problems they encounter for themselves and their children. We call it, the money and power angle. While the use of the terms money and power together is not new: in fact, Jay Coakley (2007) pairs those terms in ways that define American sport in particular, the explanation of these concepts in terms of parenting may reveal additional insights into why parents exhibit such stress and frustration at such an early stage in their children's sport development.

It was reported in Newsweek (Wingert and Lauerman, 2000) after the killing of a hockey dad, that out-of-control adults are prevalent in many sport situations, particularly community and amateur sports. Reports of parent spectator antics and aggressions have been frequent since this report, and even though many similar events have occurred through the past several centuries, the awareness toward intensity and seriousness of conflicts has been raised to a level of criminal conduct.

The existence of pre-violent and accepted conditions seemed to be noted as well in a study by the Rutgers Youth Sports Research Council (Heintzman, 2008) where over 1000 citations were reviewed spanning a period of 20 years. Evidence of parent misbehavior was noted to include anger versus rage, negative role modeling, and pride versus ownership. The Council noted in the conclusions of the study that as "gatekeepers of public park facilities, recreation professionals have a critical role in ensuring that the highest standards of conduct are upheld at events" (http://youthsports.rutgers.edu/resources/geeral-interest/parental-violence-in-youth-sports.html).

COACHES' AGGRESSION TOWARD KIDS

Adult volunteers comprise the majority of leadership roles as coaches, parent representatives, and other positions within the sport environment.

The most influential role is that of "coach" beyond which the influence of parent exerts. In looking at the role of the parent, from the time of a child's birth until school commences, the parent is the key role and influence. Once school commences and activities begin outside of the home, the next series of role models include teachers, coaches, and other leaders. Often the bond formed by these outside influences is a healthy and enduring one. All too often, however, the bond is a tenuous and unsatisfactory one if the individual who is the leader is ill-equipped to deal with children, is ineffective when dealing with conflict, is in conflict with the parent authority, or has devious intentions when getting involved in the sport program. Unfortunately, volunteer and paid coaches in youth recreational and interscholastic sport are not trained or held to the coaching standards previously expected of the coaching and teacher combination hired in the school systems. In order to teach in the school system, you needed not only a certification in a content area for teaching but also be certified to coach. Now, many schools accept those who do not have teaching certification to fulfill coaching spots, and the disconnect with the standards expected within the schools is a cause of many problems.

Hillstedt (1987) also alluded to coach difficulty in working with the parents of their athletes. The continued stress of dealing with parents who want the best for their child, often at the disadvantage of other players is difficult to deal with even when the coach is qualified and experienced. Coaches have to deal with the over-involved parent who develops a relationship with the child's coach and other power structure personnel, becomes a player-agent, and often has learned many ways to manipulate and secure favors for their child. The coach also faces issues with the under-involved parent whose apathetic approach causes problems for the player who misses practices, fails to pay, and seems to have to rely on others for transportation and encouragement. Then there is moderate involvement of a parent who has a balanced approach but may not be able to mitigate the effects of the over-involved player agent parent. Coaches try to provide an equitable situation for all, taking into account skill development and effort, winning and losing efforts, and provision of a broad range of coaching services.

There has also been an awareness of training and development needs of coaches, who have experienced stresses and strains of being not only employed, but also involved in what becomes a second occupation with all the attendant stresses and strains. Role-overload is further enhanced if the coach is also a parent. Therefore, the coach needs to provide a safe and well-organized sport programs for a team of participants, to oversee events that are under the jurisdiction of that team, to see that practices and games avoid injury that players see a degree of personal success, and that parents, spectators and players are satisfied with the experience. This type of role-overload often causes stress, frustration, anger, aggression, and ultimately violence – against player, parents, referees, opponents, those who administer the program, and families. When the system breaks down, it is often due to something that an overworked, frustrated coach did not accomplish.

The coach role is crucial to a successful operation – unfortunately, it is often an exacerbating factor due to a lack of structural controls to support the volunteer effort, i.e., an effective sport structure.

ATOD

An emerging area of study is addictive behavior and the role of sport violence engaged in by people who consume too much alcohol and then lose control over their behavior. While it is not a focus of this book to address the plethora of literature that would suggest those who engage in the sport system and consume a variety of alcohol, tobacco, and other drugs are more likely to commit violent acts, it has been noted that consumption of these substances may be a root cause of some aspects of sport violence behavior. As we explore the role of exclusion, mob mentalities, and aggression further, alcohol and other drug consumption may be one of the instigators of violence, particularly among crowds of fans.

SPORT STRUCTURE

Perhaps the most important causal factor that gives rise to violence in sport is its structure – or infrastructure. This includes the following:

1. Quality of the planning of facilities and programs for sport delivery to include a defensible philosophy and approach.

2. Quality of regulatory structures including rules, codes of conduct, program development, and control.

3. Quality of financial support to allow for adequate supervision, officiating, coaching and leading, adult education, player education, and oversight.

4. Quality of professional preparation and certification of all individuals who interact with the sport system.

5. Quality of evaluation mechanisms to provide a framework for continual improvement.

6. Quality of participation outcomes as perceived by players.

Each of the above factors indicates major organizational structuring to ensure that those who participate will enjoy the recreational sport in which they participate, will be provided with a way to progress in skill and involvement, will be able to choose to enter and exit from sport experiences without undue influence of role models.

MANAGEMENT

Mismanagement is often the cause of a violent episode. When frustration occurs with those who get angry, it is often over a failure on the part of the management system to correct a repetitive situation, improve the quality of officiating, intercede readily when situations erupt, provide adequate safety and security when indicated, and provide a proactive framework to educate those involved in the sport experience. When standard management processes break down – players, parents, spectators, referees, administrators, and many others are at risk of intimidation, bullying, injury, threats, abuse, and other factors.

The responsibility for managing sport experiences in a community is the public sector to reflect regulatory conditions around laws and education, national, regional, and state governing bodies, professionally managed public and private service delivery systems that meet the standards of accreditation, certification of staff, and best practices. In most communities, the school system and local government are the key coordinating agencies to deliver sport. Bolstered by full coordination with private services that link to regional, national, and international systems, where appropriate, the public sector must be responsible for public safety in ensuring that those who participate in any local jurisdiction activity does so safely, securely, and effectively. To do less is an abridgement of responsibility for the public good. To allow violent events to occur in facilities that are publicly owned and operated is to deny the taxpaying public safety and security.

Poorly managed sport systems have been attributed the main reason for sport problems that result in violence. Public leisure service delivery systems are not uniformly facing the responsibility for all facilities and areas that are delegated to volunteer organizations via agreement. This delegation of power and authority to volunteer organizations without providing proper oversight continues to be a disturbing reason for an escalating pattern of violence during many sporting events including practices, games, tournaments, and spillover violence affecting the community.

Mimicry

To what extent are youth and adults influenced by violence depicted in the media. Several areas of research have confirmed the role of viewed violence and the subliminal influence it has on how one perceives violence in the sport environment and how one reacts to the anger–aggression continuum.

The sport experience

Hughes and Coakley (1991) introduced and then developed the concept of excessive over conformity to the sport ethic as a feature of sport. This has been noticed in high school and college interscholastic sport, but has also been developing in sports participation in much younger ages as well. In noting the features of this over conformity, the sport ethic contains the following features:

- The athlete is expected to make sacrifices for the privilege of involvement in the sport. These sacrifices include the normally expected attendance at practices, punctuality, game involvement, and dedication, but it has also become expected that the sport will be participated in exclusively instead of participation in other sports of interest.

- The athlete is expected to strive for distinction in sport to include excelling beyond other players, do the best one can, and finding a unique niche that fits well into the team network. This can also include behaviors that identify one as an individual, and sometimes their behaviors also define one as a spectacle.

- The athlete is expected to accept the risks inherent (although not always) in the activity and play through the pain. This has resulted in injurious orientations that may later preclude play. For example, doctors are now noting that the effect of concussions in football can create similar patterns in athletes to the brain patterning of those with dementia conditions.

- The athlete is also expected to refuse to accept limits. Within this framework, the athlete receives tacit approval for behaviors that extend beyond what are normally accepted behaviors. Problems such as cheap shots, sneak attacks, disregard for playing rules, and a sense of entitlement can cause many problems and issues with violence.

Given the scenario of typical expectations of the athlete, athletes who demonstrate these attributes are more likely to receive approval by a coach, parent or other role model. Those with lower self-esteem react to the expectations of external pressure more fully, and this over-conformity can cause excesses that result in violence. Accordingly, over-conformity results in an arrogant and entitled athlete who believes that the tacit approval for excesses can extend beyond the playing environment. This arrogance, or hubris, can lead to a belief that one is not accountable as compared with the average "mortal" and can engage in activities that otherwise would be viewed as criminal in any other circumstance.

The other focus of the sport experience is why violence occurs outside the playfield. In a study of hooligans in England, it was noted that violent outcomes are the result of mutual interactions, between the crowd and other agencies, such as police (King, 1999, p. 269). Looking further into why these altercations occur, it is necessary to understand more of the theoretical approaches and solutions to crowdedness and facility management. In many cases, the control of large crowds is also a problem beyond the sport environment – when large numbers gather, there is always potential for frustration that mounts in the heat of competition, as a result of feeling confined, and also if there is anger that erupts over winning and losing. Much was learned about emotional contagion associated with crowds that could become riotous when there was a perturbation such as a loud shot, an issue with weather, a perceived threat, or a particularly charismatic speaker or leader. Crowd issues are normally explained when, upon hindsight, there has been a failure in security coverage, crowd behavior control, a facility that places players, referees and fans in a too close proximity to each other, when large crowds are denied access to the facility, and when the facility is overcrowded and hazards such as collapsed bleacher, roof breakage or other such calamity occur. Crowd control issues are frequent in Europe football matches where those who can enter the facility and those who cannot clash. Known as hooligans, the disenfranchised marginal group loiters outside the contest taking in whatever they can through the fence, in pubs nearby, or through sneaking in. Ultimately, clashes occur from rowdy hooligans and upset fans who interact more from a class issue than a sport issue. Nonetheless, it has been an issue that has led to deaths, stampedes, and other factors associated with the sport contest. Often, in these forms of contests, alcohol is a primary factor in the escalation of the problem. Ultimately these altercations mar the overall sport experience for everyone.

Investment

Finally, a factor that causes frustration and problems with parents and children is the degree of investment that is made in sport. To engage in sport

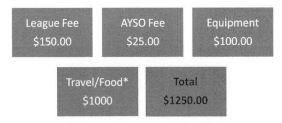

FIGURE 5.2 *Estimated cost to provide one child under twelve one fall season of soccer in a Metropolitan area of the United States.*

participation is to make an investment not only in child participation, but also personal participation, and commitment to professional, intercollegiate, and interscholastic teams. In order to illustrate the financial pressure involved in participation, the illustration in Fig. 5.2 should suffice in providing enlightenment. The cost to provide one child with one activity for one season is described here.

This covers one child only for a 10-week season – over $125/week. If more than one child in a family enrolls, the cost increases geometrically. As children increase their competition levels, costs increase, and eventually, affordability is an issue, regardless of the socioeconomic level of the family. The pressure to continue increases, the pressure to afford these costs increases, and that can result in frustration on the part of the parent that can serve to view the child as an agent to ensure the efficacy of the investment instead of the child who should only have responsibility to commit and enjoy the opportunity.

Costs to participate in increasingly expensive sport activities take away from other efforts to spend a family's discretionary dollars. Vacations may not be taken, travel responsibilities may increase, distances may require overnight commitments, and the family structure may start to unwind. In addition, while the justification to spend this money may be for an eventual college athletic scholarship or success on teams in high school, there is no guarantee of either. In the case of the possibility of athletic scholarships, less than 1% of all athletes receive a college scholarship for sport at any level. Secondly, the player-participant may receive an injury (Figs. 5.3 and 5.4) that prevents continuance in the sport, or may suffer burn-out due to too much– too soon, or may simply drop out. Parents involved in altercations seem to be involved in an endless circle of effort to support their children, a difficult and frustrating situation. Parents would do well to plan financial involvement ahead of the growth curve of children's interest in sport – setting a limit of what is available, and then backtracking when the child wishes to pursue

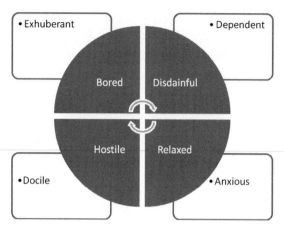

FIGURE 5.3 *Personality types and potential for anger and aggression. Valdez, P., and Mehrabian, A. (1994) Effects of color on emotion.* Journal of Experimental Psychology, *123(4) 394–409.*

something else. In the solutions chapter, the role of organizations and of role models will be discussed to see what can be realistically done to mitigate the concept of the player as an investment instead of a child.

Aside from the role that the parent plays in the financial investment in a child's sport, the more global problem exists in the day to day decision making of administrators for the overall investment in sport within a community. Community financial investment in sport is big business, and

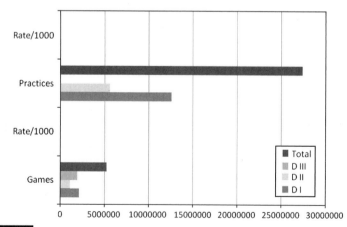

FIGURE 5.4 *Game injury rate for 15 sports as per National Collegiate Athletic Association 1988–2004. Hootman, J.M., Dick, R., and Agel, J. (2007) Epidemiology of collegiate injuries for 15 sports: summary and recommendations for injury prevention initiatives.* Journal of Athletic Training, *42(2), 311–319.*

often those who benefit really are not paying attention to community societal needs. Instead, the glamour of a new stadium complex with convention facilities precludes community development for improved facilities. In addition, the extent to which the public uses these facilities is extremely limited; therefore, frustration can amount to problems between those benefiting from the project and those who do not. Further, the entire global economic system involves sport development that includes gambling, stock ownership and many other dealings that can create investment problems. While the degree to which these problems trickle down has not been studied, there have been publicized incidents of point shaving, throwing games, and other irregularities that can feed the sport and violence scenario both during a playing contest and outside of the actual playing process. While it is not a focus to investigate the status of this form of deviance, local investment in private facilities by investors with prurient interests for those they are associated with may affect the quality and effectiveness of ethical sport behaviors.

SUMMARY

There are many factors that enter into the cause of the highly visible and very disturbing trend of sport violence. Family factors, anger and aggression, and situational variables are blended in a continually escalating manner, and the result is a series of issues that often are difficult to understand in hindsight. The positive fact is that all these behaviors, if properly anticipated may be mitigated to some extent by realizing that there are solutions to be considered. In future chapters, these extended understandings and future solutions are explored.

REFERENCES

Anderson, C.A., Benjamin, A.J., Bartholow, B.D., 1998. Does the gun pull the trigger? Automatic priming effects of weapon pictures and weapon names. Psychological Science 9, 308–314.

Coakley, J.J., 2007. Sports in Society: Issues and Controversies, 9th edn. McGraw Hill Higher Education, Hightstown, NJ, p. 676.

Crowley, M., 2007. Field of screams. Reader's Digest. October 2007, 43–48.

Ferguson, A., 1999. Inside the crazy culture of kids sports. Time 154 (2), 52–60.

Gilbert, B., 1988. Competition: is it what life's all about? Sports Illustrated 68 (20), 45–55.

Heintzman, G., 2008. Parental violence in youth sports: facts, myths, and videotape. Retrieved from: http://youthsports.rutgers.edu/resources/general-interest/parental-violence-in-youth-sports, 8/26/08.

Hillstedt, J.C., 1987. The coach/parent/athlete relationship. The Sport Psychologist 1, 151–160.

Hughes, R., Coakley, J., 1991. Positive deviance among athletes: the implications of over conformity to the sport ethnic. Sociology of Sport Journal 8, 307–325.

Jackson, G., Deiser, R.L., 2008. Research update: the danger of anger. Parks and Recreation 43 (6), 22–27.

Jamieson, J., 2009. Personal written statement.

King, A., 1999. Football hooliganism and the practical paradigm. Sociology of Sport Journal 16, 269–273.

Miller, T., 1997. Sport and violence: glue, seed, staff, or psyche? Journal of Sport and Social Issues 21, 235–238.

Miller, A.G., 2004. The Social Psychology of Good and Evil. The Guilford Press, New York.

Mull, Bayless, Jamieson, 2005. Recreational Sport Management. Human Kinetics, Champaign, Il, 354 pp.

Nixon II, H.L., 1997. Gender, sport, and aggressive behavior outside sport. Journal of Sport and Social Issues 21 (4), 379–391.

Segave, J.O., 1997. A matter of life and death: some thoughts on the language of sport. Journal of Sport and Social Issues 21 (2), 211–221.

Semyonov, M., Farbstein, M., 1989. Ecology of sport violence: the case of Israeli Soccer. Sociology of Sport Journal 6, 50–59.

Shields, E.W., 1999. Intimidation and violence by males in high school athletics. Adolescence 34 (135), 503–522.

Siegenthaler, K.L., Gonzelez, G.L., 1997. Youth sports as serious leisure. Journal of Sport and Social Issues 21 (3), 298–314.

Smith, D., Steward, S., 2003. Sexual aggression and sports participation. Journal of Sport Behaviour 26 (4), 384–395.

Stanczykiewicz, B., 2008. Parents beware: affluent kids are at risk. The Indianapolis Star, Tuesday, October 7, 2008, A8. (http://youthsports.rutgers.edu/resources/geeral-interest/parental-violence-in-youth-sports.html).

Case Study 5.1

The information below reveals a pub crawl event organized by a sport club. Discuss the management issues inherent in this event. What would you do similarly or differently?

LaCrosse Shitshow BAR CRAWL

1. 4 pts Walnut St. Tap (11:00): Drink of choice & 1 shot of choice (per person)
2. 4 pts. SPORTS (11:35: Spin wheel twice & 1 drink of choice (per person)
3. 4 pts. Bar 1 (12:15): Drink of choice & 1 beer chug or shot (per person)
4. 3 pts Bar 2 (1:00): 3 Pitchers of Beer (per team)
5. 5 pts. Bar 2 UPSTAIRS (1:35): 3 large A. M. F. (per team)
6. 6 pts. Bar 3 (2:10): Spin the Wheel
7. 10 pts. Food Place 1: Anytime after 2:40 and a whole burrito with chips and cheese (can order water on the side)

EXTRA POINTS

2 pts: Grab a boob
7 pts: Taking a body shot
9 pts: Getting as body shot
4 pts: Taking a shot with bartender
5 pts: Make out w/a townie
15 pts: Get any girl's bra
10 pts: Puke and rally
20 pts: Get any girl's underwear
8 pts: Make out w/ your coach
5 pts: Get a girl to buy your drink
13 pts: Making it to upstairs
16 pts: Make out w/ bartender
17 pts: Making it to Bar 3
22 pts: Change clothes w/ coach

RULES

2 pts: throwing things across bar
5 pts: smart off to your coach
5 pts: not leaving bar on time
5 pts: drunk dial your girlfriend
10 pts: not showing up to next bar
20 pts: getting kicked out of bar

DISQUALIFIED

Start a fight (sober ref's call)
Going home with your girlfriend

SPORT STORIES 5.1

The problem of youth sports and violence, in part, stems from inadequate role models and a lack of community consensus on proper response when an incident occurs. While I had many excellent coaches growing up, my primary role model was my dad, Roger Jamieson. He had played baseball his whole life and when he hung up his cleats for the last time, he went about coaching his boys. He understood the purpose of sports, competition, and winning and losing graciously.

In the spring of 1963, when I was a ten year old rookie and substitute player on the Indians, a Little League majors team, we were battling the Pirates one evening. The game was close going into the final innings; our team being behind by a run. The Pirates manager, Mr. Kennedy, has his star player and son on the mound. We had two men on base when our star player, Force Chamberlain, came up to the plate. Force, age 12, was huge and looked like the Babe to us.

The umpire behind the plate was a 16 year old high school athlete named Champ. Force knocked one right out of the park along the left foul line. It landed on the adjacent field in foul territory. From our vantage point, it looked like it left our field fair and then hooked foul. We, on the bench, erupted and cheered as our hero had won the game for us. Our celebration was short-lived, as the umpire called the ball foul. He alone had the only correct angle and the authority to make the call.

My Dad called time out and asked to approach the umpire. As soon as he did, Mr. Kennedy came bounding out of his dugout, yelling and all fired up, erroneously sensing my father was going to bully the teenage umpire into changing the call. My dad remained calm and put his arm toward Mr. Kennedy in an attempt to quell the anger. My dad then turned to Champ and asked him if he realized that if a ball left the park fair and then landed foul, it was a fair ball. Champ state he knew the rule and judged the ball as leaving the field foul. My dad has no qualms about the call.

Before leaving the plate, Dad turned to Force and firmly said, "DO IT AGAIN." The next pitch, Force knocked it out left-center. Clearly fair and farther than the last hit. The ball came to rest on Field One's third base dugout. My dad, a grown man and highly decorated veteran World War II Marine officer, submitted to the 16 year old's call. It was my dad's job that night to represent his team and ask the right questions about a questionable call. Mr. Kennedy lost his temper assuming my dad was trying to cheat his son out of a win.

I have stood on countless sidelines since that time, either coaching my own kids or simply being a parent spectator. It only takes one or two hot-headed malcontent parents (more commonly the father) to disrupt a game heckling a ref or coach or opposing team player. Typically they ride or chide a ref over calls of no consequence. The root cause for this behavior is multi-faceted, but its primal source is overprotection of their child. The ref, in their eyes, is interfering with the child's chance at success and perhaps monetary gain through scholarship. Many Boomer parents have difficulty allowing their child to experience sports without their interference. But I remember my father and his approach to sports and realize that long after we forget the score of the game and the events on the field, we will still remember how people conducted themselves and what type of example they made for their kids.

Jay A. Jamieson, M. D. (2009)
Team Physician, Sprague High School Wrestling
Salem, Oregon

CHAPTER 6

Fan–Sport Environment Interaction Disorder

"Serious sport has nothing to do with fair play. It is bound up with hatred, jealousy, boastfulness, disregard of all rules and sadistic pleasure in witnessing violence. In other words, it is war minus the shooting."

George Orwell

Splat! Splat! Splat! Three distinct explosions are heard within seconds. As the pageantry of hearing a young lady dressed in Red Wings attire sings a beautiful rendition of the Star Spangled banner to the game one crowd of Stanley Cup enthusiasts concludes, three octopi thrown from the stands hit the ice and explode. Due to the small pieces of gunk that the NHL officially describes as "matter" hitting and lubricating the ice the league has attempted to restrict the tossing of these sea faring animals onto the ice. Fans are eager for the league to allow them to continue this tradition and the Red Wings themselves sold t-shirts with "Al the Octopus" surrounded by a mug shot and the words proclaiming, "Don't Punish the Tradition". Whether just a tradition or a remnant of our blood thirst as people, the terminal nature of this act is of great concern to people and organizations that care about animal rights. Why is something so awkwardly violent part of the sports environment?

The Detroit Red Wings custom goes back to the 1950s, when two brothers running a local fish market threw an eight-armed creature onto the ice at a playoff game for good luck. "They get all the credit for it or the blame," said building manager Al Sobotka. Back then, a team had to win eight playoff games to attain the championship. Now it's 16 games." (Detroit News, May 23, 2008) Al himself has been threatened by the NHL with a 10,000 dollar fine if he swings or throws an octopus onto the ice and has personified the mascot fight literally and figuratively. A ritual such as throwing beings to their death if they are not already dead is an interesting dynamic of the sport fan dynamics.

A New England Patriot victory over the home town Minnesota Vikings featured a fan being arrested after he threw a beer onto the field that hit football quarterback Tom Brady. A 31-year-old father, Brad Reiland tossed the beer in reaction to the 17-0 lead that the Patriots had just taken over his team at the Metrodome. After Tom Brady completed a touchdown pass to Ben Watson, the fan committed the act and was then arrested in the bathroom while trying to scrub paint off his face. Reiland apologized and stated he did not remember much of the incident because he was intoxicated. Reiland had to pay a disorderly conduct fine and nervously awaits the day when he will have to explain his action to his now 4-year-old son.

In Cleveland, NFL referees are aimed at over and over by fans in a near riot as they throw beer bottles onto the field in a reaction to a call in the game. With caps on, the beer bottles became missiles with fatal consequences. Similar incidents have led to a policy of removing bottle caps from the plastic bottles and not allowing fans to have the caps. This allows physics to work in favor of safety, as a bottle without a cap cannot sustain its volume throughout the flinging from fan towards their target. Alcohol is still a popular choice for fans to throw as it essentially started the Pacers-Pistons riot and is often less of an instigator in countless other cases of athletes getting beer poured on them or thrown at them.

Does this behavior trickle down to other organizations? I myself was hit in the arm with a dead sparrow spray painted blue while a member of the Jamestown High School Blue Jay hockey team after scoring a goal against our rivals. This was not nearly as bad as when our home fans would repay our rival Minot Magicians for their antics by throwing a live rabbit onto the ice of the John Wilson arena. The brutality of a rabbit hitting the ice was something of a morbid nature as its back legs were instantly broke from the fall onto the surface. The schools tried very hard to eliminate such behavior from the fans and at best were able to set strict enough codes where most fans chose to throw stuffed animals for the convenience; however, there were always the exceptions.

Ice hockey games have been delayed as fans throw pennies onto the ice. Interestingly, the pennies melt through the ice in a clever way. Unfortunately, pennies can be a career-ending injury if a knee is blown out when a metal skate blade hits them. Fans who wish to throw items in a positive manner at a hockey game are allowed to throw their hat onto the ice if a player scores a hat trick, which is the traditional term of endearment given when a single player is credited with scoring three goals in an ice hockey game. Fans willingly throw their favorite hats to a player on the ice. Fans themselves seem disruptive and willing to join in anarchy and disrupt the flow of the game or take aim at an opponent with a projectile, sending violence towards the opposing player.

Animals and objects often end up on the playing surface of sporting games. What is the satisfaction fans feel from this? In one way, the fan is extending a part of them onto the surface that they cannot get to themselves. By transferring themselves through the bleachers and onto the restricted area where the focus of their fanaticism is, they are in a way receiving pleasure in this deviancy. Fans who identify and cheer for their teams may lose focus and behave in ways that they would normally not do in order to shift, or change the outcome of the match, or perhaps to get the attention of an athlete that they are watching. There is a certain power in breaking a boundary that is both physical and perceptual, that fans who witness sports, and especially violent sports seem eager to test.

Sometimes words themselves penetrate the boundaries between fans, players and coaches. When asked about how he responded to chants to fire him that were shouted from fans, NFL coach Brad Childress took it in stride and did not seem to mind. The Minnesota Viking fans who were frustrated by coach Brad Childress and an offense that had not lived up to their expectations, chanted in unison, "Fire Childress" on several occasions. Coach Childress claimed that he did not hear the chants when asked about them by reporters. When asked about the fans' reactions at his Monday night game his response was one that reinforces the thoughts that there is a consistent interaction between fans and coaches that at least verbally ties them together in an interaction and penetrates the boundaries of participant and fan.

"It's funny because I can remember Andy (Reid) and his chief of security walking off and I obviously can't tell you any of the things that were said because they are not printable," said Childress, who was the Eagles offensive coordinator before taking over in Minnesota in 2006. "But they used to have a running joke. Anytime I walked with them there was a running joke: What's the worst thing somebody has to say today? And that would be walking on and off the field for the pre-game warm-up. God forbid a loss.

"That was absolutely maybe some of the most vulgar things that you've heard in your life. But it's amusing. It's what we do, though. You can't take it personally. I have problems when they boo our team but that's their prerogative. They pay a lot of money to get into that game and if that's what you're there for, as opposed to support your team, that's up to them."

Words across a median can even be more hurtful when directed with severe hate. When I did some research on Barry Bonds and his chase for breaking the all time home run record for most home runs in a career I was alarmed at the reaction he got in several baseball parks he visited. Fans near me at both Wrigley field on July 19, 2007 booed and taunted him as he hit two homeruns to move closer to Hank Aaron. In my section many remarks were made that could be interpreted as racist, while others were aimed at his alleged use of performance enhancing drugs. In St. Louis he received a little better treatment, but in Cincinnati, Reds fans near section 112 did not mind yelling "nigger" at him when he jogged past us to his place in left field. Only when a security guard who was female and black was working in our area did the racist comments cease. After the game a cursory search of the internet confirmed the interesting notion that Hank Aaron and several reporters also felt as though fans in Cincinnati were as tough on him and equally as crude. A fan I talked to at the St. Louis series told me that he felt the fans here were softer on Barry because they were fed up with their own perceptions that the media was attacking Barry in a way that reminded them of how the media turned on Mark. He also claimed to have been to many Cincinnati Reds games when Aaron was chasing Ruth and mentioned how vulgar Reds fans were.

To simply say that Cincinnati is the lone culprit is also wrong. Though there is no defense for such blatant public displays of racism, fans being disrespectful and launching epitaphs of hatred is nothing new to most cities. Sometimes players respond, and sometimes they let it go. Images of hockey players going into the stands to fight people reminiscent of the Paul Newman classic movie, Slapshot, is an image that leagues are trying hard to avoid. After a couple of prospects are hit in the head with an item thrown from the stands, the three brothers jump into the bleachers with their skates and full gear on and start punching people in the crowd.

The fight follows a plot that includes fighting, violence and deviant fun that has always ranked highly in terms of classic sports movies. Maxim ranked it number one in terms of all time "Greatest Guy Movies". As they say, "Why is this the ultimate Guy Movie? Because Paul Newman and the rest of the Charleston Chiefs live the life every real guy dreams of: They drink beer, get laid, play sports, gamble, watch TV, avoid relationships, and successfully put off adulthood. And at the end of the film, their immaturity is rewarded with a Main Street parade in their honor! *Slap Shot*'s got it all: sports, humor, male bonding, violence, more sports, plus some not-strictly-necessary-to-the-plot naked females. What's not to love"? (Maxim, 2008)

SPORTS RIOTS AND HOSTILE INTERACTIONS
INVOLVING FANS

Hockey fans are notorious for supporting their team and slugging it out with them if that's what it takes to win. As it turns out, the toughest goon in the movie Slapshot was based on a real character. Though the movie is guilty of reinforcing poor behavior for hockey fans, it was not the sole inventor of the concept by any means. In fact a deeper look at the making of the movie reveals an interesting connection between the media and the sport as it was at the time of production.

"Goldie Goldthorpe didn't get to play himself in Slapshot but everything about him, from his looks, to his antics, to his bodacious blonde afro, was copied and immortalized on film. A legend at 18 because there was a time when he had to be released from jail to play for the Thunder Bay Vulcans, Goldthorpe's history is a riotous collection of fights, suspensions and hockey hijinx. The man has seen and done it all. Like the time he was thrown out of a minor-league game for fighting only to run back onto the ice in his street clothes and shoes to start another fight. Or the time he jumped out of a penalty box and went after the referee, tackling him around the ankles before biting him on the leg. Or the time he went to jail for beating up a player on the tarmac of the Green Bay airport in Wisconsin. That player, by the way, was one of Goldthorpe's teammates. Then there was the time he broke a security guard's leg when an on-ice fight spilled into the stands. For whatever reason, Goldthorpe had more than one skirmish in the stands and not always with unruly fans.

"I was in the WHA at the time. I was watching a (North American Hockey League) game between Binghamton and Syracuse," says Goldthorpe, who had also played in the NAHL. "There was a brawl in the warm-up and Bernie MacNeil is mouthing at me and I said, 'You wanna go?' So I started pounding him (near the players' bench) then he moves and I knock out a security guard (who had gotten too close to the action). The police escorted me to a dressing room." Goldthorpe was involved in another off-ice brawl and this one likely cost him a role in Slapshot. In an NAHL game between the Binghamton Dusters and the Johnstown Jets, a nasty spat spilled into the seats with Goldthorpe smack dab in the middle of it. As fate would have it, the brother of actor Paul Newman was at the game doing research for Slapshot. Afterwards, when things had calmed down, Newman stopped by the Binghamton dressing room to talk to the players. As he walked into the room, Newman's brother was showered with broken glass and sticky Coca-Cola. The man who had thrown the bottle at the wall just above the doorway was none other than Goldie. "It was an accident but that was it. They thought I was an undesirable," Goldthorpe admits. "They thought I was too wild and I'd beat up Paul Newman." (www.hockeyfighters.com, 2009).

The nostalgic days of a hockey player beating a fan with his own shoe is not far away. In the 2007 Stanley cup playoffs, the notorious Philadelphia fans had taunted the young Pittsburgh Penguin team early and often. After winning in front of their crowd, the Penguins began to taunt the crowd and attempt to rile them up. "How much money do you guys make" was said by George Larque. "Hows it feel yeah!" Is exclaimed by Evgeni Malkin as he jeers into the crowd. A series of Penguins laugh at the crowd after both George Laraqu and Jarkoo Ruutuu leap towards the glass in a mocking gesture. Ruutuu taunted the Devils players and coaches in an earlier series, but instead in this series, he focused his pest like on ice antics on the fans (Youtube, 2008). The smack talk here is exactly what can trigger a thrown beer cup and lead to another malice.

In Europe, fans of football are not as likely to be looking to fight players as they are each other. The term hooligan is used by security to describe the well-known violence that is inspired by soccer games in England and other countries. The violence has been referred to as "the British Disease" and has been blamed for all types of vandalism, beatings and killings surrounding matches. Though this form of sport rage goes back to the early 1800s it began making headlines and attracting media attention in the 1960s and continues to evolve as gangs have grown with the times and now use internet websites for message posting and to communicate with other gangs to arrange fights.

Hooligans often travel to the opposing teams' city to vandalize their opponents' town. The Hooligans representing each team would square off and fight their battles, often expressing local, regional or national teams. What started as a battle of fists sometimes has become a battle of weapons. Perhaps even more alarming is the propensity of Hooligans to go after the police or security who tries to break up their fights. Many times the police who attempted to stop the fighting or vandalism was victimized and even killed.

Two terrible disasters inside the stadium attracted even more attention to hooliganism. On May 29, 1985 a Liverpool, England team played the Juventus, Italy soccer team in front of 60,000 fans. The crowd later described as "mostly drunk" began chanting, lighting fireworks and waving flags. When the fans of Liverpool stampeded towards their rivals police were unable to control the crowd. A retaining wall that separated the two rivals gave out under the pressure and collapsed down on the crowd. Thirty nine fans died, many of who were stampeded while attempting to run away from the wall.

The Hillsborough disaster of 1989 occurred in a cup semi-finals game between Nottingham Forest and Liverpool. An overfull stadium was bulging and a line of 2000 or so people needed to get into the game. The police felt as though they needed to relieve some pressure and allowed the fans to rush in and they swarmed into an already over-capacitated terrace. The weight collapsed the area and 93 football fans were crushed to death as policeman ran onto the pitch to stop the game.

These incidents were the cornerstones of several movements to control fan violence in the UK. The Football Spectators Act of 1989 Allowed courts to impose restriction orders on convicted fans to prevent them from attending matches abroad involving England. The Football Spectators Act of 1991 created three new punishable offenses for fans: throwing missiles towards the pitch or spectator, taking part in indecent or racial chanting, as well as going on the pitch or its surrounds without lawful authority. The Football Intelligence Unit was created to identify and track all known Hooligans and their intentions. They compiled a database of anyone convicted of any football-related misdemeanor, with those on the list being banned from traveling abroad to watch football and, in serious cases, from attending matches in Britain. Not to fall behind, Hooligans are using mobile phones and the internet to change locations of the fight, and are seen traveling by bizarre routes to outwit police and continue their craft.

In other parts of Europe, sports clubs are also organized at a local level. Because players play in the same community throughout their lives the competition can become intense. Local community members feel a greater sense of pride as fans because they can identify with the teams from their hometown. Though violence is evident in some popular European sports such as rugby and soccer, there are not as many reported problems with violence reported to media and authorities in every country.

A referee was struck by a fan with a water bottle in a top level professional hockey game in Norway. After an initial stoppage of play and removal of the fan the game resumed. After the game the situation was resolved with a phone call between the fan and the referee. After the fan apologized and they talked for a while everything was forgiven. The referee was quoted as saying he would not press charges and that he forgave the fan (Rebellion Hockey, February, 2005). This situational example provides insight into the sporting relationships in Norway and some differences with the North American Model.

Identity and personal stake in teams

Identity and being able to identify with an athlete or team has been a reason that many people feel obligated to engage in an altercation with an opposing team in Hooligism, and this is also seen in other sports where fans have a strong community tie with a team. Parents and family members of the players have an inherent stake and tie with the team. Just as in the cases of parents coming down to the defense of their children, a recent NCAA basketball game featured the rage of an angry sibling looking out for his brother on national television. "Jonathan Xavier came down the stands and jumped over the Providence bench during a nationally televised game on Jan. 17 to confront a referee. He was upset no foul was called after his brother, Providence guard Jeff Xavier, was hit in the face by a Marquette defender's arm while he was driving to the basket." (ESPN, 2009, p. 1). It would make sense that family members should stand up for each other, and it appears that the sports milieu is not immune to the emotions that accompany them in a competitive environment.

Often fans can have other motives, such as when pornographic star Brittney Skye ran on the eleventh hole of the US Open in June of 2003. The eventual US Open Champion, Jim Furyk was hitting an impressive putt, at the Olympia Hills, Illinois golf course. Skye snuck underneath a boundary rope that is designed to separate fans from the players attempted to present Furyk with a flower. Skye was topless and had the URL of the online casino written on her chest and back. "She was right there, 4 feet away, with a flower of some sort," Furyk said. "It was a total shock. I turned around and just went, 'Whoa!' You don't know how to react" (NBC6, 2003). The sponsor, GoldenPalace.com had supposedly informed her that she would not be arrested but asked to leave the golf course. To her surprise, she was instead taken to jail. The situation was described as embarrassing for the married Furyk, and the consequences for Skye included a night in jail, six months probation, and a 1000 dollar fine. Skye was quoted by Sports Illustrated as saying, "…that she was supposed to deliver flowers and a hug to (Tiger, Ed.) Woods but bagged it at the last minute because he was "playing so poorly." Skye instead decided to grace the front-running Furyk with her presence. Other than being detained for several hours for disorderly conduct, Skye had a blast at her first golf tournament. "I'm definitely a fan now – I didn't know it was so entertaining," says Skye, 25. "Some of the players are sexy. I would love to have Tiger, Jonathan Byrd or Fredrik Jacobson in one of my movies" (Shipnuck, 2003). It seemed that combining sex and golf was a publicity blitz for all involved.

Sex in sport is even more controversial when it involves athletes and aggression. The notion that many athletes support the belief that women constitute "groupies" in sport worlds is very problematic. If athletes are not respecting their fellow community members it is likely that they would consider a criminal act against a non-athlete to be less of a problem. If institutions support athletes regardless of their behavior, this problem will only get worse. Institutional failures to hold athletes accountable for deviance and criminal acts must be identified and corrected before serious harm occurs.

Support from fellow athletes for using physical force as a strategy to attain something they want is a dangerous tenet to have in your organization. Hubris and group thinking that athletes are superior to the common person can precipitate a hostile environment. Perceived cultural support for domination as a basis for status and identity among athletes can lead to the over-conformity that can plague a sports organization. Athlete's immediate reference group, the structure of the game, rules from officials and the predispositions we feel go along with being a member of the sporting culture of a chosen sport are significant factors in the violence between athletes and fans.

There is very little research available on how watching sports may influence violence in everyday relationships of the fans. It does appear that spectators at non-contact sports have low rates of violence relative to fans who view contact sports. Spectators at contact sports have rates of violence that constitute a problem in need of analysis and control; however, rates today are lower than rates in the past. Perceived violence on the field is positively related to crowd violence.

Historical, social, and political issues underlying spectator orientations are a major factor in sport violence events. Rivalry games are usually filled with stories of past events and seem to bring out the best and worst in the fans and players involved. In the cases of college teams, a shared recruiting battle can launch a long period of resentment. Eric Gordon's controversial signing with Indiana University was met with a great deal of anger and aggression by Illinois fans who had thought they signed the NBA bound basketball recruit. When Eric played against the team he had originally signed with, he was met by a chorus of boos and insults. His coach, Kelvin Sampson, was also the target of fan comments, before a less than cordial attempt at a hand shake and discussion with Illinois coach Bruce Weber after the game proved that the conflict was also felt between the coaches.

Crowd dynamics and conditions are another component of under-standing crowd violence. The composition and size of the crowd are key variables. Warmer temperatures, cramped seating, the age of the fans, their motivation for attending, or even a sudden change of weather can instigate an altercation. Snow on the ground in Seattle led to a snow ball fight between the fans and a football player for the Seahawks. New York Jets defensive end Shaun Ellis was fined $10,000 by the NFL for throwing snow at fans following the team's loss at Seattle.

Alcohol consumption by spectators presents a unique challenge for sports officials. Beer can be sold easily and generates a nice profit. Many sports teams and leagues are sponsored by alcohol and beer advertisements. At the same time, the problems with having intoxicated fans in the crowd are abundant. Riots and anger can erupt if beer is offered and then taken away, whether purposefully, or even if the beer simply runs out. Many major sporting events have already limited the consumption of alcohol at sporting events, and even the times in which it can be sold. Usually sports are not allowing booze to be purchased towards the end of the game. This helps with driving issues as well as people who are going to over identify with the end result of the game or have been drinking for too long.

The meaning and importance of the game as well as the relationship between the two teams are another component to consider. Teams that do not play often may not be a big rivalry, however, if it is for a major trophy or championship it could be the start of a fierce game that will lead to violence. Alternately, if two competitors with a history of bad blood are playing in a sport, it would probably be violent regardless of what place the teams were in. This is especially true if each side is supported by fans who have a strong personal identification to the team.

Altercations and group dynamics in the competitive spirit

Crowd control strategies at event as well as local by-laws protect against field encroachment should be put into place in order to deter acts of violence. The rules are coupled with punitive legal responses to those involved in anti-social fan behavior. Heightened police presence at the end of play and at big games makes sense. Hi-tech surveillance systems and control rooms that monitor terrorism alerts are the norm at most large facilities. Families are enjoying their own areas in some stadiums, while other stadiums are considering banning people under the age of 18 from watching certain sports.

Facility improvements such as remodeling stadiums to put teams and fans on opposite sides of the field are becoming common. Protective tunnels and permanent canopies are being used to shield players from fans, along with walls, nets, plexi-glass and a wide assortment of barriers. Court rooms and jail cells inside stadiums are allowing people to go through the criminal justice system while still at the game. This is a constant reminder of the seriousness of misbehaving at a game. Having a fair and systematic way to process the crimes and social problems that occur at a game is a visible way to let fans know that misbehavior will not be tolerated and sends a message of a necessity for compliance to those who go to the game looking to misbehave.

Despite these attempts at controlling fans, incidents are still occurring. The brawl that happened in Detroit made all of the headlines. Unfortunately, many smaller instances of fighting are common place at many sporting events all the time. Chicago Cubs Fans vs Chicago White Sox fans are one example of a rivalry that seems to always involve fights and misbehavior.

Since the teams began playing each other in Interleague play, the loveable Cubs, have been anything but loved by White Sox fans. The White Sox winning a World Series, while Cubs fans continue to wait has served as a catalyst for many fights between fans at bars, in homes, in streets and of course at the stadium. The internet is full of clips of fans fighting each other in the stands in the name of baseball fandom.

The role of the media is hard to ignore in these instances. What role do these images have in future actions? Does watching a movie about hockey fighting when you are young make you more likely to fight or approve of fighting when you are older? What about shows such as Sports Center that show fights over and over again, or shows like Jim Rome is burning that reinforce the tough image of pro-athletes and the fighting mentality? Movies such as Slapshot seem to influence other violent sport movies, as they may have even reinforced the notion that other sports would be more fun if they were violent and sexual. In the 1990s the movie Happy Gilmour appealed to a new generation of sports fans who enjoyed hockey, violence, sex, through the context of a seemingly "boring" sport.

What role do movies that glamorize sex and violence as being part of sports such as "Happy Gilmore" have in actual events that occur? In the movie Happy Gilmour, a violent former hockey player brings a rough style of playing golf and the media supports the deviant actions of the Adam Sandler character. Fights with Bob Barker, alligators, several fans and an intense rivalry with a morally corrupt competitor provide some of the entertainment. In order to get "tougher" for hockey tryouts Gilmour allows a pitching machine to continuously hit him. The violence is coupled with sexual content in the form of jokes of topless women attending the PGA events out of excitement for the violent and exciting style of golf that the character plays. The idea of nudity and golf becomes even more apparent in the part where Gilmour signs a young lady's breast with his autograph and then repeats the action for an elderly lady by signing her breast.

The movies of Adam Sandler also include several football movies that provide entertainment by using sports violence and sensational action to tell a sport story. In Waterboy, his character Bobby Boucher is a ferocious middle linebacker who delivers bone crackling hits and overly aggressive antics throughout the movie. The Hollywood version of the football game glorified the big hits and top plays while giving images of a rougher, dirtier, and sexy version of big time college football. In the longest yard, Sandler's character uses the violence of football as a cathartic break for his fellow convicts and spends most of the movie fighting people, swearing and breaking all kinds of rules to beat the guards on behalf of the inmates in a remake of the original classic. Just as the Bad News Bears became an icon to a second generation of overachieving little leaguers, the remake of the longest yard engrained the rough images of football in a prison to another generation of sports participants.

Commercials on television are also apt to glorify rough and violent sports, such as when Miller Lite's famous super bowl commercial showed sports fans arguing over what to watch between golf and football at a bar. Miller Lite challenged people to remember that they could have great taste and less filling beer, just as they showed a parody of what would happen when one wanted to combine both golf and football. In the clip, "Davis" prepares to tee off he is smacked by a bunch of American football players who block his drive as if they are blocking a kick. They knock him to the ground and stampede him. The commercial continues and shows more rough plays and the golfer blitzed to the ground again and chases him all over the golf course. At one point he does dodge several football players and stops to taunt one of them by grabbing his face mask (http://www.youtube.com/watch?v=NA97kzai-Ew&feature=related).

In another famous NFL Superbowl commercial, fans are introduced to a mythical linebacker named Terry Tate, who is sent from Reebok to work for a pretend Feltcher business firm. Tate brings the violence of the football field to the real world, by transferring his skills into a business setting. Tate patrols the office in a series of commercials where he is the office enforcer. He uses a ferocious full body tackle to knock an unsuspecting co-worker to the ground sending his papers flying. Tate yells at the man that his break was over 15 min ago. Tate's angry approach and plethora of tackles to make people file cover letters on their tps reports has and then goes on to explain in an interview that he likes to use intimidation to enforce company policy (Youtube, 2008).

The role of media in human development is an area that has received some emphasis. Many social and psychological factors presented by the media can influence the sports environment. Proponents of Social Learning Theory argue that what we are exposed to in the media will influence our behavior (Bandura, 1973). By mere exposure our actions and behaviors can change to conform with what we believe to be acceptable. In situations where we do not have our own experiences to judge the social consequences of a decision, it would be possible that outcomes we had seen through vicarious situations in the many forms of media may be substituted for our experience. Our personalities are shaped by what we see through the media (Bandura and Walters, 1963).

Considering that the average human engages in sports throughout their life time it is understandable that the person's attitudes and choices will change for a myriad of reasons. In most countries, the average person is also bombarded with media of all types throughout their lifetime. These images will have some consequences on the moral development of these individuals in sport and in life (Gough, 1998). Early exposure to violence for young people should be avoided. Unfortunately, violence seems engrained in our culture early on from both a participant and spectator point of view.

Children under the age of two do not watch a significant amount of television and if they do they will receive messages based on images, not plot or intended materials (Bearison et al., 1982). One way that media can influence children is through story books. When parents put children to bed at night they often read them books (or let them watch videos based on these books). It has been well-documented that story books can effect the cognitive development of children (Bandura and Walters, 1963). Books are often known to be powerful influences of society. Books have been banned by dictators as well as parent–teacher committees throughout history for their power in shaping our culture. Despite overwhelming evidence of influence, there is little if any research on the role of children's books on the recreational sports development of an individual.

This is not a new issue of violence in children's books. At a time when books did not even mention sports there were violence issues. Brothers Grimm and Hans Christian books have been terrifying children for ages. The big bad wolf, trolls witches and other assorted evil characters that love to eat children have had a long history of scaring kids. Plots that seem gruesome or inappropriate for kids remain top sellers in all forms of media. Violence in the media surrounds children in a multitude of ways and it is evident from this research that it starts very young.

Though it does not have a direct connection to sports, the images of death and violence could not have been good for the development of the individuals who read these types of storybooks and then are subjected to constant violence on television the remainder of their lives. In one research study on the effects of violent electronic media, the authors found support for a family context hypothesis. They proposed that family conflict is positively related to violent electronic media use because family tensions will be reflected in children's interest in media with violent content (Vandewater, 2005).

Most marketing and steering attempts are specifically designed to influence the people that view them. Just as their influence exerts itself in all realms of life, the media influences sport in that same fashion (Whannel, 2000). Sports Marketing is the specific application of marketing principles and processes to sport products and to the marketing of non-sports products through association with sports. The media has a natural obligation to report on sports. This process itself is not very objective and allows for biases and even a difference in moral and ethical reporting for all media sources. The power issues, politics and money involved are often cited as a reason that sports are reported in the way we see them. Professional sports organizations must use the marketing mix to protect their image and brand name. The media can be a strong influence on sports attitudes and behaviors (Morra and Smith, 1996).

Sport marketing in the media can be used to build and maintain a system of economic reinforcement for those who control the resources and allow them to continue to dictate the demand for the sport they hope to continue to sale. Violence is used to hook people into trying a product or getting their attention long enough to see the other values in the game. The violence baits a potential consumer into trying the sports experience in hopes that they will support the organization in the future. Fans who enjoy the team will buy tickets for the game, products and view games on television or other media sources.

Tactics that build the commitment of the fan to the team for commercial purposes will also create strong bonds of identity with the team that can create deeper problems down the line for the fan who is strategically linked with the team. Sport Environment Interaction Disorder in fans is being enabled by the representations that the media markets towards the fan. The social consequences of an entity that has become so proficient at building consumer loyalty and commitment are being seen in venues all over the world by fans who are acting outside what is acceptable to our laws. People are ignoring laws and what seems like common sense in order to get closer to their teams and athletes, and facing the ramifications.

In this sense, Sport Environment Interaction Disorder can be classified as a Social Dysgenic disorder. In this concept, many psychological problems spring out of interpersonal interactions and most of psychological problems involve human relationships. The phenomenon and theories associated with social dysgenic theory are seen in the sport milieu and provide a rich collection of observed applications. Aggression, rage, and the power relationships that are present in sports as well as the modeling, conformity and the role of the "self" seem to have a similar and often apparent connection with the theory as it is described in non-sport situations. The concepts and context in which they were intended are usually relevant despite the differences in the environments that many of these theories have been formulated and tested in.

Sport Environment Interaction Disorder is in essence a unified theory of bringing together the multitude of theories that are contributing to understanding why fans act the way they do. The development and acceptance of many traits and characteristics that have been problematic and plagued the rightful and ethical way in which people are expected to act, is why the theory has a negative connotation. It is through the social therapeutic approach of personal and community interventions and the structuring of the sport environment by qualified professionals that we hope to provide a cure for the many symptoms, issues and problems that plague communities and organizations who have been saturated with problems between the stake-holders and people passionate about sport.

A multi-disciplinary approach is needed in order to gain a broader perspective of how the media influences violence and uses it for commercial gain. Semiology, "the study of meaning production" has been the traditional way to study media influences (Barthes, 1967). Because different people can gather different meanings based on the images they are presented it is important to factor in as many useful variable as possible. The issues call for researchers to look for connections that fuse ideas from different knowledge bases that explore the connections between violent sports actions and media influences on fan behavior. Peer influences of fans are of note, as fans can over react to one emotional fan in a negative way. Parents, coaches and educators need to address proper fan conduct and include performance contracts if needed.

Fan interaction disorders will continue to cause harm to society as long as it is not addressed in all disciplines that influence the development of our communities and individuals as a society as we seek to support our teams as fanatics in a more positive manner. Sport can be an amazing spectacle, rich in personal and community benefits when administered properly. Violent sporting events do not seem to have much support for being healthy for communities; however, it is even more clear that violent behavior from fans should not be tolerated by sports enthusiasts who appreciate the sanctity and ethos of fair and ethical sport.

SUMMARY

Fans of sports have been a vital component of athletics and a necessary part of the game. Their emotional and monetary support of the team has been both a positive and negative in the rise of elite sport. The rise of elite sport itself is both a negative and a positive factor in the overall leisure environment of communities. Without stakeholder and community interest, sport would be scaled down and nothing like what it has evolved into today. Fans themselves have changing roles, depending on their connections and identification with teams. The relationships fans have with the team can dictate the level of involvement in aggressive or deviant acts as well as the situational factors that the fan is experiencing while watching the game. If spectators view on the field violence they will be more prone to act aggressively at the stadium and for some time when they leave. Violence and shouting by the crowd are often said to have little effect on play, but the authors of this text book have shown considerable support for players, coaches and officials being aware and effected in some manner by the crowd, however, the significance of the relationship would depend on the spectators amount and means of violence, as well as the athletes own psychological abilities to allow the act to actually effect their play.

The public nature of sport has an inherent attraction to the community. Fans, sport and violence continue to have a dynamic interaction that occurs within different settings in venues all over the world. Fans and their support have made Alex Rodriquez's alleged steroid use in private, a public matter in 2009. Fans and their support of Chariot racing led to a political riot in Roman times. The role of the sport fan needs to be examined and continuously researched so that we can better understand the behavior and collective identity of those who make up the organization, and the community to which they belong.

REFERENCES

Bandura, A., Walters, R., 1963. Social Learning and Personality Development. Holt, Rinehart & Winston, New York.

Bandura, A., 1973. Aggression: a Social Learning Analysis. Prentice Hall, New Jersey.

Barthes, Roland, 1967. Elements of Semiology. Jonathan Cape, London.

Bearison, D., Bain, J., Daniele, R., 1982. Developmental changes in how children understand television. Social Behaviors and Personalities 10 (2), 133–144.

Detroit News, May 23, 2008. Octopi will fly as cup final approaches. Retrieved May 27, 2008, from the Detroit News website: http://sports.yahoo.com/nhl/rumors/post/Octopi-will-fly-as-Cup-final-approaches;_ylt=AtzasHgsCr2MPMQhXS.RuUU5nYcB?urn=nhl,84159.

Duquette, B., Tragis, J., 2009. Veteran youth hockey coach Wolter to be honored. Retrieved at http://newsminer.com/news/2009/feb13 2/15/2009.

ESPN, 2009. Providence Friars fan who rushed court held without bail. Retrieved January 27, 2009, from the ESPN website: http://sports.espn.go.com/ncb/news/story?id=3864193.

Gough, R., 1998. Moral development research in sports and its quest for objectivity. In: McNamee, M., Parry, S. (Eds.), Ethics & Sport. E & FN Spon, London.

Hockeyfighter.com, 2009. The man behind the legendary film character. Retrieved January, 18, 2009 from: http://www.hockeyfighters.com/Forum/phpBB2/viewtopic.php?p=32282&highlight=zealot.

Jamieson, L., 2009. Interview with Dave Jamieson. Current and long time youth baseball umpire. January 18, 2009.

Jamieson, David L., 2009. Personal account of violence in sport, February 2.

Maxim Magazine, 2008. 100 Greatest guy movies ever made. Retrieved December 15, 2008, from: http://www.filmsite.org/maxim100.html.

Morra, N., Smith, M., 1996. Interpersonal sources of violence in hockey: the influence of the media, parents, coaches, and game officials. In: Smoll, F.,

Smith, R. (Eds.), Children and Youth in Sport: A Biopsychosocial Perspective. McGraw-Hill, Boston.

NBC6, 2003. Streaker stalks U.S. Open champ: Jim Furyk calls incident an 'embarrassing situation'. Retrieved December, 28, 2009, from: http://www.nbc6.net/sports/2272724/detail.html.

Rebellion Hockey, February 3, 2005. Hooligans assault official in Norway's top league. Retrieved February 4, 2005, from: http://www.hockeyrefs.com/intheheadlines/02032005,2.htm.

Vandewater, E., 2005. Family conflict and violent electronic media use in school aged children. Media Psychology 7 (1), 73–87.

Whannel, G., 2000. Sport and the media. In: Coakley, J. (Ed.), Handbook of Sports Studies. Sage, London.

Youtube, 2009. Hockey fights with fans. Retrieved May 28, 2008, from Youtube website: http://www.youtube.com/watch?v=9tHJRyNG0ZI, http://www.youtube.com/watch?v=NA97kzai-Ew&feature=related, http://www.youtube.com/watch?v=tbSpAsJSZPc&feature=related.

FEEL GOOD 6.1

The Good Coach

Jordan Wolter was honored as Alaskan Coach of the Year for 2008. His hockey record includes college hockey at the University of Minnesota – Duluth (1979–81) and St. Cloud State (1981–1984). He then played for the Alaskan Gold Kings at which points he began coaching the FAHA Squirt team from 1986 to 1987. He coached two other teams and then spent three years with Lathrop High School hockey as their varsity coach. He then became the first coach for the Northern Alaska Association Grizzlies. He then became assistant coach for the University of Alaska Nanooks from 1992 to 1996 and then returned to FAHA. He started the Ice Puppies for young players and has coached all levels of the Arctic Lions and the Grizzlies. In 2005, during the hosting of the USA Hockey PeeWee National Tournament, he organized an outdoor 3 on 3 pond hockey tournament. In addition, his twin 15-year-old sons play hockey and Jake scored the winning goal for the nationals. In addition to serving, he and his boys are involved in community service work.

(Duquette and Tragis, 2009).

SPORT STORIES 6.1

I was umpiring a Pony Baseball game (11–12-year olds), when a coach ran out onto the field a couple times during live play. I had to remove him. This in itself was nothing, as he was simply over-exuberant and got a little carried away. After the game he approached me and very politely asked why I had "thrown him out of the game." As I tried to explain what he had done he disagreed and wouldn't listen to my comments so I said "enough, I don't need to argue with you" – he came unglued, and a couple of guys had to separate us. I thought it interesting that the League hierarchy asked me what his "penalty" should be, and I told them to him sit out two games and umpire two games. They did that. With over 35 years in Pony baseball as a coach, fan, umpire, league official, this is one incident that I recall.

David L. Jamieson (2009).

CHAPTER 7

The Role of Exclusion/ Inclusion

"Things might be simpler if we were all Polka-dotted."
Anonymous

The sport experience involves the ability of one to access and progress through a series of advancing goals until one either moves on to another venture or continues to the highest level of success. Along the path, known to many as the line from beginning a skill to completing a sport, obstacles may present themselves, thus breaches "an unbroken line" during the progression. In effect, for a number of reasons, this excludes an individual from continuing on the continuum to the final goal. If a player simply wishes to try other sport experiences, stepping off the "line" is perfectly fine; however, it is considered an ISM when a dedicated player ceases to continue due to some factor that excludes him or her. Thus exclusionary factors are discussed this chapter, and are presented to provide ways to avoid these issues, for it is exclusion that can be pointed out as a factor that creates frustration and striking out at the system, ergo, violent episodes.

WHO GETS EXCLUDED AND WHY?

This chapter will review many groups that are excluded or treated in such a way that they either experience many barriers and frustrations to cause difficulties or they drop out of sports altogether as a result of a systematic

CONTENTS

process that diminishes their importance as a group or individual within that group. The concept of exclusion refers to a systematic process of marginalization that results in denial of access. Categories of those who experience prejudice or the result of a faulty belief system vary according to societal groupings and location within a country or world theatre. The dynamics of exclusion may vary from society to society, but the results are the same – a particular group is placed at a disadvantage over something about which they have little control, and this disadvantage is the result of attitudes and beliefs that place them in an inferior or non-existent role within the world of sport participation. The disadvantage may be caused by a number of factors, the most common being either gender or the color of one's skin; however, it would be simplistic if those who fall into these groups are the only ones experiencing marginality and disenfranchisement. The main issue of exclusion depends on a faulty belief system of those in charge toward those with less where with all to counteract the exclusion that results. The basis by which people are disadvantaged includes the following.

Race

Many groups have been racially discriminated against in most countries around the world. These include those of African, Hispanic, Asian, Native, Caucasian, Pacific Islander, and many others who are categorized by the color of their skin. In America, there has repeatedly been a focus on African-Americans who were brought over from Africa and enslaved in the early years of the development of the United States. African-Americans were treated cruelly and were forced to work for the Caucasians in power at the time. As the country developed, slavery ended, and since that time, African-Americans have worked to achieve equality and involvement in American society, part of which is shown through sport involvement. Issues that have been fought for have been equal education, employment, compensation, and ability to participate within and among others. Within the sport realm, access to equal opportunity for sport is uneven with respect to race, with some sports attracting excellent athletes of a particular race and others having very little diversity. Coakley (2007) refers to racial ideology or the high expectation placed upon various races to excel in sport. For example, it is noted that African-American men are raised to believe that it is their "biological and cultural destiny" (p. 289) to play particular sports. Due to cultural or racial striations in cultures known for segregation and discrimination, sport opportunities have not extended beyond those sports for which there are facilities. Often these facilities are lacking since public investment in densely populated or remote areas is inferior to the investment made in more affluent neighborhoods. This bias regarding provision of better services for those who already have ample access and opportunity is apparent when conducting supply and demand data for communities. Often an affluent community will have many duplicated services, or as many as the market will bear in terms of fees and charges; whereas, a more densely populated, inner city community may offer only a handful of services due to lack of buildings and infrastructure. This disparity is depicted dramatically in the movie Hoop Dreams in which Arthur Agee and William Gates are followed from eighth grade through college to identify their path toward their goal to reach the NBA. Found on rundown outdoor basketball courts by scouters who cruise these areas to detect early talent, through a well-known basketball private high school feeder program, through different pathways to college, the lives of these two individuals could not be more starkly represented with respect to challenges with education, their daily lives, and their 3-hour round-trip commute to high school. Overcoming such barriers has been a testimony to the resilience of many inner city athletes who have been able to bridge the constraints and excel both academically and athletically; however, many are left behind. In areas where there are either no facilities such as pools, tennis courts, indoor community centers, and programs or such facilities have deteriorated, there is little opportunity for residents of those areas to swim, bike, experience adventure, stay fit, and pursue a large choice of activities.

In response to the Tiger Woods phenomena, interest in opening up opportunities for those previously unable to play golf has been instigated and been successful in developing thousands of would-be golfers. The appearance of an individual athletic success in a sport not usually available to people of color, golf is becoming a popular sport and one that has been made much more accessible, affordable, and available.

Exploration of causal factors surrounding marginalized groups such as African-American and Latino adolescents was conducted in a study by Jemmott III et al. (2001). In this case fighting behavior was studied to determine if there were predictors of adolescents' intention to fight by exploring attitudes toward fighting, perceptions of approval toward fighting, and whether they are confident of avoiding fighting. This study in comparing the theory of planned behavior with intention to act to the potential of fighting behavior was useful as a potential predictor of other disenfranchised groups as well and their potential for intervention prior to fighting and more violence, particularly in the sport setting.

Studies involving race and fans have been conducted to learn if individuals who are victims of racism are also discriminated against and treated differently in response to fan behavior. Back et al. (1999) studied the existence of racism in English football (soccer). It is suggested that the term hooliganism is one means of bundling reactions to behaviors that result from reaction to racial discrimination. A proposal to develop a framework for analyzing racialization in football was completed to include ways the context of culture, institutions, occupations, and sport may reveal the deeper discriminatory issues beyond the violent acts of those who disturb football events.

Further exploration of the ideology of all races, their differentials and the ultimate result when there are clashes would be a useful way to structure programs that educate to increase understanding of different groups and avoid issues of conflict and violence.

Ethnicity

Aside from the more obvious characteristics that describe what we attribute to race, ethnicity refers to a particular culture that could include a wider range of racial characteristics and other characteristics such as rituals, religion, daily life pursuits, and other factors. Persons of varying ethnicities often have a history of war, conflict, and other strife that can ignite a battle in the sport environment. An example includes the historical strife between British, Irish, and Scottish over differences in living, British domination, religion, mores, and other factors. These historical rivalries and hatreds often interfere with competition, progress toward excellence, and education. Ethnic minorities are classified less according to skin color, although there are variations of color that may be discriminated against, and more by cultural factors including religion, rites, and other daily living characteristics that are perceived by whomever is in power as "different". Such groups may vary according to how a particular country defines who is in power and who, as a result of an ethnic difference, may be culturally marginalized. Such is the situation with Native Americans in both North and South America, indigenous populations in Australia, certain types of Asian cultures that may come from a country not considered Asian, such as the Russian Asian population in China, and those discriminated against by a religious difference such as Judaism, Muslim, Christian, and other spiritual cultures. There has been considerable effort to improve an understanding of diversity according to ethnicity in the United States, a recent effort to change names of intercollegiate athletic teams to eliminate an impression of using Native American cultural tribes as names, mascots, and disrespectful images of the true culture. For example, in 2007, the University of Illinois successfully changed the mascot for the team who performed an Indian ritual dance before fans. Other campuses have also reviewed their approaches to honoring those who may have displayed discriminatory practices, naming issues, and other evidence to make sure that no group is isolated according to superficial stereotyping of their ethnic contributions to society.

Ability

Anyone entering the sport scene enters with an ability-set that is different from anyone else. Often, with hard work, differences in ability change at varying rates and all become skilled enough to contribute to the sport that is selected. Unfortunately, however, one's ability does not often matter when those who selecting teammates or group people by ability may not have the training to determine ways to balance sport involvement so everyone learns. If the activities are offered by a park and recreation department, for example, those in charge of either working with a volunteer organization or programming the activity itself are not necessarily trained and educated in sport to the extent that those in kinesiology, physical education, or sport management are. As a result, many different definitions of ability and grouping of abilities may not yield a positive result. Athletic groups that are mismatched by ability can be problematic for ability to develop the teamwork that grows with compatible readiness and ability. Those who are too skilled for the level of activity may become bored and frustrated; while those who have a skill level below the expectation may experience discouragement. Those dynamics bode poorly for a good experience. In addition, reliance on volunteers to run such programs without adequate training and expert oversight results in problems that center on frustration by coaches, parents, players, referees, and spectators.

The other aspect of ability concerns those who suffer from a disabling condition. Even if the Americans Disability Act requires accommodation of activity for those with disabilities, this group still remains marginalized in the local sport setting. The path for those who need accommodation to progress through an increasingly challenging sport experience is tortuous or non-existent. Often, programs for those with disabling conditions are separated from those without identifiable conditions; therefore, it is often difficult to fill such programs even if an attempt is made.

The third area of ability is the perceived ability or inability that may be an inaccurate assessment of what the interest in an effort toward the sport is on the part of the participant. Because of the rise of serious leisure, there seems to be less and less time to help individuals to cultivate skill. The best example of this is a personal one – one of the author's children signed up for football at age 8, and in the first practice was placed with a boy of 9 who was twice his size and weight who was instructed to "hit him hard." After three such efforts, when he was knocked head over heels, it was considered reasonable by the parents to have him drop the program and wait a few years to start up. In talking with the coach who had played as a quarterback for a Division I football team, he indicated that his reasoning for doing this drill was "to make the boys tough". In addition, the practices consisted of two-a-days for 2½ weeks with league play beginning after that. Obviously, such a short time to learn with such disparities in age, size, and maturity only exacerbated the possibility for injury, frustration, quitting, and other factors. One could ask: "And for what? A trophy for the Super Bowl-like end of season tournament for 8-9 year olds." This was more likely the one activity that many participants dropped long before they could realize their skills and move forward.

Gender

One of the most tracked issues in sport is that of gender disparity. Due to the effective and highly visible Title IX legislation in the United States and similar goals and efforts in most developed countries, and other countries' ideological quest for equality, sport opportunity for women athletes, coaches, administrators, faculty, athletic directors, officials, and students has grown rapidly. Regardless of issues with the implementation of Title IX, girls and women in secondary school and college experience many choices for sport, and if a similar sport is not available, it is possible to participate with men's teams. Position opportunities for woman have also been on the increase; however, there are still issues with career progression and compensation.

Sport and violence occurs in girls' and women's programs for some of the same reasons that evolve in boys' and men's programs. Incidents of anger and aggression that result in violence occur in contact sports that are played by women; however, it was noted earlier, that women's issues with violence do not tend to spillover to the extent of men's engagement in violence outside of the context of the contest. That noted, there have been some very highly publicized incidents in America and one in France that show that intentional violence does occur and the potential exists for some of the self-time issues on the rise with women's sports.

Texas cheerleader murder attempt

A mother was charged and jailed for attempting to arrange the killing of the mother of another cheerleader. In a distorted and twisted plot, this mom attempted to put out a contract to murder this person who bothered her because her daughter was so successful. The plot was foiled because the person whom she attempted to hire turned to the police to act.

Ice skating rivalry

In the women's figure skating world, Nancy Kerrigan and Tanya were rivals for top awards in national and international competition. Prior to the Winter Olympics, Nancy was injured in an attempt to debilitate her before the competition, and it was found that Tanya Harding had masterminded this effort.

French father's support scandal

The father of a girl tennis competitor placed a drug in the drinks of her competitors to reduce their alertness and ability to compete. His involvement was not found until someone succumbed to the drug and passed away. He then was charged with murder. These episodes that occurred in women's sports are examples of the lengths people will go to intentionally to improve their chances either themselves or for their children.

Another aspect of gender as an ISM is the role of women in the power structure of sport.

Welch (1997) noted the evidence of violence against women by football players by compiling information on 100 National Football League players who had been cited for off-the-field aggression against women. Types of citable problems included sexual assault and domestic violence committed by these individuals. Welch sought to learn if there was any correlation between player position and the violence against women. Noting that these individuals are regularly involved in collisions within the game, such activities were seen to comprise evidence of spillover effects. It was also suggested that misogynist behavior or dislike of women seems to increase due to the training of football players to physically dominate those in their relationships.

Another aspect associated with gender is the role that women play in the theatre of football and other highly visible sports – cheerleaders, support personnel, and concomitant hyper-masculinity associated with the marketing and implementation of professional men's sports. Foley studied American football in Texas (2001) and referenced young women in cheerleader roles as being seen as objects rather than significant factors. Another factor was the powder puff football game where senior girls dressed up as football players and football players dressed up as girls, again dealing with gender diminution to the overall important male role of football. These forms of reproducing power and gender are seen across many sports; however, football is the most visible and influential in creating strong male and female role modeling that is a precursor to the power and money role differentiation beyond the field.

Consideration of gender issues crosses male and female studies, particularly the development of feminist and masculinist critical research that is designed to serve as a basis for change in society. Feminist theory suggests that as researchers find ways to support the improvement of sport opportunities for women and girls, one must also contribute to actions that will effect change. To this end, feminist research has caused military programs to realign their sport programs to accommodate the demand by active-duty women in bases around the world. In promoting solidarity among the troops which are formed by men and women, bases are encouraging the development of new programs and better facilities that will encourage the current 11% of the force that is female to participate and have opportunity for an equally wide range of sport as that of their male counterparts (Sherman, 1997). In addition, sport development programs are following the escalating interest in specific sports such as hockey which has grown astronomically in the past 15 years (Elliott, 1997; Thompson, 2007; Morin, 2008). Starting with the instigation of intercollegiate hockey in the late 1990s, hockey participation has skyrocketed to the point where there are teams for all ages in most places. Currently, according to the most recent estimates, over 59,000 women and girls are playing hockey with the greatest number coming in women 20 years and over. The issue of whether supply is keeping up with demand is a challenge as more teams are formed and demands for ice time increase.

The role of media in the provision of more opportunities for women was discussed in a commentary on increased air time given to report softball, hockey, and the Olympics. In addition it was noted that the Women's College World Series netter over 1.6 million viewers which increased the number of girls interested in signing up for softball. The way in which this coverage featured successful women athletes as role models for those interested in playing these sports was also seen as a positive improvement in portraying women as athletes. Further, Malcolm (2003) studied how female athleticism is constructed by looking into girls' recreational softball. It was noted that the age group studied tended to exhibit exaggerated displays of femininity; however, these displays are typical of this age group and not attributable to the selection of the sport itself. It was suggested that other age groups of women may be more appropriate to study to learn how a female athlete develops, and how that development is either similar or different to athleticism that develops in boys and men.

Unfortunately, the picture for women in the employment world is not as rosy. In 2003, Wilstein noted that "women and minorities are losing ground with jobs in professional and college sports" (p. 1). The reason for this problem was attributed to the grading of professional sport associations who appeared to be lacking motivation to hire women. Other than the Women's National Basketball Association which was graded A, the National Collegiate Athletic Association received a B, the National Basketball Association and the National Hockey League both received a C, baseball a D, National Football League with a D−, and soccer an F. The rating was a wake-up call to those who need to be more aware of hiring practices; of course, it was not clear what the percentage of women to total hires was.

An increasing interest in the study of masculinist issues has also occurred. In order to understand the issues of masculinity and sport, several studies have addressed what factors might be prevalent with boys who commit violent acts in general. Benedict et al. (2002) studied several books that depicted men and boys involved in killing sprees, committing sexual abuse, harassment, and violence in Canada's junior hockey system, gang rape conducted as a part of hazing and initiation into groups, violence against women, and other types of male criminal behavior. The books that were analyzed, while not considered academically sound were credited for exposing the problems inherent in sport, and they contribute to a look at potential subculture in male sport. A research study that explored the masculine ideology with respect to aggression and violence indicated that "masculine gender role stress" (p. 97) contributed to heightened aggression and violent and could serve as a predictor of potential violence. Also, exploration of male sexual orientation similarly refereed to perceived gender role conflict when one does not like sport. Plummer (2006) noted that "sportophobia" (p. 122) links sport to expressions of tensions of male gender and sexual orientation. When interviewing gay males and their aversion to sport, particularly team sport because of the behavior of their non-gay teammates, bullying and other forms of ostracism caused negative feelings in the interviewees that caused them to ultimately develop a dislike for sport. This study similarly refers to gender role delineation for males in sport similar to females in sport and added meaning and sensitivity to what comprises a common problem of identifying masculinity.

Recent study even links hypermasculinity to war efforts in Iraq. Stempel (2003) studied 1048 Americans to learn of the relationship between televised sport and militaristic accomplishment. This linkage of sport to nationalism, particularly when a country is at war, provided a unique explanation of masculinity and images of what that constitutes among those who support war. The similarity in patterns of aggression and other forms of violence between sport and war was also deduced.

Religion

Violence in sport is equally prominent in sports rivalries that stem from religious differences. In fact, sport involvement is often encouraged by churches in order to gather youth and provide wholesome activity. Church leagues, however, get involved in the same activities as those not in church leagues. There are similar problems with altercations, often accelerated by the difference in religion. In many countries, religious rivalries that have gone on for centuries will cause eruptions in sport interactions. Further, more recently, churches and religious prohibitions against sport involvement on certain days or barring women involvement are causing strife and confrontation. The effort of women to gain ability to participate in sport in Arab nations is an example of religious prohibition and gender expectations of the role of women within the culture and faith (Ambah, 2008). Faith-based organizations are also playing an important role in connecting sport involvement to cultural relief projects by involving their parishes in efforts to improve neighborhoods and the plight of those who have economic difficulties.

Potok (2008) notes the role of theology, ideology, and approaches to hate and violence from a cultural perspective in Intelligence Report, a watchdog magazine for the observation and awareness of hate groups. He alludes to the rise of religious orders that deny that the Holocaust exists and identifies racism coming from blacks as part of this order. This is particularly noteworthy due to the many hate groups that couch their ideology in religion and commit heinous crimes in the name of their faith and as a justification for their behavior.

Studies of gender per se also have pointed to issues of conflict that may occur. Reuter and Short (2006) investigated injury and comparisons among non-contact sport according to gender, perceived risk and previous injury. There were shown to be significant differences among males and females and across sports in terms of fear of injury in that women were more fearful of injury than men. Both groups' experience with injury indicated a positive relationship with a previous injury and the fear of re-injury. Within this result, it showed that the fear was greater in baseball and swimming. The study also showed that males were less confident about the ability to avoid injury than females. It was suggested that this result may be due to a perceived greater competitiveness in men rather than women that would result in higher risk of injury. The potential pressure that athletes put on themselves was cited as a potential reason for fear and lack of confidence with regard to potential for injury. If other pressures are added, it is suggested that fear and confidence issues may be even more paramount. As for sports that had rates of injury, it was found that baseball was perceived to be the most at risk for injuries, and that track athletes perceived the highest rate of re-injury.

Gender and sex roles according to the development of fan behavior were explored by Wann and Widkill (2003) through a survey of 264 respondents. Masculinity was the dominant predictor of fan motivation except when aggregate scores for family motivation were calculated. It is ultimately meaningful to factor in the role of fandom into the efforts to handle fans at sporting events in terms of gender variables and possibly family variables. Further, James (2002) notes differences between what males and females appreciate when viewing men's and women's basketball games. Men appeared to appreciate the aesthetic appeal of both games, while women appreciated the aesthetics for women's basketball only. This study was valuable in showing the differences in reasons why individuals attend sport events and what they find most appealing.

As with all studies of gender roles in sport, differences and similarities, perceptions and problems all have significant contributions to the dynamic of game or contest view, and also have implications for how management deals with differences that can create a variety of situations. It is helpful to study fans in detail and understand motives not only from a consumptive aspect but also from a proactive aspect in planning events and contests that are ultimately appealing and positive rather than generators of issues and violence.

Social class

As mentioned in the information shared about entertainment and portrayal of sport experience, social class and status make for interesting comparisons in terms of access to opportunity, issues with haves and have-nots, affordability, handling intense practices, games and travel, building sport abilities, and handling interscholastic and intercollegiate competition. Those with little resource except for a basketball court put all their energies into being discovered by scouts who visit the inner city and follow children from as early as middle school through high school. In the documentary Hoop Dreams, a nine-year effort to follow two aspiring players, the path began in a run-down inner city basketball courts and ended in college effort to get to the NBA. Both of the lives of Arthur Agee and William Gates were shared including family life, love life, and travel to a catholic high school which involved a 1.5-h commute each way, educational barriers, and many other issues. Compared to children in the suburbs who have many opportunities to grow athletically, the miraculous progress of these two was noteworthy. Having membership in a social class gives access to many doors, and it often is the network offered by these connections that smoothens the process of achievement of goals.

Studies of hooligans and gangs revolve around the issue of social class gaps and lack of access to amenities of those with power and money. The use of the term hooligan refers to those who are considered groups that disrupt sporting events and other gatherings. Often viewing sport from the outside of the stadium, these individuals have caused the majority of problems in European and European model-based sport, particularly soccer.

Hooliganism has brought much despair to European football. The scene of stampedes and bleacher collapse and riots was no greater felt than in the 1989 disaster at Hillsborough, Sheffield, UK. Crowd frustrations and a penned in quality to the stadium caused 96 deaths due to a stampede. The resulting investigation and criminal charges were flawed as well, leaving many to wonder why the system failed (Scraton, 2004). In commenting on this social issue, it is apparent that those who are avid fans of sport but are also excluded or placed in inferior positions when viewing sport are at a distinct disadvantage and are also endangered by poor facilities and overcrowding. Those who afford better seats or seats at all are much safer at these events.

In the United States and many countries gang groups disrupt sporting events or create unsafe environments that affect the safety of those who participate and enjoy attending sports. The most recent gang survey revealed that there are approximately 26,500 gangs and 785,000 gang members in the United States who contribute to various gang-related crimes. Sport involvement and access has often been seen as a solution to mitigating gang or youth crime by providing intervention in the form of better uses of time. Special intervention is necessary to secure children prior to recruitment into gang activity; however, once someone is in, the main way to get out is crime, pregnancy, death, or a job. That groups of gangs look for ways to prove their loyalty in the disruption of lives and groups makes this issue difficult to handle within the sport environment.

Sexual orientation

Sexual orientation is seen as an important issue that has become higher in prominence in recent news. Fairness and equity toward those who become aware of a sexual orientation that is not the traditional heterosexual orientation are being argued in courts, in the streets, schools, churches, and practically every institution in America. Other countries have varying orientations to those who are homosexual and behaviors vary according to a range of acceptance to outright oppression. In addition, there has become a confusing separation of what is male and female, given rise by those who consider themselves bisexual or transgender. Early studies of these groups reveal similar experiences to other marginalized groups.

In sports, there has been a similar concern from those who feel that they have been victimized due to their sexual orientation. Further, Higgs and Schell (1998) suggest that athletes who are homosexual tend to select sport to play out that side of their being, and then display another persona in the work place or other areas of society. This reference to a double life was described as segmented into a front and back stage lifestyle. The claim that a person is gay or lesbian can create a violent reaction from peers who encounter these claims. Those who make these claims, or "come out", face bullying, aggression, violence, and other issues by their peers. The violence against those with a chosen sexual orientation that is against the heterosexual norm found in a masculinity-run sport model has been reported consistently in the news. The hatred toward homosexuals is similar to earlier hatred toward racial, ethnic, and other groups. The 2008 depiction of Milk, representing a gay city councilman in San Francisco during the 1980s represents the resentment that can lead to violence when one is openly gay. In addition, the military policy of "don't ask, don't tell" has had a tendency to keep gays and lesbians from feeling safe if they wish to state their orientation. Thus, it is important to recognize the dualism that exists in the roles established by those who are not the heterosexual norm. In the study by Higgs and Schell, it was noted that heterosexual women who play sports find little or no conflict with their athletic self and their heterosexuality. The softball environment, therefore, was seen to provide an opportunity for those who did not wish to "come out" to express their homosexuality. The management of this lifestyle, while not problematic as a heterosexual, did appear to have more concern about how to display their sport life. Also, while straight players had little or no difficulty expressing work and leisure differences, those who were homosexual felt that there was always the chance that their reconstructed lifestyle could be found out and result in marginalization and humiliation. While this study fell short of truly and deeply analyzing the nature of the differences between the two sexual orientations, and the athlete's leisure life, it is suggested that the interpersonal dynamics of the sport setting is much more complex than heretofore imagined. The obvious conflicts experienced by homosexual women, could also give rise to anger, frustration, and aggression in such a way that intra- and inter-team issues may provide a stage for violence.

In sport there is the perception that women who enter the sport environment may be predominantly lesbian, while men who enter sports are fully heterosexual. There are inaccuracies on both sides; however, there are prevailing power structures that exist that may preclude participation based on myths and fears surrounding one sexual orientation. Fears and ignorance lead to problems with the stigma attached to participation in sport; therefore those who declare themselves openly gay or lesbian may suffer the judgment that follows either from their peers, i.e., teammates or from a continued judgment outside the sport involvement. The former tends to occur if the players are male, and the latter occurs if the players are female.

Violence against women and men on the basis of sexual orientation has been well-documented outside of the sport arena. The Southern Poverty Law Center has documented anti-gay and lesbian violence along with many crimes that fall into the "hate" category. Crimes against homosexuals abound in areas where there appears to be ignorance and fear about these groups – homophobia that results in a desire to eliminate the fear.

Age

Generational violence based on age has been well-documented when considering crimes against the elderly, the establishment, authority, and other issues that erupt with violence. Unhappy youths engage in crime, often to prove themselves and challenge the authoritarian adults with whom they must contend. Taking it a step further, in sport, older athletes challenge younger newbies to become a part of a team through a series of hazing techniques that are often humiliating at the least and violent causing death at the most. Hazing refers to the ritualistic collection of activities that form an initiation into a group. These activities occur in any organization that has some form of membership acceptance with teams and sport organizations it comes with the new athletes who have made a team or sport group, with others it may be a fraternity, sorority, gang, social club, service organization, or other group. Hazing activities can be mild ways to place the new individuals through a ceremony that formerly results in welcome and acceptance to the new group. Hazing can also be brutal, wrenching, and life-threatening to those who are new and can cause illness, extended psychological issues, injury, and death.

Hank Nuwer from Franklin College has maintained an advocacy role against all hazing. In his website, www.stophazing.com, he chronicles the hazing incidents and the ultimate criminal action taken against those who performed acts of hazing that resulted in death. Many graphic resources are shown of people who have been left to die from a hazing ritual, have quit and sued a group, or who are trying to justify behaviors.

This topic is placed in the age section to note the power and authority of those who are older over those who are new or younger – athletic team hazing is a very fearsome and dramatic experience for young children. Hazing often involves tacit approval of a coach when those who are a few years older are left with the responsibility to "initiate" the new teammates into a ritualistic effort to build a team. Quite often, these rituals involve the following activities:

1. Being taped to an equipment cage.

2. Hauling water and equipment to practices and games.

3. Being required to do extra drill runs, and additional work beyond a particular practice.

4. Being attacked by fellow teammates.

5. Being kidnapped and taken to remote areas, often without clothes.

6. Have the appearance of or actual sexual contact by teammates.

7. Physical and mental intimidation and threats, some of which are carried out.

8. Drinking, chugging, and other dangerous games.

These incidents can result in many problems that fly in the face of team building, often backfiring and causing the athlete to quit, parents to sue, and injury or death. When the teammate tries to get the behavior to stop by telling a parent, he or she often gets shunned or continually harassed by those who initiated the behavior.

Anti-hazing laws and policies have abounded since several well-publicized deaths have occurred or many graphic events have been documented. Most noteworthy was a girl's volleyball team in Illinois that had an orientation that occurred near parents involved spraying the new teammates with water, feces, food, and other slop. This became a call to end hazing.

A personal experience and positive outcome involved the hazing of freshmen men's soccer players in the Midwest. The new players had been taunted and threatened by a group of senior varsity players for weeks. One by one the new players were dragged through mud, taped to equipment cages, chased or threatened. Those who have successfully eluded these threats were encountered at a team meal held at a home where parents and the coaches were. Outside, two players had shock collars placed on them and were run through the invisible fence used for pets. A parent noticed this, reported it to the school, and the offending players were suspended. The coach gathered parents and indicated that no hazing would be permitted from that point on, noting that he questioned his behavior as well due to his willingness to assign tasks to freshmen at practice that differentiated them from the rest of the team. He indicated from that point that he would cease to treat any player differently on the basis of age or newness to the team that all were the team, and all would share the burdens and development of team work. Further, he and other coaches from the school initiated a code of conduct that to this day is signed by all players entering athletic competition at the school. More information concerning solutions such as this will be articulated in the organizational solutions chapter.

There are many ways to define difference – while the above examples are those that are discussed and analyzed the most, many less obvious issues affect those who wish to play, participate, lead, or manage sport experiences. What about mild visual impairment, those with learning disabilities, left-handed participants, those with psychological disorder, and many others? If there is exclusion, what is to stop people from analyzing and excluding other groups for the same misguided reasons? Suffice it to say that exclusion does not work, inclusion is the solution.

What does an ISM cause in the sport environment? Regardless of the disparity, real or perceived power differences may lead to social formations that vie against each other. The remainder of this chapter covers typical scenarios in and around sport that involve stratification and conflict within, among, and outside marginalized groups.

POWER STRUGGLES AND INEQUITIES

The Mighty Ducks movie series chronicles the rise of a hapless team of pond hockey players from Minneapolis-St. Paul to a respectable tournament winning team. At the core of this rise is the wild and rich lawyer assigned to the team for community service for drunk driving. The class differences between the Ducks and other rivals are a consistent theme throughout the drama of their development. The D series themes have been apparent in innumerable sport films that have reached the top 50 all time favorites. These entertainment oriented plots in both non-fiction and fictional movies such as Varsity Blues, Slap Shot, Angels in the Outfield, Rudy, Hoosiers, Hoop Dreams, Friday night Lights and the like portrays the clash of the haves and have-nots. In depicting the long shot possibilities of typically young players or an older, end of career athlete, one is able to see the kinds of power struggles experienced between the protagonists and antagonists. Conflicts over homes, uniforms, behavior, entitlement, and athletic prowess fill the screen with the difficulties experienced when you just don't "fit into the sport" hierarchy. Ultimately in true "Cinderella" fashion, the long shot team wins, and everyone is happy. By reviewing all of the ways in which class conflicts affect the sport environment, movies and news reports reveal the following:

1. Bullying behavior is apparent between teams on the basis of social stratification.

2. Those without resources have little help to progress in the sport environment.

3. Teams with privilege have a head start in sport due to the availability of resources, facilities, and high level programming.

4. Breaking into higher levels of sport can be very difficult, if not impossible for those who have no monetary resources.

5. Opportunities for competition are not evenly distributed throughout communities, and often that distribution is to areas where people can pay for sport opportunities.

6. Evidence exists of positive and negative deviance, or playing that is acceptable to most even though it would not be tolerated off the sport scene.

7. Cheering for the underdog is one of the most appreciated aspects of sport involvement, and viewers love an unexpected winner, or one winning against the tide.

8. Power and money appear to be the keys in sport success.

9. The role of adults in youth programs is exaggerated but is also indicative of actual sport experiences.

10. Class friction can give rise to violent acts – fights, cheating, intimidation, and many other manifestations of re-violence of violent behavior.

11. Contact sports seem to be the most popular viewing experiences.

12. The role of race, gender, and other ISMs (Fig. 7.1) is alive and well as sub-themes within the movie entertainment industry.

Thus, it can be noted that sport as a mirror of society is portrayed through the entertainment industry, and one may learn much from an analysis of both real and fictional accounts of the sport experience. As such, though fictitious and exaggerated for the benefit of entertainment, the subtext of most sport cinema is based upon very real experience.

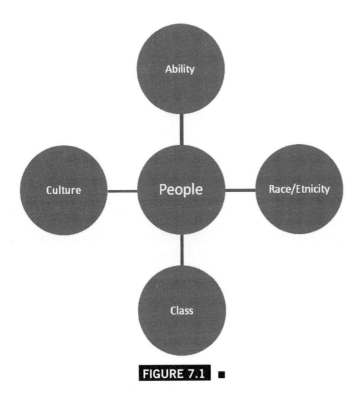

FIGURE 7.1 ∎

GANGS, INTIMIDATION, AND VIOLENCE IN SPORT

Why here in this text would the authors take time to write about gangs? It is suggested that there is a societal link between those who gather for a positive role in sport and those who gather due to disenfranchisement to handle their group with crime and antisocial activities. Also, gang activities occur with increasing frequency across the globe, and often these activities are anti-athlete, anti-athletic events, and anti-groups. It has been noted that there are labels applied to school groups that tend to define their role within the social structure – jock, nerd, gang, prep, retro, Goth, etc. The placement of groups along a strictly defined continuum may cause conflict between groups that fan out across school events and activities. Such is the plight between hooligans, spectators, and players in Europe. Attempts to deal with hooligan gangs who cause problems at events have been a challenge and come from social class differences and exclusion. Gangs exist around the world, and their defining commonality is exclusion – many gangs exist according to racial, ethnic, religious, hatred, or ideological definitions. All, however, have much in common with other forms of groups that are perceived to be more legitimate – a team, a social group, a fraternity, sorority, adult service organization. These are commonalities easily noticeable by those who are in such groups:

1. Each group has rules limiting membership.

2. Each group requires an initiation process to gain membership.

3. Each group agrees to a certain code or mission.

4. Groups perform ritualistic tasks and common rites such as handshakes, talk, and other symbols of inclusion.

5. Groups have certain rites that could be classified as hazing.

6. Groups exclude and often bully or intimidate others not in the group.

7. Members have to prove undying loyalty to the organization.

8. Handshakes, songs, repetitive chants, dress, appearance, speech, and other factors visibly define the group.

9. Actions of the groups such as activities, graffiti, logos, and fun define the group.

10. Many groups participate in criminal behavior.

11. Loyalty to the group defines all members.

12. People join the group because of a need for friends.

Gangs occur in every community, whether they are gang wanna-bees or they originated there. Gang activity has increased throughout the world and their prominence and sizes seem to be fluctuating depending on the existence of unemployed individuals with nothing to do.

It is the belief of the authors of this book that gangs and other groups really are not different from each other along the lines of similarity described above – the activities of groups bound by loyalty to a certain area whether it is sport, drugs, crime, or other factor often result in criminal behavior. In addition, those in gangs are part of a community that attends sport contests and influences the safety and level of violence that escalate among players, fans, referees, and other factors. The fan interaction chapter will further enlarge upon this aspect. Suffice it to say that disenfranchised groups can be a societal factor in causing violence in and around sport areas. Further, these groups may use sport facilities as a place to carry out visible and dangerous activities in the name of their group. This particularly applies to terrorism issues – where sport venues or large gathering of people are often targets for these groups.

In garnering safe gathering places, security measures have increased at all arenas and playing areas around the world, but particularly in the United States. Increase in security at Conseco Fieldhouse in Indianapolis is a case in point: bags are checked, people are routed through a security area, and crowd behavior is watched and dealt with. Security personnel view over 100 TV screens spanned out over all areas of the building including loading docks, and anyone visiting the building at any time must have an appointment and be met by the individual who is meeting with them.

GAINING CONTROL OF ISM ISSUES

Regardless of the group in question, it is imperative that there be an improvement in dealing with how groups affect each other, and how those who tend to build a case against a group are dealt with. In a well-publicized local issue dealing with racism against players of a local high school, the offending school was not permitted to host any home games for a period of time. In this incident, players from the opposing school were hounded and spit on with epithets referring to their race and ethnicity. While previously similar incidents went unreported, the principal of the opposing team's school took immediate issue with this, reported it to authorities who govern high school sport, in this case the Indiana High School Activities Association, and sanctions were applied rather quickly. Fortunately, nothing has been repeated.

There are many groups and individuals who base their philosophy on hatred of one or more groups. These individuals may be disruptive to a team or group of athletes, or they may attack based on the fact that there are athletes at school. They also may form groups around intense rivalries and cause many problems. As a young girl of 9, the author observed the annual football game in Paterson, New Jersey – Eastside versus Central High Schools. When the game was over, gangs thronged onto the field and broke up the wooden goal posts and carried them off. These activities escalated until some youth were pushed off the top of the stadium to injury and death. The next year, the game was held at an undisclosed location in secret with no fans.

In addition, random acts of violence in the schools have often pointed to disenfranchised youth who retaliates against the success of athletes by targeting them for their often ill-played-out massacres. Columbine High School killings occurred because two students were particularly incensed against athletes and felt they needed to die. Obviously being in a group is important and being accepted is a part of a positive high school experience; therefore, those who do not gain acceptance are marginalized, bullied, and hurt. These individuals often turn to methods of retaliation that are unpredictable and spontaneous. The dynamic, as it relates to sport, is that these self-same individuals may have been completely turned around if there had been a role for them in some group that worked along more positive lines.

WHAT ABOUT INCLUSION?

It would be irresponsible to conclude this chapter with only the exclusivity that abounds in traditional sport experience. Included here is an introduction to Chapter 9 which focuses on the role of organizations in providing solutions to the issues surrounding sport and violence. There have been many more issues around inclusionary tactics to involve groups whose interests and attempts to participate in sport have been elusive. Those who have been successful in addressing these concerns have included professional players, enlightened national organizations, and philanthropic people. The following examples will enlarge on these efforts.

1. Tiger Woods' widely publicized successes on the golf course have allowed him to introduce golf to a wider ranging group of interested kids. His golf programs include transportation to golf courses in areas where access is difficult due to distance and affordability. He has revolutionized golf education by making sure that youth get access and learn.

2. The National Collegiate Athletic Association (NCAA) has initiated programs to improve the general population of athletes by having

them attend Yes clinics in towns where the Final Four for sports are held. These clinics feature athletes attending the final four and include clinics for a large group of aspiring athletes. In addition, NCAA is rewarding their athletes when they are positive role models in their CHAMPS programs.

3. USPORT, a grant awarded to collaboration between Purdue and Indiana Universities, provides sport education to developing countries. The programs are designed to expand sport infrastructure in these countries and provide alternative to poverty-stricken youth to participate in specific sport experiences that are provided by those who have become trained through the USPORT training.

Those excluded may be included. It is the premise of raising the issues in this chapter that there is no valid reason for excluding any individual on the basis of an ISM. An ISM prevents all from participating and being of value in sport and culture. The creation of an ISM is the creation of a tacit approval to harass, hate, and bully. In no circumstances should there be tolerance or acceptance of any group benefiting over another group on the basis of hate or discrimination. To do less encourages marginalization and violence between the divided parties and as a result of being disenfranchised from sport opportunity.

It has been noted that the myth created by an individual to mock or separate another group is often out of ignorance. Those in leadership positions can affect change in dramatic ways by confronting the ignorance that so often divides groups. Quite often, when these issues have been confronted by courageous people, they have opened new opportunities for expansion of sport and cultural interaction. The most pointed example may be the focused targets toward the Muslim world. As it has become more understood, sport opportunities have increased. One noted accomplishment within the Muslim society itself has been the effort on the part of women to gain opportunity to compete. In an AP news release in the Washington Post, it was noted that a women's soccer team is fighting Saudi restrictions on female athletes. Their accomplishments gained them the opportunity to compete internationally, and now they are attempting to have this restriction lifted (Ambah, 2008).

It is expected that a combination of individual efforts made such as this and organizational efforts noted in the examples above will be a very effective force in ending the prevailing hegemony of male dominance, power dominance, and ideological dominance. Something about sport involvement seems to bridge gaps, change people's perceptions, and improves quality of life.

AN END TO HEGEMONY

With increased doors opening and opportunities increased, particularly when they are funded through new sources, the traditional male dominated sport structure will give way to more inclusive combinations that provide new insight on how to mitigate the negative aspects of sport and increase those experiences that are more fulfilling, safe, and fun.

It is expected that this power structure will no longer be able to sustain itself with male dominance and will give way to wider power structures of inclusion. While intensely corporate and bureaucratic, new mechanisms will facilitate this change in a faster manner.

Power dominance

Money dominance, i.e., corporate conglomeration support, will give way to other mechanisms such as those gained by more philanthropic ventures – What about an Oprah campaign, or one that is fueled by more concern about world hunger, the environment, the plight of youth, and end to genocide? Wealth is distributed among a much wider range of philanthropic people who have little to do with sport, or who have ability to change the nature of an outdated structure.

Ideological dominance

In a world that has nations that defeat the goals of one-half of their population, i.e., women, enlightenment gained through viewing broadcast media can change the system to open up to sport involvement. The role of women will continue to be challenged by women and those who care about the plight of women across the globe. It will become increasingly impossible to prevent women's involvement in sport, and it will become a source of pride to countries as they open their restrictions and enjoy the successes that accrue to their nation. It has happened before, why not again?

SUMMARY

In summary, an ISM is just that – a myth about a particular group. It is easily changed with education and enlightenment – more difficult to come by in the dark. It is highly important to open up and create an inclusive environment – this change may reduce in particular, violence against the very groups one is attempting to restrict – this opening up will add a resource to the sport world that will engender expansion and inclusivity. A bit idealistic, but stranger things have happened in the sport world.

REFERENCES

Ambah, F.S., 2008. A drive toward the goal of greater freedom: women's team fights Saudi restrictions on female athletes. The Washington Post, Tuesday, April 15, 2008, A9.

Beam, J.W., Serwatka, T.S., Wilson, W.J., 2004. Preferred leadership of NCAA. AQ3 Division I and II intercollegiate student-athletes, Journal of Sport Behavior, 27 (1), 3–17.

Bredemeier, B.J., Weiss, M.R., Shields, D.L., Cooper, Bruce A.B., 1987. The relationship between children's legitimacy judgments and their moral reasoning: aggression tendencies, and sport involvement. Sociology of Sport Journal 4, 48–60.

Brekken, Ted K.A., 2009. Personal account of violence in sport, February 2.

Cudney, S.R., 2000. Heroes, hoboes, and the question of ethics. Journal of Sport and Social Issues 24 (4), 370–379.

Dupuis, M., Bloom, G.A., Loughead, T.M., 2006. Team captains' perceptions of athlete leadership. Journal of Sport Behavior, 29 (1), 60–78.

Elloitt, H., 1997. Speak softly and carry a big stick. Ambassador, 24–29.

Farber, M., 2006. Tiny happy people (holding Sticks). Sports Illustrated May 15, 51–58.

Foley, D., 2001. The great American sport ritual: Reproducing race, class, and gender inequality. In: Andrew, Yiannakis Merrill J., Melnick (Eds.), Contemporary Issues in Sociology of Sport. Human Kinetics, Champaign, IL, 478 pp.

Garland, J., and Rowe, M., 2000. The hooligan's fear of the penalty. Soccer and Society, 1(1), pp. 144–157.

Jemmott III, J., Jemmott, L., Hines, P. & Fory, G. (2001). The theory of planned behavior as a model of intentions for fighting among African American and Latino adolescents, Maternal and Child Health Journal, 5(4), 253–63.

Karns, J., and Myers-Walls, J.A., 2009. Ages and stages of child and youth development: a guide for 4-H leaders. http://www.ces.purdue/extmedia/NCR/NCR-292.html.

Malcom, N.L., 2003. Constructing female athleticism. American Behavioral Scientist 46 (10), 1387–1404.

Miller, A.G., 2004. The Social Psychology of Good and Evil. The Guilford Press, New York.

The Four Faces of Anger. www.stressdoc.com/anger3.htm. Retrieved 1/28/09.

Morin, S., 2009. Play like a girl. USA Hockey Magazine 31 (1), 30–33.

Nixon II, H.L., 1997. Gender, sport, and aggressive behavior outside sport. Journal of Sport and Social Issues 21 (4), 379–391.

Office of Juvenile Justice and Delinquency Prevention, 2008. Fact sheet highlights youth gang survey. Juvjust https://www.exchange.iu.edu/owa.

Paul, R.J., 2003. the impact of violence, scoring, and regional rivalries – discrimination and the NHL. Journal of Economics and Sociology. Variations in NHL attendance.

Roberts, S., 2008. For the U.S., a new red alert. Sports Illustrated 109 (6), 88.

Weinstein, M.D., 1995. Masculinity and hockey violence. Sex Roles: A Journal of Research. Plenum Publishing.

Scraton, P., 2004. Death on the terraces: the contexts and injustices of the 1989 Hillsborough disaster. Soccer and Society 5 (2), 183–200.

Sherman, R., 1997. Fighting for women. Athletic Business, September, 53–59.

Singer, R., 2008. Policing dietary do's and doughnuts. U.S. News & World Report 144 (18), 29.

Stewart, K.G., Ferguson, D.G., Jones, J.C.H., 1992. On violence in professional team sport as the endogenous result of profit maximization. Atlantic Economic Journal 20 (4), 55–65.

Thing, L.F., 2001. The female warrior. International Review for the Sociology of Sport 36 (3), 275–288.

Thompson, H., 2007. Mothers know best. USA Hockey 29 (9), 40–45.

Ramsey, G., Rank, B., 1997. Rethinking youth sports. Parks and Recreation 32 (12), 30–34.

Welch, M., 1997. Violence against women by professional football players. Journal of Sport and Social Issues 21 (4), 392–412.

www.stophazing.com

Young, K., White, P., 1995. Sport, physical danger, and injury: the experiences of elite women athletes. Journal of Sport and Social Issues 19 (1), 45–62.

Case Study 7.1

A prominent parent, wife of an internationally famous entertainer writes a letter to the editor exposing some questionable practices in the local football league. When her son tried out as a new player, he was placed in line to play a position as middle linebacker, and the parents of a child who played that position last year filed a complaint. Then her son was told that he would be sidelined due to the fact that the former player had quit as a result of not being assigned the position. The coach who made the decision is not faced with the editorial and people with many opposing opinions on how to handle the issue. In order to provide a suitable answer to both parents, what should be done?

SPORT STORIES 7.1

At one of Matty's games, a Jamestown parent was so heated up that he had one leg over the glass about to go out on the ice because he felt the ref did not blow the whistle fast enough when a Jamestown player went down with an injury.

Dr. Ted K. A. Brekken, Ph. D.

CHAPTER 8

Spillover Effects of Sport and Violence

That tiger didn't go crazy….That tiger went tiger.
Chris Rock, Comedian

Popular American comedian and actor Chris Rock told this joke during the Never Scared tour on HBO after learning about a tiger that attacked entertainer Roy Horn of Siegfried and Roy. Though Chris Rock had the primary goal of being funny, he makes a great point in regards to the nature of violence. Just as the tiger has natural tendencies to be violent, the human spirit has a violent past that also included fighting for survival and resources to survive in a tough and unforgiving world. Various levels of social control in the spirit of progress and civility have created an environment where humans must control their actions and behavior or be subject to social ramifications. Legal code and informal influences have shaped these interactions to meet the needs of a changing world. How these laws or rules are used in an athletic contest has created a wide assortment of paradoxes and fundamental issues that need to be examined in the unique circumstances that surround the individual and aggregate differences in each sporting activity.

Sport and violence represent two contrasting ideals. Sport in its purest form is an aesthetically pleasing performance of human kinetic intelligence. Sport can provide numerous benefits to those who participate in the activity as well as those that perform a support or spectator role. Violence on the other hand is something that is very natural, yet has an entirely different meaning within each society. Violence is inherently wrong and damaging other human beings has been seen as a way to shock the normal values of most cultures.

CONTENTS

Culture itself has many meanings, and it seems whenever two different individuals get together you can find a culture that has distinct opinions on what is acceptable violence and what is not. Thus when criteria is presented for evaluating what is acceptable violence, one of the primary constraints is often simply agreeing on the definition and interpretations of what violence actually is and what should be allowed. When thought of in terms of the unique cultures within the world of sports it is hardly surprising to learn that little can be agreed upon when it comes to identifying and categorizing what is natural and accepted violence. Without initial success few attempts at examining this problem are able to sustain their efforts long enough to arrive at any solutions.

SEXUAL ABUSE AND VIOLENCE: THE SURFACING OF CRIMINAL COMPLAINTS AGAINST ATHLETES

Grouping all athletes together as one large aggregate group creates problems that are often associated with trying to analysis any crime pattern in terms of multiple offenders. A great deal of caution should be given to any crime report that claims to be able to predict an individual case based upon information and statistics that are prevalent among some type of group that that person can be associated with. At the same time, being able to make some broad assumptions based upon patterns in crime data would support some generalizations about athletes in regards to crime in order to develop solutions and programs to help athletes as a group.

When looking through crime statistics for patterns it becomes obvious that many factors that are associated with crime are prevalent to those who consider themselves athletes. Many of the most important theories of criminal justice discuss tendencies in criminals that would seem apparent to anyone who is an athlete. Life course theories drawing from a view that crime is something that changes within our lifetime, explain how everyone goes through times when they are more likely to be criminal. Criminal thinking has an onset stage when people are beginning to consider crime. Adolescents and those going through puberty will experience a shift that makes them more likely to be criminal simply because they are the right age for committing crime. Crime statistics will show that most people have gone through these stages and begin settling down when they are about 22 and will settle into an adult role.

When thinking about athletes, it makes sense that athletes should have a higher than average crime rate according to this theory simply because so many athletes are between the ages of 14 and 23 years old. When a person grows older they are less likely to consider themselves as an athlete and would have a low chance of having the opportunity to be a full time athlete. Thus the cohorts we think of as "athletes" are always welcoming in new young people just reaching onset. Meanwhile the vast majority of those who have matured during their athletic years to the age where desistence is common, no longer consider themselves athletes because they will find a profession other than sports. Additionally elite athletes that are able to persist as athletes well into the age where crime rates go down for their age bracket will not be experiencing a normal life. The unique dynamics of being an athlete create a less than ordinary maturation process for young athletes, especially those that are not able to get the education and mentoring necessary for their own personal success.

A second major crime theory is that of a biological pattern amongst criminals. This has been demonstrated in the past as looking for bad genetics and sometimes this theory is used to describe why someone with a large forehead may be more likely to commit crime. It is fairly logical to think that those with big hands, long arms, huge muscles, or other large features would be motivated to play sports. Size and dominance can cause fear and anxiety in other individuals. Media and cultural impressions of a large attacker is the norm that has been conditioned into the average person. Biological changes can often determine athletic success, as those that peak early will be given athletic chances when they are young. Reaching puberty early is a good way to be a good athlete and make the team. Unfortunately, those that reach puberty faster are often left with questions and uncertainty that is often shown in the form of deviance, and if they are an athlete this may show up on the playing surface.

Recent attempts at measuring crime have been less simple. Increased academic work into how the environment, community, and all kinds of micro- and macro-level forces push, pull and intertwine together to create criminal opportunity. Within nearly every theory there is an application to athletes that can be found. At a professional level athletes have away games and travel to other cities to play their matches. This is nothing earth shattering, however when you plug this into crime patterns you find that this can be a problem. Problem in the home environment has an effect on family cohesion and is a major issue with athlete arrests. These breakups of marriage can be the cause and result of intense training and team obligations. This weakening of family ties and lack of a stable home where the entire family is together has put an elite athlete into a cohort that has some of the key characteristics indicative of a fatherless family. Of course the money and fame helps with some issues, but it can also be a double edged sword in terms of exposure and accessibility to the formal legal structure.

Finally, the importance of understanding the measure of crime is important. In *The Mismeasure of Crime* the myriad of issues involving accurate crime reporting and statistics is examined with a critical look towards assumptions and problems with consistency (Mosher et al., 2002). The authors conclude that the data and the analysis of crime data have been far from consistent and cite numerous examples. "All social measurement involves human decisions, interpretations and errors" (Mosher et al., 2002, p. 5). This lack of consistency in reporting and interpreting statistics along with intentional and accidental manipulation of these figures makes it difficult to truly examine this question with any validity.

It is apparent that statistics cannot be taken for fact for many reasons. If a new sport is popular in a poor neighborhood it can be seen as a great thing for the community and the sport. That being said if you are trying to keep crime statistics down for your sport, you would want to eliminate this sport from being played in the ghetto and only allow your sport to be played in the suburbs. By offering sports only in suburbs the statistics could be manipulated to show that your athletes were not committing crimes. In this way your sport looks like a clean sport. By this logic, rising crime rates amongst athletes could be indicative of a sport penetrating the ghettos and helping the community in many ways that are not showing up in the arrest records.

Like the television show, Twist of Fate, each year rookie players are given substantial salaries. Sometimes they make mistakes with their money as they attempt to live within a new lifestyle where they have access to cash and power. Despite recent attempts to educate players on proper behavior, incidents continue to occur. The irony in these programs was even more apparent when the NBA announced that Mario Chalmers, a Miami Heat point guard drafted in the second round out of Kansas, along with his former Kansas teammate Darrell Arthur, a rookie forward now with the Memphis Grizzlies, were asked to leave the rookie symposium because of disciplinary violations. According to ESPN.com marijuana was found in a hotel room, though the NBA cited the program's prohibition on guests in the hotel rooms during the symposium as the reason for the expulsion. Interestingly, number two overall pick Michael Beasley initially denied being part of the incident and continued to stay for the rookie program. Afterwards, Beasley confessed his involvement and had to pay a 50,000-dollar fine, which was significantly more than the 20,000 dollars that both Arthur and Chalmers were fined.

Beasley's initial lack of accountability and disregard for the seriousness of the investigation were cited as reasons for the additional fine. Perhaps this empowerment is what leads many athletes to challenge law enforcement. This was cited as a huge problem by observers of Chicago Bear running back Cedric Benson. Benson was operating a boat with 15 passengers aboard when he was stopped by a River Authority officer for a random safety inspection. According to the authorities he failed a field sobriety test and was uncooperative when the officer tried to take him to the shore. Cedric did have some witnesses that contradicted the police account. While the incident was being investigated, Cedric was released by the Bears after he was charged with a second DUI in Austin, this time driving a car.

The rape allegations that are often made against American athletes, such as the Duke Lacrosse team, Mike Tyson and Kobe Bryant are not only a North American problem. An 18-year-old woman claimed she was raped by four members of the English Rugby team. This alleged 2008 incident in an Auckland hotel where the team was playing was the latest in an increasing number of problems involving rugby players. Rugby personality, Hamish McKay suggested that the rape allegations will give the English team a competitive edge on the sports field. He claimed that the charges will make them angry, and hungry to win. An embarrassed coach quickly banned women from the hotel and banned sex from his players (Foster, 2008).

The ego of the athletes may pressure them into criminal behavior and further defiance of law enforcement. What can explain how someone like Pac Man Jones can continue to make poor choices when he has so many reasons to follow rules? How was he in the position to be arrested six times and have been involved in 12 matters requiring police intervention when he knows the risks. Rushes and buzzes can be exhilarating for the athletes. Risk and the deviancy of their actions along with the thrill of a trying not to get caught off the field seem to be very similar to making a dangerous and illegal play on the field and getting a thrill from the official not calling the penalty.

Money and power can also create opportunities for athletes to become victims. The summer of 2008 featured Indianapolis Colt wide receiver Marvin Harrison allegedly involved in a shooting at his car wash. No greater reminder of an athletes' vulnerability can be found than the tragedy surrounding the death of Washington Redskins young safety, Sean Taylor. His home was broken into and he was unable to have a gun, so he tried to defend his family with a knife. Unfortunately the intruder had a gun and Sean was killed as a result of the break-in. Further evidence and a trial found a former employee with inside information and knowledge of the home guilty of the crime. The Redskins and other NFL teams wore Sean's number 21 as a patch to commemorate the tragedy.

This event was hardly an isolated event. On Jan. 1, 2007 Denver Broncos cornerback Darrent Williams was shot and killed in a drive-by shooting early in the morning, as his limousine was sprayed with bullets in downtown Denver. Ironically, "In December, Williams spoke of returning to his hometown this offseason to talk to youngsters about staying out of gangs.

Williams, who has two young children in the Fort Worth area, recently talked to Criss (ed. His High School Coach) about establishing a free football camp for youth players." (Pasquarelli, 2008).

It had only been a little more than three months ago, on September third of 2006 when the NFL had last dealt with a shooting controversy. San Diego Chargers linebacker Steve Foley was shot twice near his Poway home. An off-duty Coronado police officer had followed him for several miles after suspecting him of driving drunk. The officer shot Foley and used a great deal of force. The linebacker missed the entire 2006 season due to injuries. In July of that same year, Cowboys defensive back Keith Davis was shot in the head and right thigh while driving in his car on a Dallas Interstate. Police suspected that it was a car-jacking attempt.

Before those incidents, in the 2005 NFL season, Philadelphia defensive end Jerome McDougle was shot in the abdomen during a robbery attempt in Miami. He missed the entire season due to injury but returned for the 2006 season. Even ex-players were attacked as 37-year-old David Lang, who played for the Los Angeles Rams and Dallas Cowboys, was shot following an apparent argument with an acquaintance. On Independence Day of 2004, Chargers defensive back Terrence Kiel was shot outside a Houston mall in an attempted car-jacking. Kiel was shot once in his ankle, once in his knee and once around his stomach, though he was able to recover in time to play that season.

Pittsburgh Steelers linebacker Joey Porter was one of six people shot outside a Denver sports bar. Porter was shot in the left buttock in 2003, though he recovered from his wounds. Carolina Panthers running back Fred Lane was shot and killed by his wife, Diedra, during a domestic dispute in 2000. Lane's wife is serving a prison sentence after pleading guilty to manslaughter charges. In 1992, Indianapolis Colts defensive end Shane Curry was shot in the head and killed outside a Cincinnati nightclub after a dispute regarding a blocked vehicle.

Football players were not alone in making the head lines for being shot at. Bryshon Nellum, a 19-year-old track star at the University of Southern California, was shot three times in the legs while walking outside a restaurant with some friends. Police were unsure if he was specifically targeted to be shot in the legs; however, gang signs were reported to be flashed before the 2 a.m. shooting. The November 2, 2008 shooting has threatened his ability to remain one of the fastest young track stars in the world.

Fans have even let the contests that seemingly do not involve them lead to violence. When fans over-identify with their sports teams crazy things can happen, and unfortunately, fans at home have access to guns. An Escambia County, Alabama couple got into an argument over the Alabama/LSU football game that ended in shotgun blasts. Dennis Smith, an avid LSU fan, called Michael Williams, a fan of the Crimson Tide, after the game and an argument ensued that ended in shotgun blasts, according to Conecuh County authorities.

Dennis and his wife Donna Smith, went over to Michael's house and continued the argument. After a physical altercation, "Smith retrieved a pistol from his vehicle, and threatened Williams, who armed himself with a shotgun and fired two blasts, striking and killing Dennis Smith, officers said. Donna Smith then threatened Williams, who shot and killed the woman, they said. Investigators said alcohol was believed to have been a factor in the killings…" (Baggett, 2008)

The thought that a football game watched on television can incite the desire to kill another human is a scary reminder of the engrained sense of violence we have within ourselves. Whether or not the killing was entirely over the football game may not be completely clear, but the lethal ramification of this action is something of note, even if it appears to be extreme. Though the brutality does not fit into our acceptance of what should happen when two fans are arguing, the images are not without duplication in the media, and of course the many international and local examples of extreme violence in the sport setting that have been given throughout this text makes this story not as surprising too many people as it really should be.

SUCCESS, SACRIFICE AND DROPPING OUT OF SPORTS

The roots of this violence surrounding sport are deep and embedded in much of our sport programming for youth. The performance ethic refers to emphasizing measured outcomes as indicators of the quality of sport experiences, such as winning. In this model, fun is thought of in terms of winning or losing or getting to be better. Parents are looking at the sporting event as an investment and their notions of sport participation as an investment for the child's future. The benefit of sport is not always one that rewards the parents directly in the sport through success, but should be instead measured by the overall development of the person that is provided by sport participation through a lifetime of leisure activities.

As public access to sports has been reduced, private sports organizations are becoming the norm. Private and commercial sport groups often emphasize the potential for children to gain material rewards through sports. Parents who see the high salaries that professional athletes receive are enticed by these endorsements. As a result, children often "work" long hours and become like "laborers," hoping to reach the rewards that their parents are investing in. These programs are not governed by child labor laws, and allow athletes to put an inordinate amount of physical stress on their bodies, and emotional stress on their individual psyche.

How youth come to view the sports world early on is crucial to setting their sporting disposition. The view of the sport ethic in America is of specific need for study. The sport ethic is a set of norms that many people in power and performance sports have accepted as the dominant criteria for defining what it means to be an athlete and to successfully claim an identity as an athlete. Athletes at a young age are taught to strive for team and personal distinction. In order to reach some type of distinction, an athlete must display skill, dominate an opponent, or do something better than everyone else. This central component to the sports ethic is where competition finds an inherent and perpetual home.

The sporting ethic in the United States is full of many other tenets that seem to link into the problem of over competition. Athletes are taught that great athletes are quick to make sacrifices for the game. Coaches, parents, siblings, teammates and the media are there to reinforce the idea that athletes play through pain in order to achieve success. Athletes are taught to be tough like warriors and to limit the amount of weakness they show. They are taught to accept no limits in the pursuit of their goals. When an adult coach asks a young ice hockey player to lie down in front of a fast moving and incredibly hard hockey puck, they eagerly let it hit them for their team, and are often congratulated by their peers more for this act than scoring a goal, especially if the player is injured.

The adult influence on youth sports can be very problematic, as ethical issues arise because of the changing role of the adult–child relationship in sport. The increased supervision and structure of formal sport that have replaced sandlot baseball and other forms of child sport that resembles play is one area of concern. Children themselves will have less experience in solving conflict and arguments in sport and in life if they are not in situations where they have to resolve things within a peer group without an "outside leader" to mitigate. Self coping and compromising skills would be used very little if all problems are solved by an authority figure. Interpersonal decision making skills, improvisation, cooperation, and problem solving are key components of the informal games that were once popular in the American culture.

Modern life styles have also caused several changes to the structure of sport. The urban life style has made some youth over-exposed to activities. The wide variety of leisure pursuits available along with the educational and other potential skills that a child could participate in has left many with a full schedule. This scheduled hyperactivity can often leave little time for young people to develop positive uses of their time when they are not scheduled to do something. In this manner, boredom when time is unscheduled could lead to a need for excitement and ultimately, deviance.

Basking In Reflective Glory (BIRG theory), is a phenomenon that explains the need that some parents feel to dictate the leisure choices of their children. Having a common sport to share with your child is a very appealing concept. It makes good sense for parents to place their children into sports that they enjoy or had enjoyed as a youth. Parents are apt to pass on the tricks, skills, mental game plan, aggressive tendencies and strategies that they learned through their passion for the sport to their children. Their own expertise is often the reason that they end up being their child's informal coach as soon as their child shows even a glimpse of interest in the sport, and sometime they will follow it up with being the formal coach if it is in their child's perceived best interest.

Other factors like genetic attributes would even reinforce many of these notions by helping to place people in sports where their bodies would be a good fit. For example, a family that has a history of being very tall would possibly have a long line of family members who have enjoyed basketball. Children who grow up in Texas in families who love football will often play the same position as their family members for this reason. Many offensive lines were made with familial ties to high schools and many young football players are taught early to bulk up and beef up for a future as a blocker for their parents favorite high school, college or even professional team.

If the child has the same passions and drive this situation may work out very well. Unfortunately, when looking at cases of burnout, or worse, parents living vicariously through kids' experience, can often be found as a reason that too much pressure was placed on the athlete. The child that is already on a path of a systematic pursuit of becoming a professional through serious sport and leisure should be a concern to those who care about that person's long-term moral, personal and even athletic development. Participation in sport should not be viewed as a career for young athletes.

Long lasting benefits of active sport participation are numerous. Unfortunately, there are also some long-term problems that are occurring to athletes because of their sport. Elite athletes in many sports experience physical problems that require them to either play through incredible pain or quit their sport. Many female basketball players in the United States have had their knees shredded while cutting, jumping and playing basketball, and must endure long-term issues when walking. Shoulder and knee problems are common for football players, and even non-contact sports like baseball feature chronic knee problems for those who spend a lifetime playing catcher.

Perhaps even more alarming are the ramifications from the long-term effects of concussions. With high rates among collision sport athletes such as

American football, to the odd concussions of heading a ball in International football, the propensity of young people experiencing concussions is high. Women's ice hockey has some of the highest concussion rates of all NCAA sports even though the rules limit and restrict player contact. "Sport that limit or restrict player contact such as soccer, basketball, and women's ice hockey still has a majority of their game injuries associated with player contact. A review of the playing rules in these sports to determine the effectiveness of the non contact emphasis seems warranted." (Hootman, 2007, p. 314).

The problems in studying the long-term effects of concussions on each athlete are obvious when thinking in terms of American Boxer, Muhammad Ali. Because of his Parkinson's syndrome he has many communication problems in interviews. A great deal of his mental state is related to the disease, but to say that all the punches to the head did nothing to damage his brain is also a pretty big stretch of the truth. The problem has always been isolating and measuring the effects of concussions, without the results being tampered by the effects of the disease and other confounding variables that all boxers may be subject to such as punches to the head, lack of sleep, absentee parenting, lack of B vitamins, or many other variables that may have an effect that works against or in conjunction with the disease that is taking the brunt of the blame for his current state.

According to recent research done on the brains of deceased National Football League football players by Boston University, the long-term effects of concussion are more severe than previously thought. "The findings are stunning. Far from innocuous, invisible injuries, concussions confer tremendous brain damage. That damage has a name: chronic traumatic encephalopathy (CTE)" (Smith, 2009, p. 1). Concussions that were once thought of as part of the game and a minor injury are only now being understood in terms of their long-term issues as many ex-athletes are having severe problems with brain functioning.

On Tuesday afternoon, researchers at the CSTE released a study about the sixth documented case of CTE in former NFL player Tom McHale, who died in 2008 at the age of 45, and the youngest case to date, an 18-year-old multi-sport athlete who suffered multiple concussions.

While CTE in an ex-NFL player's brain may have been expected, the beginnings of brain damage in an 18-year-old brain was a "shocking" finding, according to Dr. Ann McKee, a neuropathologist at the Veterans Administration Hospital in Bedford, Massachusetts, and co-director of the CSTE.

"We think this is how chronic traumatic encephalopathy starts," said McKee. "This is speculation, but I think we can assume that this would have continued to expand."

CTE has thus far been found in the brains of six out of six former NFL players.

"What's been surprising is that it's so extensive," said McKee. "It's throughout the brain, not just on the superficial aspects of the brain, but it's deep inside."

CSTE studies reveal brown tangles flecked throughout the brain tissue of former NFL players who died young – some as early as in their 30s or 40s.

McKee, who also studies Alzheimer's disease, says the tangles closely resemble what might be found in the brain of an 80-year-old with dementia.

"I knew what traumatic brain disease looked like in the very end stages, in the most severe cases," said McKee. "To see the kind of changes we're seeing in 45-year-olds is basically unheard of."

The damage affects the parts of the brain that control emotion, rage, hypersexuality, even breathing, and recent studies find that CTE is a progressive disease that eventually kills brain cells.

(Smith, 2009, p. 1)

HUBRIS AND CELEBRITY PRIVILEGE: ATHLETE'S FEELING ABOVE THE LAW

Athletes that continue to focus their personal efforts on acquiring sport specific skills and knowledge are typically absorbing the traits of the sport culture and develop within a subculture of similar athletes. Each individual begins to identify and have a strong bond with the athletes and stereotypes of the sport. The group of peers will encourage the athlete to persevere in spite of injury, fatigue and even through concussions. When the athlete fails to live up to the expectations of themselves, their teammates, their parents, or coaches they may choose to quit the sport or drop out instead of continuing to participate.

When athletes and teams fail to meet their goals many coaches are left in difficult situations as leaders. When priorities and team agendas revolve around athletic success, it becomes hard for all those involved to deal with not achieving their goals. The manner in which a coach deals with the failure will set a distinct barometer for the team to gauge their own actions. How a coach deals with controversy and hardship is a life lesson taught over and over again in countless sporting moments. As an early authority figure in the athlete's life, it is crucial for that role model to set a positive example that should reinforce good sportsmanship and citizenship.

There are many good coaches who rarely make the news for their ability to role model. Unfortunately, many authority figures make the news for things that would not be considered a positive role model. When Cory Petero, a 36-year-old assistant youth football coach loses himself in the heat of the moment and faces charges of child abuse for shoving a 13-year-old opponent of his son's to the ground, it is difficult to fathom how this would effect those who witnessed this event. When a major brawl occurs at Madison Square Garden in New York City resulting in countless images of chaos between the Knick and visiting Denver Nuggets to be broadcast internationally over a plethora of media sources, again one must question the role of leadership, especially when such outcomes are becoming frequent despite the tighter security and control promised after the fallout from the Pacers-Pistons riot.

Ironically, the exact role of head coach Isiah Thomas in this brawl was something of a mystery. Though not formally fined or suspended, the video images of his lips warning Carmelo Anthony from going "to the paint", or "to the hole" were often cited as a cause or at least indication of some involvement by the coach. His attitude reflected the fact that the bigger issue may have been the disrespect by the Nuggets for running up the score, itself a questionable and sometimes ignitable topic on sportsmanship. A heated exchange by both Thomas and Nuggets Coach George Karl filled with vulgarity and insults during individual interviews was not a classy or professional way to deal with the aftermath from the brawl, and has done little to divert attention away from the violence and fear associated with the fight. Sadly, the precedent and mannerism in which the professional coaches have handled the situation has created an unfortunately poor model for other coaches, especially those in youth sports.

Coaches have distinct power to influence the players in their team as well as anyone who is able to observe their behavior. As athletes seek guidance, the role of the coach can be diverse and challenging. Coaches are privy to information and serve the interests of many stakeholders other than just the athletes. Occasionally the multitude of tasks and responsibilities of a coach may put them in situations of conflict that requires immediate use of positive leadership. The intense pressure for coaches to win games, and gather accolades for their team can create a wide variety of paradoxes for a coach who is also looking out for the individuals they may coach. Many of these dilemmas strike at the moral foundations of the coach's character.

It is acceptable to acknowledge that winning is a goal in sports, but that there is a second, more important goal of using sports to teach life lessons when effective programming is implemented on all levels. Coaches are often held accountable for the behavior of their players on and off the court. Having a coach who is aware of their own educational opportunity to help mentor athletes is a goal for the Positive Coaching Association spokesperson Phil Jackson. The former coach of Michael Jordan, and several NBA championship teams' states, "You win not only because you win games but because you build character in the athletes you coach" (Positive Coaching Alliance, 2006).

Deviant issues involving coaches are occurring in communities throughout the world and frequently are reported in the various media sources. Morality and winning clashed in a national debate when Covenant School of Dallas, a private Christian school beat Dallas Academy 100-0 in girls' basketball. Micah Grimes, the head coach was fired for the incident and an apparent lack of remorse for running up the score when he failed to apologize and stood by his girls' excellent performance. The school was disappointed by the coach and did not feel that a team should beat another team by such a score out of sportsmanship.

Despite stories involving coaches losing all ethics in pursuit of victory as they pressure to win; little has been done to regulate the hiring, training and supervision of coaches. Even with headlines boasting of gross negligence, financial crimes, sexual misconduct and other surprisingly common allegations against coaches, many organizations do not allocate enough resources to properly screen and interview each applicant to ensure the integrity of the coaches' resume.

Considering the overall structure of most sports organizations, it is perhaps very fortunate that even more problems with coaches of an even greater significance have not been more prevalent. The current legal culture of America and the inherent risks in recreational sports has created a demand for accountability by those supervising both professional and recreational sports. It has been stressed that the coach fills an important place in the organization, often serving as a role model. The cost to educate and train this person is expensive, and the cost of conducting a job search and screening process adds to the overall expense. Though having qualified personal serving in sports organizations would cost more in salary, the importance of providing a safe and educational setting for developing young citizens is a cost a community should be able to sustain.

The screening of the role models for our future citizens should not suffer because of obstacles such as short-term costs. If the youth of the community cannot pay for their own essential needs such as security, and education, then the community needs to subsidize this expense. To neglect the overall quality of extra-curricular activities would further hinder the development of the community. Communities who are filled with people who have learned citizenship, work ethic, teamwork, and positive goal setting from a qualified adult may be rewarded in ways that are not easily measurable in typical terms of civic effectiveness. An understanding of community leadership, networking and inertia would provide some insight into the positive effects of personal development in sport when transferred to a community setting.

When a community cannot supply ample supervision and leadership for its youth, the youth must find supervision and leadership from sources that have not been purposefully selected by design. Marginalized groups of individuals seem to find a way to unite. In many areas of the United States, peer groups that often consist of juveniles have filled this void with a dangerous alternative, Street Gangs. Poor overall social conditions, a low quality of education, a lack of recreation opportunities and a larger number of the population feeling excluded has helped gangs explode in popularity in the United States.

Often people may be labeled a gang member because of their ethnicity, race or some stereo-type that is not rooted in the person's actual status. A practical definition of a gang is that it is a group of individuals who associate on a continuous basis, form an allegiance for a common purpose, and are involved in delinquent or criminal activity. This definition is simple and functional and it can encapsulate many themes associated with gangs. It allows the police departments to take proactive law enforcement action normally before the gang gets an organized structure. The gang may range from a loose knit group of individuals who hang around together and commit crimes together, to a formal organization with a leader or ruling council, gang colors, gang identifiers, and a gang name. A gang should also be distinguished from an ethnic group or any lawful association in that it presents a security threat to someone.

American gangs create the same types of problems that hooligans create in terms of the sport culture. The social force that a group of people can use to influence what we would think would be a rationale thought process of an individual is very powerful in the context of sport. Group think, hubris, and the desire for people to be liked by others can have terrible ramifications when not guided or supervised. The common roots are evident when considering the way that street gangs and sports teams often use to initiate new members into the larger group.

Hazing

The common term used to describe the harassment of participants when joining a new organization has been known as hazing. Hazing is defined as, "any activity expected of someone joining a group that humiliates, degrades, abuses, or endangers, regardless of the person's willingness to participate" (Hoover, 1999). Hazing is an action or situation which recklessly or intentionally endangers the mental or physical health or safety of a participant or an act that destroys property for the purpose of being admitted to an organization. It is especially important to note the importance of ignoring the participant's willingness to participate.

Because the participants are going to be influenced by their desire to join the organization, they will be tolerant to some forms of abuse and may not realize that the hazing is something that could be separated from their overall decision to join. The courts have had to take this definition so that people who are hazed who do not fight back or object to the maltreatment they will receive can be protected from accidentally waiving any rights by submitting to be hazed simply because they are willing to do almost anything to join the group, thus the legal definition generally states that in hazing, upon which the admission or initiation into or affiliation with or continued membership in an organization is directly or indirectly conditioned shall be presumed to be "forced" activity, the willingness of an individual to participate in such activity notwithstanding (Delaware State Code 9302).

Cases of hazing have been documented at an alarming rate. Shocking stories of rape, abuse and torture have highlighted the news. What is often seen as a good thing or something of a cherished tradition, have devastating consequences as these acts occur and evolve. Teammates using their power of seniority have forced under classman to perform sex acts. In some cases athletes have been molested by teammates and even gang raped with objects. Nakedness, alcohol and pain are three common themes that are used to teach young athletes respect, but each of these three themes are also key ingredients for disaster in a program.

After a terrible hazing incident at Alfred College, a large study was conducted by the university to research the national problem of hazing. The football team canceled a football game, expelled a veteran student athlete and suspended six others for an alcohol related hazing incident on campus. As a response to this incident as well as a death of a fraternity member nearly 20 years earlier, the school conducted a landmark survey on hazing in sports. The study has the purpose of identifying the breadth and depth of initiation in college athletics, identifying perceptions of appropriate initiation behavior and identifying strategies to prevent hazing (Crow, 2002). The questionnaire found that

- 45% of the 2027 respondents knew of, heard of, or suspected hazing on their campuses;

- 80% reported being subjected to one or more of the listed hazing behaviors, yet only 12% characterized or labeled those activities as hazing;

- 65% participated in some form of questionable initiation behavior;

- 51% claimed to be involved in alcohol-related initiation activities, including 42% who consumed alcohol on recruiting visits;

- 21% participated in unacceptable (dangerous) initiation activities, including 16% of female respondents;

- 60% said they would not report hazing to school officials.

Athletes who were at the greatest risk of being hazed were male swimmers and divers, lacrosse players, and soccer players. Athletes in a state with no anti-hazing law were also subject to a higher rate of being hazed. Fewer women were involved in hazing than men, however it should be noted that when women were involved they were more likely to include alcohol and alcohol-related events.

The punishments and penalties for violating hazing statutes often consist of fines, jail times, and the potential to have degrees and certifications withheld. The most common penalty is usually a 3–12-month jail term and $1000 fine in the United States. Many states are currently using anti-hazing legislation to tighten these penalties. Several states have made hazing a felony and are increasing efforts to combat the problem. It is important that administrators, coaches, and concerned stakeholders encourage the organization to not to wait for the law to respond to an incident, but to instead be proactive in combating hazing.

We encourage organizations to send a clear anti-hazing message by developing a written anti-hazing policy. Educating administrators, coaches, and players on the issues and problems surrounding hazing is important and should be a continuous activity. Each athlete should sign a contract that makes them accountable for hazing that could occur and makes sure they understand their expectations. Organizations should expect responsibility, integrity, and civility in their athletes. Screening recruits for behavioral problems, establishing a recruitment visit policy, and involving high-level administrators in the recruiting process should help in selecting athletes who will represent the team in a positive manner.

An organization that makes an athlete's behavior on and off the field part of the coach's evaluation will do well to minimize hazing incidents. Programs should offer team building initiation rites by training coaches on the importance of initiation rites and the proper ways to conduct them. If a team requires organized initiation rites prior to each season, and incorporates initiating into team goal-setting it can better control the process and discourage players from using their own creativity to haze younger teammates. If there is any issues with hazing it is vital to establish a record of strong corrective action. Immediately notify law enforcement of suspected hazing in order to help the athlete and organization get the support or discipline they need so that the organization as a whole can become healthy again.

It is important that any organization eliminates these instances of hazing so that the more important goals of the group can be met. After the Minnesota Vikings and rookie head coach, Brad Childress, established a policy against hazing, some of the veteran players were a bit unsure of what was going on. Veterans like Fret Smoot had been subject to the common practice of hazing and had memories of being tied to a goal post and doused with water, and are now happy to use their veteran expertise to return the favor. Despite a long history of hazing within the Vikings organization and across the league, Coach Childress was committed to make his rookies feel better, and be able to produce on the field without the fear of hazing.

When Childress announced his policy, Smoot considered that chances it would work with the following quote, "Awwww, never!" Smoot recalled saying when he first heard about the rule. "But he did it. He really wanted us to focus on winning, and I respect that. I just wish he was my coach my rookie year." (ESPN, 2006, p. 1). Other veteran players were also unsure of the ramifications of not helping to prepare their young players for the season and perhaps were pining to challenge the orders, but the coach remained firm on his stance. The no-nonsense coach sees hazing not as harmless fun, but as a potentially divisive force. "You better be inclusive," Childress told his players. "You better pull people into the pile, because if that guy can help you win and you're a seven-year player and you think that doing something to him or making him get up and sing or alienating him is going to help you, no, it's not" (ESPN, 2006, p. 1)." If the ritual has lost its appeal at this level, one would defiantly have to reconsider what value if any, hazing has in any organization?

SUMMARY

The role of athletes in society is one that is constantly being defined, adapted and manipulated. When the athlete does not abide by the rules of the social norms, their actions are often highlighted to serve as an example for other people. Stakeholders who support these athletes place a higher standard of living for the athletes. America and many other countries enjoy having heros and encourage people to aspire to be like these examples of success.

The sense of accomplishment and worth that athletes feel from their sport can be problematic when they become separated from the average person. Proving to others that one belongs to a group can become an issue when new members will do anything to fit it. Crimes against non-athletes as well as crimes against teammates can occur so that a particular person can fit into their new team. When an athlete who is expected to be a hero fails, the fall from good graces can be catastrophic. Whether it is a sports-based hero or any other, there seems to be an attraction to the story of the fallen hero that seems to permeate through the culture as well?

Sometimes fans themselves will identify so much with a team or a sport that they will commit crimes against the athletes for a myriad of different reasons. Jealousy, fame, a need to connect with the celebrity, greed, power moves, and a many other social or psychological reasons have been given by many fans who behave as they do towards athletes. An innate need to fight, be violent and release aggression is often seen as a reason for violence by sports spectators. Unfortunately the spillover effects are intense and carry high consequences, as the examples in this chapter have demonstrated.

REFERENCES

Baggett, C., 2008, November. Football dispute leaves 2 dead. Retrieved November 10, 2008, from the All Alabama Website: http://www.al.com/news/pressregister/metro.ssf?/base/news/122631213873770.x ml&coll=3.

Brekken, Ted K.A., 2009. Personal account of violence in sport, February 2.

Carlson, J., 2009. Personal account of violence in sport, February 2.

Crow, B., Rosner, S., 2002. Institutional and organizational liability for hazing in intercollegiate and professional team sports. St. John's Law Review 76, 87–114.

ESPN, 2006. Kids are all right: vikings ban hazing of rookies. Retrieved January 10, 2009 from the ESPN website: http://sports.espn.go.com/nfl/news/story?id=2547145.

Foster, P., and Rayner, G., 2008. England rugby rape claim; sex ban for players. Telegraph. Retrieved February 1, 2008 from http://www.telegraph.co.uk/news/worldnews/australiaandthepacific/newzealand/2164911/England-rugby-rape-claim-Sex-ban-for-players.html.

Hootman, J., Dick, R., Agel, J., 2007. Epidemiology of collegiate injuries for 15 sports: summary and recommendations for injury preventive initiatives. Journal of Athletic Training 42 (2), 311–319.

Hoover, N., 1999. National survey: initiation rites and athletics for NCAA sports teams. Retrieved December, 20, 2006 from http://www.Alfred.edu/news/html/hazing.html.

Mosher, C., Miethe, T., Phillips, D., 2002. The Mismeasure of Crime. Sage, Thousand Oaks.

Norton, P., Burns, J., Hope, D., Bauer, B., 2000. Generalizations of social anxiety to sporting and athletic situations: gender, sports involvement, and parental pressure. Depression and Anxiety 12, 193–202.

Pasquarelli, L., 2008. Williams killed when limo sprayed with bullets. Retrieved December 10, 2008, from the ESPN Website: http://sports.espn.go.com/nfl/news/story?id=2716385.

Positive Coaching Alliance, 2006. [Official Web Site of Positive Coaching Alliance] Retrieved February, 2, 2006 from the Positive coaching Alliance Website: http://www.positivecoach.org/.

Shaughnessy, J., 2008. Living her dream. The Criterion XLVIII (36), 1.

Smith, S., 2009. Dead athletes' brains show damage from concussions. CNN, Retrieved January 21, 2009, at the CNN website: http://www.cnn.com/2009/HEALTH/01/26/athlete.brains/index.html.

FEEL GOOD 8.1

Making the Team

Samantha Peszek went to the Olympics in Beijing with one of the greatest girls' gymnastics teams ever sponsored. Her road to that treasured sport included her faith, in that she prays before competition, and manages a hectic schedule with aplomb. A student at Cathedral High School, she is a part of the first US gymnastics to win the World Championships and become part of the Olympic dream. After missing a month of school to go to the World Championships, Samantha went to school early, skipped lunch and stayed later to complete all her missed work. In addition, according to friends, she is very humble, having to be coaxed into bringing her gold medal from the world championships to school so they could see it. Her Olympic involvement is the stuff of dreams, and although she had to miss out on competing during the team championships, she was a part of an excellent USA showing. Her personal qualities such as her ability to set and meet goals, her humble personality, and her drive are all admired as being excellent characteristics for her high level athletic accomplishments.

(Shaughnessy, 2008)

SPORT STORIES 8.1

One time a pitcher purposely threw at a batter (with his 60-mile fastball) because the previous guy hit a homerun. That was actually pretty funny in its harmless audacity. Like a tiny dog that barks ferociously.

Dr. Ted K. A. Brekken, Ph. D.

SPORT STORIES 8.2

Once when I was catching in softball, the runner kept leading off third, finally, I threw the ball to the third basemen, really hard. Unfortunately, it connected to the baserunners head. Ow. I don't think I intended to hit her, I just knew I had to get the ball there fast. Another time, when I was pitching fastpitch (one of the last times), I had a heckler in the bench behind home plate. Something snapped in my concentration and the ball stuck a bit, went sailing over the backstop and hit the heckler. No kidding. It was a ball.

Carlson, J. (2009).

CHAPTER 9

Specific Solutions to Mitigating Sport and Violence

"Both males and females agreed that if severe sanctions are not present to control violence in sports, violence will likely occur, and that violence will occur if it is recognized as an implicit part of the game"

(Lance et al., 1998, p. 8).

While root causes of sport violence are varied and complex, all sport experiences hold one entity in common – the facilities used for sport have an undeniable connection to the public domain, either through direct programming of events or through an indirect method of making facilities available to other groups to handle programming. Therefore, when violent events are involved it is simply a failure of public management. What was just said?? To reiterate – when all is said and done, it is a failure of management when sport violence episodes erupt. And why not?? When food is recalled off the myriad of store shelves because it was sold to consumers and someone became ill, it is the failure of the corporation and the public oversight of that corporation that caused the tainted product to be made available to the extent that someone became ill or worse.

So it goes that when sport experiences become "tainted" by some ill specter of violence, it is the self same deep pockets that are really responsible, i.e., the starting point is the point where non-profit and pressure groups are given authority and responsible for the programs and the next layer – the public sector for why this tainted product was marketed and sent to the public without appropriate controls. All sport experiences, meets, and contests are ultimately governed by a public leisure service delivery system, and it is

CONTENTS

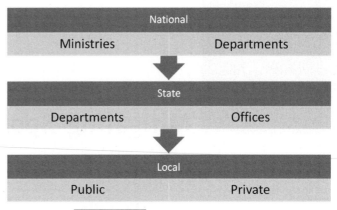

FIGURE 9.1 *Chart of organizations.*

important to point to the root cause as being this very system. Unfortunately, it is this sector that does not appear to be as fully aware of what these groups are doing. Programs are offered by many public, non-profit, and commercial businesses on these grounds; however, it appears that there is little oversight of these programs or outcomes.

The uncoordinated proliferation of services makes for a labyrinth of sport programs and many mixed messages. In looking at how many organizations may be involved in full service sport systems, (Fig. 9.1) depicts three major levels of delivery occurring at the national, state, and local areas.

THE SPORT HIERARCHY

Each community has many organizations delivering sport and leisure services; however, without a common regulatory process, there are no guidelines of commonly accepted delegation of these programming experiences. One of the reasons for this is the passing of sport offerings from the school sector to the governmental sector. Schools have been regulated by the states in which they reside and further by national educational policy guidelines; however, no such guideline across the board regularly process exists at the national or state level to regulate youth sport and subsequent activity. It appears that the local leisure and sport service delivery system lacks the guidelines that give rise to learning a sport, competing in a sport, and creating a consistent process for children to advance to higher skill levels and competitive involvement. Further, the public, leisure service delivery systems abdicate their responsibilities when addressing this advancement and allow pressure groups to manage these responsibilities.

In order to address sport and violence issues at the local sector, the following must happen:

Proposal number 1

All entities offering sport at the local level must agree on standards and processes in the offering of sports programs. These standards must include governance policies, rules and regulations, educational and experience requirements of all personnel, including volunteers, a policy that reflects the developmental aspects of the participant and the appropriate programming level, standards and processes for competition, alignment with national governing bodies for specific sport involvement, supervision and oversight of practices and contests, training updates for referees and all staff, outcome assessment of players, and advancement guidelines for progress through what should be an unbroken line of sport opportunity.

RESPONSIBILITY FOR A SAFE, CIVIL SPORT ENVIRONMENT

Each individual who becomes involved in sport, whether they are volunteers or paid employees has a keen responsibility to agree to safety and civility expectations to ensure a positive sport experience for all. All must agree to provide this, and then all must agree to confront issues as they arise. There are varying degrees to which a participant perceives an environment as safe or dangerous; for example, many tourists select places based on real or perceived safety issues. If an area is reported to be a high crimes area, or if there are repeated problems with negative publicity concerning issues that could raise concern, individuals will simply avoid the site. It becomes highly important to develop a compendium of items that are standard practices for anticipating problems that may evolve into violence. A safe, civil sport environment consists of the following factors:

1. All programs must have a framework that ensures that it is being offered with developmental appropriateness, supported by regulatory sport organizations with regard to rules and conduct, and that facilities meet high safety standards. For example, rules adapted from state high school associations or written for recreational sport involvement must be judiciously applied to the program. Other standards include crowd control maximums, supervisory load, police enforcement, first aid availability, and staff oversight.

FIGURE 9.2 *Chart of Organization Information.*

2. An educational approach to all of those involved in sport: players, referees, staff, coaches, parents, spectators, administrators. This approach features materials that are produced in writing and distributed, posted, and enforced. Figure 9.2 shows examples of information that has been shared by agencies who sponsor sport programs through orientation sessions and on-site availability.

3. There must be an educationally sound enforcement mechanism for those who do not follow a safe and civil approach with each other. This can be in the form of a warning, a citation, or removal from the premises.

Proposal number 2

A uniform code of conduct must be developed for all those engaged in sport. This code should guide all aspects of any sport and be directed to players, participants, coaches, leaders, parents, employees, regulatory personnel, spectators, sponsors, and enforcement personnel.

Codes of conduct exist in many organizations; however, there is no standard code that has been adopted to mitigate violence, reduce harassment, and behave properly as a spectator. A general code developed by ordinance and enforced by consequence is absolutely important to set a standard of sport involvement for all sports in all communities. Then, individual organizations may also adopt more specific codes that allow for standards to be followed that may be unique to that sport.

Table 9.1 shows a standard code of conduct which emphasizes the minimum number of items that need to be agreed to. These items should

Table 9.1	Standard Code of Conduct

Philosophy

"All sports programs offered by Highlands Ranch Community Association are based on fun and participation. We realize there is a competitive situation when two teams are playing each other, BUT winning is not our primary goal. We expect coaches, spectators and team members to participate with this philosophy in mind. HRCA has a zero tolerance policy for coach, player and spectator misconduct.

(Source: Highlands Ranch Community Association)

Mission Statement of Organization

To provide a non-competitive introduction to the game of youth baseball. The objective is to develop a basic understanding of the simple fundamentals such as hitting. It is the intent of our program to provide a positive and enjoyable environment where every child has the opportunity to develop their skills and enjoy the game of baseball regardless of ability.

(Source: Bloomington Junior League Baseball Association)

Enforcement Practices

This facility and program operates with a "zero tolerance policy" that means there is no acceptance of verbal and physical abuse of any person participating either through play or other involvement, including spectators.

Standards of Play

- Proper sports environment.

- Programs based on the well-being of participants.

- Drug, tobacco, and Alcohol free environment.

- Part of a participant's life.

- Training.

- Parent's active role.

- Positive role models.

- Parental commitment.

- Safe playing situations.

- Equal play opportunity.

- Drug, tobacco and alcohol-free adults. (Source: National Alliance of Youth Sports)

Specific Conduct Measures

Code of Ethics Pledge – Agreement to abide by the rules. Separate pledges for Coaches, Parents, Spectators, and Players.

(Source: www.nays.org)

Penalties

All penalties and rules within games are called by the supervising referees. SA bench minor penalty for unsportsmanlike conduct shall be assessed whenever a player, coach, or spectator argues with an official.

Continued

Table 9.1	Standard Code of Conduct—*Cont'd*

Disclosures

A report of potential risk and injury should be provided for all activities and there needs to be a warning for any items that may not be in the general awareness of the participant.

Consequences

If rules are not followed, statements as to consequences need to be provided to include warnings, citations, police response or other actions that will be taken.

Due Process

Those involved in conduct violations shall be given due process – an opportunity to be heard by a group of peers selected for reviewing incidents and making recommendations on violence mitigation.

Pledges of Participants

Coaches' Code of Ethics Pledge –

I hereby pledge to live up to my certification as a NYSCA Coach by following the NYSCA Coaches code of ethics pledge.

I will place emotional and physical well-being of my players ahead of any personal desire to win.

I will remember to treat each player as an individual, remembering the large spread of emotional and physical development for the same age group.

I will do my very best to provide a safe playing situation for my players.

I promise to review and practice the necessary first-aid principles needed to treat injuries of my players.

I will do my best to organize practices that are fun and challenging for all my players.

I will lead, by example, in demonstrating fair play and sportsmanship to all my players.

I will use those coaching techniques appropriate for each of the skills that I teach.

I will remember that I am a youth coach, and that the game is for children and not adults.

(Source: www.nays.org)

apply to all those involved and be signed for every program and every contest.

THE SPORT MANAGEMENT PROFESSIONAL

According to a community standard for youth sport management, developed by the National Alliance of Youth Sports (United States), each community should have a trained and educated youth sports administrator to handle sport experiences. European countries suggest in their national guidelines that a Sport Council be the main authority for sport clubs at the local level, and that opportunities be developed that work with sport specific governing bodies. Many other countries simply enable club development with the incentive of training and funding. It is suggested that this regulatory effort does not often go far enough to ensure safe and equitable practices throughout a community.

In order to best illustrate the issues associated with sport management, Richard F. Mull, former Director of the Division of Recreational Sports highlights major issues associated with the role of a sport management professional. He, further, invented the term, recreational sport. Mull alludes the importance in programming with social control and response to societal expectations in mind. In a discussion with the authors, he expressed that the leisure programming model should consider the ugly factor.

> *"The ugly factor only raises its head 5% of the time. It's not everything. But you don't program for the 95%. You program to protect yourself against the ugly factor, then the other stuff just kind of comes naturally. We would have all kinds of events, and 95% of the time there was not a problem. They knew that we had a student system to govern them in a fair way. If they did not behave properly there were consequences and this created a control." (Orr 2007)*

Mull also comments on the following areas of concern:

1. Parents often have more influence than the sport management professionals.
2. Systems need to be in place to handle violence and other issues.
3. Training and education are needed for officials and staff.
4. Disciplinary action needs to be handled with the rules of due process.
5. When something happens, it needs to be addressed immediately with action taken and supplementary documentation.

Mull also notes the reasons for applying the sport action model by asserting:

> *"Sport is a mini society. All sport parallels society. Everything that goes on in an hour sporting event is the same thing that goes on in society. You've got organization, you've got competition, you've got officials, control, you've got venues, you've got people, you've got personalities. You just take whatever goes on in society where people work, live and go about, you just take all of that and it contains right into and one of the elements that we take for granted in sport is the control mechanism and the process of influencing control. In society it goes off. We have our problems in society but the system is there" (Orr 2007)*

In looking at the issues associated with Mull's statements, the need to manage the entire sport experience from initial planning through resolution is evident. The management process includes thorough planning, training of all staff and officials, involvement of players and spectators in addressing the rule infractions or face disciplinary action, responding immediately to those issues with reporting, witnesses, and documentation, and resolving issues through hearing that replicate the due process system within the country. Anything less than a trained workforce that anticipates potential problems and acts on them immediately produce a chaotic sport situation that will escalate and ruin what should be a positive experience. In all cases where violence in sport has occurred, one can point to issues with management that failed.

Proposal number 3

A sport management professional who is well-versed in local level sport offerings should be hired in each community. The major purpose of this professional would be to develop a comprehensive community system that reflects quality of life principles, promotion of healthy lifestyles, and a developmental progression of sport involvement for all.

The availability of recreational professionals schooled in sport delivery is important for the development of programmatic efforts for all age groups. This professional also needs to address the gaps in programming in the community and take the responsibility to train all personnel in sport delivery regardless of agency. It is important that these individuals see their roles as coordinating functions as well as delivery functions and that any entity that is involved with sport on public property respond to the requirements to include quality programming for the safety and security of players, participants, referees, umpires, judges, coaches, leaders, parents, spectators, and any other viewer or observer. It is no longer appropriate to keep one's personnel agenda for a child or a team. It is no longer correct to encourage behaviors that intimidate, scare, or deter participation on any basis. It is no longer appropriate to allow limited knowledge to prevail. It is time to stop all violence before it starts in any sport setting regardless of what is the nature of the game or contest.

ROLE OF NATIONAL AND LOCAL POLICY

In studying sport and leisure policy, Jamieson (2004) noted that many countries have developed policy at the national level that sends strong guidelines to state or provincial and local service delivery systems. These policies address how programs should be run, monitored, assessed, and evaluated. These policies are not only directed at the education system but also at club and governmental delivery. All-encompassing policies vary depending on the type of country that exists and the nature of the ideology of that country. The background and origin of this policy development provide a guideline of how each country may respond.

Proposal number 4

A policy framework should be drawn from what exists at the international, national, state/provincial, regional, and local levels to govern all operations that have to do with the physical development of participants at all age levels including pre-school and post-school involvement.

This framework will guide development of age and developmentally appropriate activities that provide a positive learning and competitive environment for the purpose of enjoyment and advancement.

The establishment of governing boards at the local level will be to ensure that any policies and guidelines that are developed above the level of the local sector are incorporated locally and reflected similarly to their intent at advanced level. These policies shall include, but not be limited to:

1. Developmentally sound skill development.

2. Educationally certified and degreed personnel regardless of paid or volunteer status.

3. Player/participant advancement that makes developmental sense.

4. Safety and security guidelines for facilities, programs, and personnel including background checks, hazard management, and injury prevention, protection, and first aid.

5. Parent education that provides the basis and guidelines for age appropriate programming, home development, conduct codes, and enforcement of positive behaviors.

6. Criminal consequences for any behavior that is criminal regardless of sport setting.

7. Ease of access to all sport offerings regardless of social class, affordability, skill level, or access challenges.

8. Funding guidelines and training expectations.

ROLE OF ADMINISTRATORS IN SPORT ENVIRONMENTS

Those who administer sport environments need to get on the same page with each other and with those who are participating, advocating, working, and encouraging sport involvement. Schedules of learning, playing, competing, and sharing need to be part of a master calendar of facilities that meet minimum standards both of condition and number per 1000 population in defined communities. Facilities, equipment, supplies, and programs should be shared regardless of the entity that is responsible for the facility in order to encourage the widest use of the supply of facilities and area. There should be a central coordinating authority for facilities that ensures safety and security of all venues and those who participate and work in those venues.

Proposal number 5

Administrators of facilities and program must form a coordinating council to improve program quality, distribution of program services, and facility sharing to increase access and equity across the many participating groups. This group will maintain the responsibility to ensure safety and security of all programming and decrease opportunity for escalation of violence that comes from poor management of facilities and programs.

To accomplish this, those hired to be responsible for the public good, i.e., users of respective facilities must all agree to mitigate all violence issues in their jurisdiction by agreeing on the same approaches to sound management of programs, people, resources, and facilities. A unified approach will be respected if it is handled in an organized fashion. No one has the lock on facilities and programs and no one can create an unfair advantage when violence issues are at stake – there simply has to be agreement to unify communities against the problems that have torn apart families and programs and set this right.

It is important that all areas and facilities are identified as safe and secure. Further, there need to be improved ways to sense when danger can occur. After many school violence incidents, studies commissioned by the Office of Juvenile Justice and Delinquency Prevention (Wilson, 2000) identified eight principles to create safe and secure conditions for those who have been exposed to violence:

Principle 1 – Work together,

Principle 2 – Begin earlier,

Principle 3 – Think developmentally,

Principle 4 – Make mothers (sic, parents) safe to keep children safe,

Principle 5 – Enforce the law,

Principle 6 – Make adequate resources available,

Principle 7 – Work from a sound knowledge base,

Principle 8 – Create a culture of non-violence.

Each of the above principles is to be offered when working with children. They are aspects that may create a positive environment, help children to feel secure, assist in quelling fears of parents over involvement, and allow the program to development according to safer and more secure lines. From the start, it is important to start from a point of view that takes into account the concerns and fears of those whom are involved in a sport experience. Many players come from backgrounds where school experiences, home experiences, and other factors may evoke an issue with insecurity about safety.

After 9/11 in the United States and other major terrorist attacks that occurred in Bali, London, and Spain among others, major sport and gathering facilities created security systems that protect large throngs of entertainment seekers. Sport facilities have increased security, security monitoring, inspection, and observation. Further, they have reacted more quickly to incidents that begin with bad behavior and end with assault and battery or worse. For example, Conseco Fieldhouse in Indianapolis, Indiana has a turnstile inspection program barring backpacks and other containers, its security staff monitors over 100 screens directed at every square foot of building space, and intercepts rowdy fans long before the situation becomes a crisis. Other facilities have not faired as well as Conseco, as noted when the Detroit versus Pistons game at the Palace in Detroit. Failures were reported in security staffing who were not present to monitor an increasingly drunk group of fans who were close to the playing floor. Basically, poor management of this facility contributed in part to widely reported problems involving players and fans.

SPORT VIOLENCE LITIGATION

Legally speaking, sport violence is an offense punishable in a court of law in 28 states within the United States. Further, litigation against perpetrators of sport violence are also regularly charged and punished though laws created for that purpose in Europe, Asia, Oceania, Africa, North and South America. The fact that some actions have been punished in this way is increasing the number of complaints. Commit violence in the sport environment and expect jail time, particularly if you have a high profile. Simply stated, legal recourse is becoming more available for victims of sport violence.

Proposal number 6

Laws preventing violence need to be improved and applied throughout the legal and regulatory systems in every locale, state or province, region, national, and international entity to place more importance on legal resolution to violent episode and also to prevent the unnecessary escalation of violence in any sport venue.

As an example, Heinzmann (2002) suggested that hiring competent officials and quality coaches may reduce instances of sports rage. Little empirical research has been done that tested quality of officials and the effect they have on participation or participant comfort level. However, having qualified leaders present and trained on proper procedure in times of crisis would certainly make sense. The costs of training and employing officials are justified by understanding the benefits received by having quality officials as part of your program instead of inadequate officiating. It is also plausible to require a supervisor or official at every event offered, simply on the grounds of risk management and control of potential problems created by aggressive participants in any sports setting.

Further, NFL official Mark Baltz believed that letting officials know they have a future in officiating and a purpose to their community was important in retaining quality officials at any level. The area of officiating needs to tie more closely with a profession in order that officials invest in it as an occupation for which they are well paid (Baltz, 200?).

Legal action may cause individuals to pause and recognize the consequences when they misbehave in a sports setting. Early detection of these problems with warnings and removals will go a long way to reducing the person to person conflicts that erode the sport experiences.

SIGNIFICANT ADULT RESPONSIBILITIES

Due to the existence of professional staff who are already running major programs, it is apparent that they cannot accomplish this all by themselves, and if the problems with sport and violence continue, it is likely that programs will cease if responsible adults do not gain control of themselves and their less mature peers. Adult-controlled sport environment is not enjoyed by youth, and many quit because they are not having fun. That should be a simple adjustment, but the first report by Michigan researchers occurred 15 years ago and accounts of violence in sport has escalated through improvement in the media distribution of such reports.

Adults who are interested in sport development for children need to take a step back and analyze as well as plan along with their children for positive experiences that are less drawn toward the scholarship and fame/fortune direction. Children need more control over the selection and continuance of activity, and they need to see their parent or guardian as supportive of ending participation as well as starting involvement. Quite often, a bad or dangerous role model serving as a coach or parent support may be negative learning that is hard to forget. There is no sport that is worth putting up with harassment, hazing, bullying, abuse, and incompetence on the part of adult role models. Children should not be prodded to enter sport when they are physically or mentally not ready. Further, they should not be pushed by their parent, coach or other adult into playing through injury, since such advice may wind up with the player never being able to play the sport again. If a child can be engaged in knowing what a good program is and is not, then that child should also be respected for dropping out.

Proposal number 7

Parent guidance and education starting with the birth of their child should provide improved choices for participation in leisure activity that emphasizes the overall health and development of the child rather than push for serious leisure. In addition, all programs that involve the starting point for child involvement should require extensive parent education as well before the child can participate. Training and education concerning wise choices with financing sport and leisure, age-appropriate choices, role of coach or leader, parental roles, and many other aspects should be identified.

In the education of parents with regard to sports, realistic expectations must be shared. For example, children's sport involvement is costly, and financial planning is appropriate. However, the parent should recognize what is affordable and positive and what is not. The following list can be important when sharing the planning of sport involvement.

1. Pay attention to the development of overall skill regardless of sport. It may be smarter to enroll a child in tumbling in order to gain overall strength and balance, or swimming to accomplish ways to be safe in the water than to sign up for t-ball.

2. Travel teams are not all what they describe. Identify if the travel experience will involve more playing time at games than staying in town. More playing time staying local will be less expensive and not measurably reduce a child's ability to advance when it is age-appropriate.

3. The decision to advance to more dedicated sport time and higher levels of ability are a commitment that a child should make with the help of qualified coaches and developmental specialists. If the child does not have the maturity to make the decision him or herself, then he or she is not ready. The child should not be pressured to make this decision, since eventually, if the playing is not inner motivated, the child is likely to burn out.

4. Affordability is important – sport should be engaged in for enjoyment and skill development. As far as excess involvement and the eventual delivery of an athletic scholarship – forget it. Parents are better off placing funds in a college savings account when their children are born – it will grow at the rate that one would receive were they to earn an athletic scholarship.

5. Academics are more important than sport, and some children cannot withstand the high demands of travel, intense physical activity, and keeping up. One noteworthy situation with a player who played two sports year round was his 1.7 grade point average after he left high school. He had to sit out a year and then go to college, which took him several years more. Less involvement in sport and greater attention to athletics would have made a great difference.

Parents and adult role models are still the most important individuals to children and those emerging into adulthood. How adults act and what they say can be powerful to a child. If a child sees a parent acting like a delinquent, it is an extremely negative message to see and respond to; however, if the child sees a parent and coach as measured and encouraging, it can be a very effective tool to help the child enjoy the sport and focus on improvements.

RESOURCES AVAILABLE FROM MANY ORGANIZATIONS

Awareness of the organizations that exist to support positive role modeling in sport is an important aspect for all who are interested in education. Table 9.2 shows the name of those who enter and participate. In addition, a few of these organizations are described in more detail due to their development of codes, guidelines, and aspects of sport involvement that have held great influence with many organizations.

1. National Alliance of Youth Sports (www.nays.com) (NAYS) – this organization has provided information that is available on the web to parents, players, administrators, referees, and many other entities

Table 9.2	Organizations Responsible for Positive Sport Environments
Name	**URL**
National Coalition for Athletics Equity	http://www.intermatwrestle.com
Coaching Youth Sports Archive	www.chre.vt.edu
Administration USA Gymnastics	www.usa-gymnastics.org
Violence Prevention and Youth sports	http://www.reeusda.gov
International Youth Sports Conference	http://www.nif.idrett.no
Sports Illustrated for Kids	http://www.sikids.com
Little League On-Line	http://www.littleleague.org
National Alliance for Youth Sports	http://www.nays.org
International Olympic Committee-USA	http://www.olympic-usa.org
Sportzone	http://espnet.sportszone.com
American College of Sports Medicine	http://a1.com
Children and Sports Injuries	http://healthy.net
National Recreation and Park Association	http://www.nrpa.org
National Collegiate Athletic Association	http://www.ncaa.org
National Intramural Recreational Sports Assn	http://www.nirsa.org
Boys and Girls Clubs	http://BoysandGirlsClub.org
American Youth Soccer Organization	http://www.soccer.org
Pony League	http://www.pony.org
Center for Sport Policy and Conduct	http://www.hper.indiana.edu
Violence in Sports	http://npin.org
Sports Illustrated Good sports	http://www.sigoodsports.com
Contact Sports and Violence Against Women	http://www.feminist.org

interested in appropriate approaches to youth sport. Within the framework of training and development, any agency or group may benefit from codes of conduct, rules, and many other resources. A coach training designed for all sports is available, and NAYS enables community organizations to see that all coaches under their jurisdiction are trained.

2. National College Athletic Association (www.ncaa.com) (NCAA) – the major organization that serves athletes in major colleges and universities, NCAA is working through its athletes to encourage better community programs and provide more positive role modeling. The web site includes information that is useful for those who are organizing sport experiences and those who would like to access the organization's programs.

3. National Recreation and Park Association (www.nrpa.org) (NRPA) – this organization represents those who work in the public sector and

delivery sport and leisure services. Those enrolled in this organization attend professional development programs on sport and training, consider the issues around sport and violence, and provide the widest range of programs and services in communities.

4. Single Sport National Governing Bodies: In response to the Olympic effort, most countries have national governing organizations (NGO's) that are responsible for a single sporting event. These organizations govern the sport, provide a system for participation, regulate the development of athletes, provide resources, competitions, and selection processes for Olympic participation. In addition, each of these organizations is responsible to promote the sport, start developmental programs, and ensure there is a feeder system throughout the development of high level competitors. In the United States, 46 organizations fall under the Olympic development umbrella; whereas, in other countries, the number of organizations varies with the number of sports that country sponsors in the Olympics.

Figure 9.3 shows an organizational chart depicting the staffing of a typical NGO, in this case, U. S. A. Gymnastics.

Each NGO has a similar purpose: to promote the sport of ____. These organizations feed into the schedules for state, regional, national, and international competitions that improve the teams that eventually compete in the Olympics. They are full-time operations with staffing and a strong relationship to those who develop sport locally.

In addition to these organizations, countries also feature many organizations that also promote sports that may not be on a path to the Olympics,

FIGURE 9.3 *Organizational chart depicting local to national staffing for one part of USA Gymnastics.*

but they have levels of competition that require some coordination and regulation. Often these organizations are eventually incorporated into the Olympic umbrella if their sport is introduced; however, many of these organizations exist for local, regional, state, and national promotion. They operate similarly to the NGO's with the main difference being that they have no tie to Olympic development. As such, they operate with many different agendas, approaches, and less standardization.

5. The Y's – (www.ymca.net): The Young Men's Christian Association is an example of one of the structures that is based on religious foundations promoting the well-being and character development of members through many activities, with sport included as a major emphasis. There are approximately 2700 YMCA's in the world with almost 21 million members. The main focus of the Y is to promote sport experiences that boost self-esteem, leadership, moral character, and many other purposes. Y's programs emphasize the role of the parent and child engaging in sport and supporting the core values of the organization. Y's often are the first step in community exposure to skill development and competition.

There are also other Y-based organizations that focus on sports and other purposes, although their role is more oriented to specific development of their primary memberships. For example, the Young Women's Christian Association focuses on the development of girls and women along many lines of effort beyond sport. Also the Young Men's and Women's Hebrew Association, now located under the umbrella of the Jewish Community Centers, are also organizations that sponsor programs of specific value to those of Jewish descent. While equally important for their roles with their constituents, they are less involved with an emphasis in sport.

6. Private and Commercial Operations: In addition to public and private membership-based organizations, there are also a myriad of private for profit and not-for-profit organizations that form to promote either a multiple sport focus or a single sport focus. These consist of clubs, retail-based operations that promote sport competitions, and sport organizations run by volunteers. These operations support local sport by sponsoring, running programs, and assisting existing operations. They make the most use of public land that is under the jurisdiction of park and recreation departments and other landholders, and they run many community programs that grow and develop into serious leisure.

7. Schools: Much of the problem that exists in sport today is the result of a failure of the educational system when divesting itself of recess,

physical education, and sport programming outside of school. Instead of coordinating this effort and transitioning those program cuts, cuts were made and people scrambled to find services elsewhere. Schools must provide leadership and encouragement in the establishment of a community sport system that reflects the needs for certification of staff and setting high standards of programming.

Proposal number 8

Organizations that can support the infrastructure of sport should be incorporated into all planning mechanisms for sport programming. These organizations are rich with resources and are able to help create consistency with other communities and organizations in delivery of programmatic services.

By becoming more aware of resources such as those mentioned above, it will be possible to coordinate services and develop best practices to mitigate violence and exclusion within the sport environment. To accomplish these best practices, there simply must be improved coordination of efforts at the local, state, province, or region, national, and international levels to ensure that the regulatory and managerial processes are supporting a safe, well-developed and civil process in sport.

Table 9.3	Eight Proposals to Improve Organizational Oversight
1	All entities offering sport at the local level must agree on standards and processes in the offering of sports programs.
2	A uniform code of conduct must be developed for all those engaged in sport.
3	A sport management professional who is well-versed in local level sport offerings should be hired in each community.
4	A policy framework drawn from what exists at the international, national, state/provincial, regional, and local levels to govern all operations that have to do with the physical development of participants at all age levels including pre-school and post school involvement.
5	Administrators of facilities and program must form a coordinating council to improve program quality, distribution of program services, and facility sharing to increase access and equity across the many participating groups.
6	Laws preventing violence need to be improved and applied throughout the legal and regulatory systems in every locale, state or province, region, national, and international entity to place more importance on legal resolution to violent episode and also to prevent the unnecessary escalation of violence in any sport venue.
7	Parent guidance and education starting with the birth of their child should provide improved choices for participation in leisure activity that emphasizes the overall health and development of the child rather than push for serious leisure.
8	Organizations that can support the infrastructure of sport should be incorporated into all planning mechanisms for sport programming.

SUMMARY

Eight propositions (Table 9.3) are presented that emphasize the need for greater oversight and coordination of the sport experience. It is suggested that every level of organization is responsible for seeing to it that a sport framework is coordinated, has developmental soundness, and is held accountable. The concepts of developing managerial strength when setting contractual obligations for private use of public land, the need for education of all those concerned with sport, the role of national organizations, the need for establishment of safe and secure environments, and the assurance that all programmatic efforts are sound are important in mitigating violence and maximizing programs for all.

The current lack of managerial oversight must give way to sound systems that can respond to violent episodes instantly and handle the aftermath in a way that reflects due process expectations in society.

It is essential that organizational leadership be developed and effected in order to make the most desirable changes in the sport environment. These organizations, particularly those holding land and facilities that are typically contracted out for services, may exert many changes to change the cycle of violence that has befallen those who participate in sport programs. Obviously increased oversight along several lines is important: improve basic adult responsibilities, and improve organizational monitoring of all programs. Following the eight proposal cited in this chapter is a start for organizational change. Understanding the need for change is the ultimate first step. It is possible to eradicate violence in these programs and move toward a much more positive environment.

REFERENCES

Anonymous, 2000. CPRS' youth development policy and strategies. California Parks and Recreation Society 56 (1), 42–44.

Archdiocese of Indianapolis, 2003. To be Safe and Secure. Archdiocese (report), Indianapolis, IN.

Bonnano, J., 2009. Due process, free speech, and New Jersey's athletic code of conduct: an evaluation of potential constitutional challenges to a good idea. Seton Hall Journal of Sports and Entertainment Law 14 (2), 397–440.

Brekken, Chris., 2009. Personal account of violence in sport, February 2.

Chavez, V.N., 2007. Youth development: creating a framework for action. California Parks and Recreation 63 (2), 26–43.

Docheff, D.M., 2004. It's no longer a spectator sport: eight ways to get involved and help fight parental violence in youth sports. Parks and Recreation.

Gibbs, N., 2001. "It's only me." Time 157 (11), 22–23.

Harmon, L.K., 2008. Get out and stay out. Parks and Recreation 43 (6), 50–55.

Heinzmann, G., 2002. Facts, myths and videotape. Parks and Recreation 37 (3), 66–72.

Hobson, K., 2006. Baby, work out!. U.S. News and World Report 140 (24), 56–70.

King, A., 2001. Abstract and engaged critique in sociology: on football hooliganism. British Journal of Sociology 52 (4).

Hyman, M., 2009. Young bodies under pressure. Youth Sports Network: Suny Youth Sports Institute. http://www.youthsportsny.org. Retrieved 1/22/2009.

Jamieson, L.M. (2004) Value of government policy in sport and leisure. Proceedings for the World Leisure Congress, Brisbane, AU, October 2–4, 2004.

Kidman, L., McKenzie, A., McKenzie, B., 1999. The nature and target of parents' comments during youth sport competition. Journal of Sport Behavior 22 (1), 54–68.

Lance, L., Ross, C., Houck, T., 1998. Violence in sports: perceptions of intramural sport participants. NIRSA Journal, Spring, 145–148.

Linbos, M.A., Peek-Asa, C., 2003. Comparing unintentional injuries in a school setting. Journal for School Health 73 (3).

Michiana High School League, 2008. Zero tolerance: verbal and physical abuse of officials (Pamphlet).

Midnight basketball and beyond…Sports in youth development. Profile, Fall, 1999, 5.

Mundy, J., 1997. Developing anger and aggression control in youth in recreation and park systems. Parks and Recreation 32 (3), 63–69.

National Alliance for Youth Sports, 2009. Time Out! for better sports and kids. Retrieved from www.tomeforbettersportsforkids.org, 2/9/2009.

Owczarski, J., 2008. Specialization can be detrimental to young athletes. Beacon News. Retrieved from www.suburbanchicagonews.com/beaconnews/sports, 1/22/2009.

Onofrietti, T., 1996. The recreation–education model: a philosophy of youth sports. NIRSA Journal, 18–19.

Orr, T.J., 2007. Interview with Richard Mull. Former Director Indiana University Tennis Center. February 13, 2007.

Price, S.L., 2008. Eight is not enough. Sports Illustrated 109 (7), 96.

Reilly, R., 2007. School for the uncool. Sports Illustrated 107 (11), 98.

Roberts, S., 2008. The prying game, (September 22),. Sports Illustrated 109 (11), 76.

Rowland, C., Stewart, W., 2008. Research update: vying for volunteers. Parks and Recreation 43 (10), 28–29.

Shalter, P., Raising your Champion. Champion Athletic Consulting, Dayton, OH Undated Pamphlet.

Sherman, L.W., 1997. Preventing Crimes: What Works, What Doesn't, What's Promising. National Institute of Justice, Washington, D.C.

Steelman, T., 1995. Enhancing the youth sports experience through coaching. Parks and Recreation, 14–18.

Steinbach, P., 2007. Face offerings. Athletic Business, 48–49.

Wells, B., 2008. How much competition is too much for kids? The Republican sports Desk.http://www.mass.live.com/sports/index.ssf/2008/12

Weems, R., 2009. Personal account of violence in sport, February 18.

Wenthe, D., 1997. Kool Kids: Corporate-sponsored free swim. Parks and Recreation 32 (11), 58–61.

Wilkins, N., 1997. Overtime is better than sudden death. Parks and Recreation 32 (3), 54–61.

Witt, P.A., Crompton, J., Baker, D., 1995. Evaluating youth recreation programs. Leisure Today, 3–6.

Wolff, R., 2001. Don't turn your child into a sports specialist. Time.

Wolff, R., 2001. Give the heave-ho to outrageous behavior. Time 95 (23).

www.nays.com

www.nrpa.org

www.ncaa.com

Young, S., Ross, C.M., 2000. Recreational sports trends for the 21st Century: results of a Delphi Study. NIRSA Journal 24 (2), 24–37.

Case Study 9.1

Intramural Sports

Sports and Violence

Event: Elite 8 of Division II Intramural Men's Basketball Tournament

Officials: 3 year veteran and one of the top rookies

Situation:

Team 1 vs. Team 2 is playing for the chance to go to the Final Four and possibly the championship game which is played in Assembly Hall. Team 1 has had controversy in their last two games. They have lost and protested each game and won. Both were because their opponents had illegal players.

This game was heated from the very beginning. Bob on Team 1 is very aggressive and has been warned by officials in other games. He has never been ejected or been given a technical foul. During this game Bob is guarding Jay. During the middle of the first half, Jay complains to the officials that Bob spit on him. The officials tell Jay that they did not see anything, but during the dead ball, they would talk to Bob about it. They let Bob know that he needs to keep his cool.

This makes Bob very mad. Jay again complains to the officials that Bob called him names and made threats against him. All this after the officials talked to Bob. This is right before half time. The officials this time call Bob and Jay over for a meeting. The officials warn both players that if they hear anything out of either of them, they would not hesitate to eject both players.

The second half starts and both teams are very aggressive to each other. The officials had to stop the game and warn both captains that if the teams did not cool it, they would start ejecting players and end the game if needed. The game was eventually won by two points by Team 2, and both teams were extremely mad afterwards.

After the game, Jay again complained to the officials and one of the top administrators. He claimed Bob had spit on him and continued to call him names and make threats against him even after the officials warned him. The administrator said that he would investigate it and he could not do anything about it at the time. This is all going on while both teams are still at the court. Jay mumbles under his breath, "If you aren't going to do anything about it, I will." He walks over to Bob and punches him in the face and takes off running. Jay was eventually apprehended and was arrested. Bob required 10 stitches in his lip.

Team 1 protested because they believed Jay was an illegal player.

Now the Intramural staff has to decide what happens with the players and the game.

Case Study 9.2

While playing basketball, I developed into what my coach called, "the enforcer." My duties included rebounding, setting hard picks, and defense. These were my official duties, but I had unofficial duties that my coach inferred. These duties included always fouling out and inflecting as much harm on targeted players from these fouls, picks, and various other basketball actions. On the rare occasion, I was called in to retaliate against a player who causes an injury to one of our players. For example, my team and I were in a basketball tournament. The second round game my team's best player was undercut by another player on the opposite team. Our players shoulder was separated and we lost him for the remainder of the tournament and longer. This happened right before half and when we got in at half time, my coach pulled me to the side and told me to take care of the situation. I asked him who I should foul hard, but he informed me to take out as many as possible. I started the second half and when the time came, I retaliated by taking out their best player. At this point, their team surrounded me and I found the idea situation to accomplish my goal. I punched the first guy who got into my face and the other teams remaining players started hitting me. The referees separated us finally then my coach grabbed me and told me to go to the locker room. I went to the locker room until the game ended. When the coach came in, he congratulated me on doing what I was told. I found out from him that I was suspended for the rest of the tournament but I had accomplished my goal of taken out four of their players, two with injuries and two were ejected for fighting. My coach gave me the game ball.

Weems, R. (2009).

SPORT STORIES 9.1

I was running a penalty box at one of Matty's peewee hockey games. A parent running the clock watched his son get checked hard enough to draw a penalty. The dad had to be restrained from going over the boards. He verbally attacked the opposing player as he took a seat for 2 min. The two of them continued to banter. I had to block their line of sight and diffuse the situation. It was tense for a while.

Chris Brekken, Father-in-law of Tom Orr

CHAPTER 10

Solutions

An old man, going a lone highway,
Came, at the evening, cold and gray,
To a chasm, vast, and deep, and wide,
Through which was flowing a sullen tide.

The old man crossed in the twilight dim;
The sullen stream had no fears for him;
But he turned, when safe on the other side,
And built a bridge to span the tide.

"Old man," said a fellow pilgrim, near,
"You are wasting strength with building here;
Your journey will end with the ending day;
You never again must pass this way;
You have crossed the chasm, deep and wide
-Why build you the bridge at the eventide?"

The builder lifted his old gray head:
"Good friend, in the path I have come,"
he said, "There followeth after me today
A youth, whose feet must pass this way.

This chasm, that has been naught to me,
To that fair-haired youth may a pitfall be.
He, too, must cross in the twilight dim;
Good friend, I am building the bridge for him."

The Bridge Builder by Will Allen Dromgoole

This poem captures the role and motivations of any thoughtful person when it comes to helping our youth and to set a motivation to help future generations that encompasses and surpasses the depth of the human heart. During the research of this book we have chronicled so many instances of human expression that penetrated the lines of acceptable behavior. Each of these incidents seemed to have its own unique aspects, yet found a way to tie into the greater themes that surrounds deviance in sports. Every incident is grounded in a specific time, place and social setting that makes its interpretation difficult. There are certain actions and reactions that are preferable for future cases, and there seems to always be a personal choice or environmental condition that was abnormal.

Understanding these incidents is seen less important to many people who embrace the natural entertainment they provide. Tantamount to both of these desires is the ability of society to take each incident as a learning opportunity. Highlighting and sanctioning unethical behavior is important for controlling public sporting events. Taking a pragmatic approach to sports violence as a problem leads one to look for solutions. The recording of solutions and best practices for sports violence is an arduous, but important task. Categorizing and study of the variables associated with violent acts in sports create a knowledge base rooted in the history of professional, recreational and youth sports. It is the goal of authors to serve as a bridge builder for future generations. In this manner events in sport violence will be archived and mined for the good in them so that we can learn from our sport history.

The value in sports history mirrors that of the greater society. If we do not learn from the errors in our sporting societies of the past, we will be doomed to repeat them in our sporting future. Thus this chapter continues the cycle of interpreting and understanding the solutions that lie within the crazy and embarrassing incidents that plague our nightly news and our daily lives. As much as we want to throw these stories away and forget about them, it is important to remember the stories of the Duke Lacrosse Investigation, the Tanya Harding incident, Michael Vick, and a backup punter who tried to stab the starter in the league so that the society is not twice plagued by such events.

It is very important that leisure management agencies consider deviant acts and plan for them. This can be handled by playing "what if" games and considering ways that they can respond to problems that could be anticipated. Specifically programming for social control is a powerful tool that recreation leaders can use to manipulate events and intervene in the social actions that occur within the program. Creating an environment that is safe and allows participants to receive positive benefits is something that should be considered when designing and implementing sporting events and other leisure programs.

By setting up programs that put a priority on sportsmanship and character development, a moral tone can be set for the organization.

Considering social benefits and personal benefits to participants in a way that maximizes the physical and psychological well-being of those involved will give participants an opportunity to learn and have a chance to succeed. If these benefits can be equitably distributed to community members the benefits can be spread in a manner that does not marginalize groups. Leisure opportunities that develop character should also function with structure and discipline so that aggression and anger that occurs can be dealt effectively and efficiently. Programmers should consider the ugly factor of the event and have a proactive approach to dealing with it when it occurs, while also using the possibility of an event as an educational opportunity to address a perceived social problem. A good example of this is the anti-hazing seminars that are popular in colleges, high schools and youth leagues around the world. If something negative occurs it should be used as an educational tool for those that were exposed to it and if there are ways to reduce harm and provide discipline than those steps should be taken.

IMMEDIATE PROBLEMS FACING DEVELOPMENT OF SOLUTIONS

Heinzmann (2002) recognized the lack of research from the academic world to explain and test what was happening when people got angry at sporting events. He stated, "We can utilize the vast quantity of social science research that has been conducted on youth crime/school violence to enhance our understanding of how the media may be influencing public opinion about sports rage" (p. 3). This statement demonstrates the need for academics to provide bias free information that uses the scientific method to provide insight into this important issue in a balanced way to the general public. Without academic challenges and scientific inquiry, the current and future study of sports rage could be set back by mistakes and nonsense theories that are presented by other sources. These ideas become accepted public knowledge when engrained into people's perception. Those who become authorities on the subject not by intelligence or experience, but simple willingness to claim an expertise through their position only makes the problem grow worse. Qualitative design facilitates are preferable because they allow the research to emerge as theory develops. Qualitative data can be collected through in depth interviews, direct observation, and written documents

(Trochim, 2001). Triangulation of these methods can more accurately measure social phenomenon and provide more support for validity. "When the findings of different methods agree, we are more confident" (Brewer and Hunter, 1989, p. 17).

Obviously more research conducted both quantitatively and qualitatively that examines the frequency, demographics, types and resolution of violence would be helpful for agencies in targeting the most likely directions for solving sport violence problems. Currently, research studies have unveiled incidents and the manner in which various subjects perceived violence. In addition, research studies involving cases of actual incidents have provided incites from a qualitative perspective. Unfortunately, however, much more research effort is encouraged along the following lines:

1. Disciplinary action to sport violence;

2. Typologies of perpetrators of sport violence;

3. Criminal acts in the sport setting;

4. Current and projected status of sport violence;

5. Typology of the ideal sport parent (coach, spectator, referee, etc.);

6. Interventions for sport violence;

7. Research of best practices that can benefit problem solvers;

8. The psychological portrait of a violent athlete (coach, spectator, referee, etc.);

9. Assessment of practices to mitigate sport violence;

10. Study of research gaps in sport and violence.

As with any social problem in society, it is important for there to be a complete understanding of the background of sport. In this closing chapter, it is important to summarize what has been shared and to focus on the most important areas to start with in order to see expedient resolution of the sport violence scenario.

CULTIVATING A VISION – A GENERAL COMMITMENT TO YOUTH

In order to address the youth part of the problem with sport violence, and violence in general, there needs to be a strategic approach that is developed in a community. An example of this major thrust is the strategy for youth service delivery that was adopted in California by the professional society of recreators – the California Parks and Recreation Society. Through study and focus, the society adopted a youth development mission and plan that operates in every city within the state. The vision statement identifies the direction this way:

> *"Initiate a community needs assessment in order to identify the value of youth programs. Use the results of the needs assessment to build a community consensus/vision that establishes youth as a high priority and supports the transition into a youth development model. After the assessment, develop, values, vision and mission statements for your youth programs that are consistent with youth development principles. Phrases to consider include 'all young people develop healthy lifestyles, 'young people are provided', 'acquire knowledge, capacities and skills to become productive, active, and socially responsible,' or 'all young people develop life skills and form attitudes to enable them to become self-directing, productive and contributing members of society." (Fritz, 2007, p. 34)*

Specific actions that were recommended, based upon research were identified from a comprehensive research report by Eccles (2002 as cited in Chavez, 2007, p. 43) that included:

- Physical and psychological safety,

- Appropriate structures that provide: limit setting; clear, consistent rules and regulations; continuity and predictability; and age-appropriate monitoring,

- Supportive relationships characterized by warmth and closeness,

- Connectedness, caring, and responsiveness,

- Opportunities to belong and for meaningful inclusion regardless of demographics or abilities,

- Positive social norms with clear rules for behavior, expectations, values and morals,

- Support for efficacy and mattering that includes enabling, responsibility and meaningful challenge,

- Opportunities for skill building,

- Integration of family, school and community efforts.

The intent in providing a sound sport environment is also to take into consideration the above considerations when developing the child. Unfortunately, it is rare to see a sport program operate with such a broad-based philosophy where youth development is top in the adults mind – whether it is a coach, parent, spectator, or administrator. Youth-based programs can emerge from this philosophy and improve all service delivery for youth.

It is not only youth who wind up engaged in sport violence – moreover, experiences in youth are often the blueprint for actions in the future. For all programming, regardless of age, similar developmental principles are needed to allow individuals to enjoy the chosen activity fully. It is suggested that all goals for all programming consider the person first, then the ideals for programming may be developed around that person's or group of person's characteristics. The difficulty in setting age-appropriate programs for those who reach adulthood is that individuals have been influenced by past experiences and tend to repeat those experiences; however, through education and reinforcement and engagement, change is inevitable. For programs to sustain the pressure without imploding, it is necessary to insert reason and intention. It is through sound planning and efforts to mitigate violence that changes will be experienced. This chapter examines several approaches and strategies that are imperative for future sport programming.

FIRST MAJOR FOCUS: THE SPORT ACTORS – SOLVING PROBLEMS AND ISSUES

Those involved in the sport scene from the time they are participants to the time they become part of the leadership are facing constant pressures to perform and push the level of sport to a higher level. Every individual who forms a part of a sport experience has a responsibility to assess the level to which they should go in encouraging sport participation, the pursuit of winning at all costs, and the ultimate benefit that results from competition and physical exercise.

Enacting a sport event is like theatre – each individual play his/her part, and one part misses a cue, the entire experience may break down and be unenjoyable for the actors and the viewers. When children come to play, they do not need to hear the result of an over-pressured person screaming for more and more – the child needs a pleasant experience and a great deal of encouragement. It is imperative that the entire sport experience be reviewed and revised to ensure that children and adults pursue sport experiences that remain safe and free from psychological and physical injury. In addition, parents and other adult role models need to take a break on the cycle of violence that leads to the levels of entanglements reported in the news. Children and supportive adults do not need exposure to such characteristically poor behavior. They need to feel comfortable and not embarrassed that adults act in this manner.

LEADERSHIP IN SPORT ORGANIZATIONS

Those in charge of facilities and programs must carry the appropriate educational and professional benchmarks that show exposure to sound development of sport programming. Those who coach need extensive training in the role of coaching that particular sport. Referees must show the results of extensive training. It is clearly within the realm of those who operate schools and sport delivery systems that standards must be raised and programs need to be re-evaluated if persons do not meet those standards.

Those responsible for national organizations must step up and insist on local quality control, so that those who progress have the best chance of improving in a way that prevents over-training, burnout, or injury. From the top levels of government to the local boards, everyone has a stake in the success of those who participate in sport – if children, they are those who will carry their success forward in a positive way; for adults – they will continue to build health and strength as a partial result of their participation. Sport and fitness experiences must proceed according to what is developmentally sound physically, socially, and psychologically.

Who begins this process? Everyone! Reforms often start at the grass roots level – however, those responsible for providing information about sport need to rewrite the books and become informed in such a way that information is the fuel to power reform.

POLITICS, VIOLENCE REDUCTION

Any nation that has ever been involved in media coverage of a violent event whether it is hooliganism, fan–player controversy, betting on child athletes, abusing athletes with medication, or any other item of a scandalous nature is a victim to the repercussions that this negative message portrays. It is the responsibility of people at the national level to address societal problems that are not easily addressed at a state or local level-items such as discrimination, hunger, morbidity, and other issues often are debated and discussed until some type of policy direction is established. Policies must be developed at the national level that addresses the coordination of services to mitigate violence, and also that addresses state and local responsibilities. Without a policy that addresses violence, these actions will continue to reflect the nature of the society in which they occur, and they will no doubt escalate to a point where sport is no longer a positive experience for players or viewers. The concept of a nation without sport is not unusual; indeed, Roman and Greek societies died for less.

As a social problem, it is imperative that countries assess the effect of violence in sport on quality of life in a community. Change must be made to ensure that improvement of management quality, training, and programming occurs. To some extent, reorganization of those agencies that are involved in sport may be necessary, or those agencies may need to be restructured to address what is necessary for improvement of sports programs. It is no longer suitable for these sport programs to be run by those with no training. The guidance and ability of professionals is a minimum standard that must be addressed.

Government policies may be structured to support programs that mitigate violence, to address consequences for those who violate behavioral guidelines, and for organizations that fail to address safe and secure environment issues. Many countries already have policies with respect to sport that identify key areas of importance. The policies that exist consist of a response to information about the needs of the country such as:

1. Health factors – Through assessment of morbidity statistics and medical records, citizens' health issues are revealed such as heart, lung, and other ailments. Targeted needs are developed, particularly those that may be prevented through a healthier lifestyle.

2. Fitness and exercise patterns – The degree to which the general population exercises in hours per week is assessed and then used as an annual comparison figure to mark success of programs.

3. Longevity issues – This is described in average life expectancy of males and females and compared with other countries and within the country to note improvement or degradation.

4. Stress factors – Particular issues concerning work, leisure, school, and environmental factors are described with respect to how the population in general is affected.

5. Facility needs – A needs assessment of facilities and areas is conducted that note factors such as ease of access, walkability, distribution across population groups, and other factors.

6. Program needs – Through needs assessment gaps and duplicated services are noted and described.

7. Special needs of a target population – Target groups that may include those from rural or remote areas, those who need special accommodation, those with specific needs as a result of advanced age, a particular indigenous group, youth, women, and other groups are identified through cultural analysis.

8. Remote, rural access – Anyone residing remotely may be accommodated with specialized services.

9. Sport development needs – Through analysis of gaps in developing sport skills that include early instruction to advanced level services is assessed to determine how to improve sport success for competition and for health.

10. National and international visibility goals – Goals established for improvement of the national image and accomplishment are set with regard to national and international competition, service, and visibility.

11. Sport system regulatory issues – Within sport, issues such as performance enhancement use, exploitation of youth, substance abuse, behavioral problems and other factors are assessed and determined for inclusion in policy and consequential guidelines.

Table 10.1 shows specific categories of country policy amalgamated from several sources. It can be seen that very little reference is made to sport and violence. There may be many reasons for this in that many countries do not experience violence to the extent that the United States, Europe, and South America do; however, there are issues in almost every country that surround the need for some policy regulation.

In looking at the existence of sport policy that emerges from many policy documents, there are areas within more well-established and developed countries that address part of the problem with sport and violence, but there is no comprehensive policy that addresses the full nature of sport violence. Some countries address managerial issues that lead to a well-managed system; however, due to failure for the national policy to diffuse effectively to the local sector, often the guidelines are not applied thoroughly. In addition, the policy guidelines refer to specific issues within a country, such as doping, substance abuse, use of hormones, and similar issues; however, that is just part of the problem.

The other part of policy development is to develop standards that are accrued from those in positions to effect change – the administrators, coaches, parents, spectators, players, teachers, referees, and anyone involved in a sport

Table 10.1	Components of National Policy
1	Policy Intention
	What are the key goals of implementing a policy with respect to sport?
2	Policy Direction
	In what way will policies be implemented? Initiated at the national level and implemented through the local, or vice versa.
3	Special Issues
	Is there a specific population, problem, or national need?
4	Funding
	What is the chief source of funding? A sponsor, government allocation, fee-based program, or a combination?
5	How will the mass population and sport elite benefit?
	Is one more important than another or co-dependent on funding?
6	Training
	Who will handle training? How will it be implemented?
7	Marketing
	What is the market plan for dissemination of information to educate and encourage?

or sport-related environment. It can start at that level. It is time for reform and change in the nature of sport delivery that assesses the full benefits for those who participate. It is time to end the cycle of violence that starts with poor organization, lack of training and education, misguided and overzealous adults, and ultimately ruined players. People need to take a step back, take a breath and make a commitment to reform the system. The following describes simple ways to get started as an anti-violence advocate:

1. Parents – Get a grip. Your child will have better success studying more and securing scholarships than hyper-involvement in sport. Your efforts may begin by starting a savings account for your children's futures that budget a portion of what would be spent for leisure activities. Invest in programs beyond sport as well, such as cultural arts, social programs, and other experiences. Assess your motives as your children become more successful in their endeavors and allow them to make choices as a part of their involvement.

2. Players – It is your life. Make choices that will broaden your life and be fulfilling. Sport involvement may take many paths – struggling in one sport does not mean struggles in others. Explore creative pursuits, use your yard, and enjoy your life. In addition, say something to adults who are acting improperly.

3. Administrators – Gain control of all sport programs using your facilities and areas by being the coordinator of training, selection of volunteers, monitoring of programs, and mitigator of violence. It is your responsibility to see to it that all activities under your jurisdiction are run properly regardless of whether these activities have contracted facilities or if you are running them yourselves. Your education should be solid, but if not take the necessary time to see that those under you jurisdiction receive the proper education and training to effectively offer comprehensive services. In addition, respond quickly to issues and follow due process in handling problems. Those of a more severe nature should go through the judicial process accorded those who commit crimes. Lobby for ordinances and laws that address the consequences of violence and enforce them through policing and support of staff.

4. Policymakers – Heed the issues present in the rise of sport violence in your jurisdictions and create legislation that effects policy development for the betterment of sport. Assist in the coordination of services in your jurisdiction in order to address better management and control over all sport development. Become learned on the progression of violence from frustration to acting out, and work with local individuals to create more education as to why this occurs. It is time for improved and explicit ways to address this social problem.

5. Educators – Take back the right to educate and offer programs that stress positive outcomes in the schools. Work with governmental officials to ensure the offering of services meet guidelines similar to those you enforce – education in specific content areas, certification, and monitoring. Children need exercise while in school, and many simple issues may be resolved with that.

TOWARD AN ERA OF RENEWED RESPONSIBILITY

The purpose of this text has been to familiarize those who study sport and those who participate in sport with the pressing social problem of sport violence. In discussing all angles of this problem, we have defined the issues, discussed the historical roots of the problem, identified the status today from an international perspective, noted societal factors that are a foundational issue, identified potential causes, noted exclusionary issues in sport that give rise to violence, inspected fan behavior, identified spillover effects into society and focused on organizational and individual solutions. Sport violence, in its many forms, is a problem that permeates the very society we live in and has become an ingrained response to many issues that affect daily living. In order to correct the pattern that has developed over the years, and taking the issues described in this chapter, the following mega-solution is proposed.

Charters

There is a need for an international charter that addresses the reality of sport violence and the code of honor that mitigates it. This charter may be appended to existing codes that operate within and among countries, for example:

- All countries that currently operated with a nation-wide sport/leisure/ health policy may include the charter to affirm efforts to mitigate violence in its various forms within a specific country.

- This charter may be appended to any relevant charter that is concerned with peace efforts within the United Nations and its ancillaries.

- The charter may become appended to any anti-crime efforts and as such classify sport violence in keeping with a country's crime prevention initiatives.

- The charter may be appended to the World Leisure Bill of Rights approved in 2000 (Table 10.2).

Table 10.2 Positive Aspects of Sport – Setting Important Goals
Fun factor
Development
Social learning
Choice and substitution
Accomplishment
Fitness
Confidence/self-esteem
Self-efficacy
Health
Happiness
Recognition
Winning
Scholarship
Olympics
Popularity
Celebrity

The organization

Organizations having responsibility for sport must reorganize to create agency/business readiness for sport violence mitigation. It is evident that many organizations have already begun to adjust the approaches they have taken toward the sport development programs under their jurisdictions. The following examples provide a framework that others may follow:

- The National Alliance for Youth Sports (NAYS) is adopting a community philosophy making youth sports safe and positive. The organizational approach involves appointing professional youth sport administrators and holding everyone in the program accountable for their behavior. This organization serves as a resource for all communities determined to get rid of the "ugly factor" and is most effective if the major facility provider is invested in this approach and accesses all of the many materials that await on the web and through those who consult. Within this website is the Parents Association for Youth Sports that is affiliated with NAYS and consists of an educational process to help children experience safe sports participation. It also encourages positive sport conduct.

- The Fun First! Sports for Kids (NRPA) program is designed to influence its member departments to help parents with kids get the most out of their sport participation. Based on the belief that parents really want their children to experience positive outcomes, they provide tools needed to see that these goals are achieved.

- Richfield, MN has developed consequences to behavioral misconduct whereby the umpire stops the game and notifies both coaches. Notification is then given to the fan, and the game is stopped until the fan is removed.

- A notification such as this one from the National Youth Baseball Association is as follows:

  We, the NYBA, appreciate your attendance at our youth events. Our participants need your POSITIVE SUPPORT, and ENCOURAGE-MENT. ABUSIVE BEHAVIOR of players, coaches, umpires, or fans WILL NOT BE TOLERATED. If your behavior continues, WE WILL STOP THE GAME UNTIL YOU LEAVE THE PREMISES.

- Law enforcement and legislative solutions also have been developed that consist of local by-laws against field encroachment, heightened police presence at the end of play, hi-tech surveillance systems, court rooms and jail cells inside the stadia, and punitive legal responses to those involved in anti-social fan behavior.

■ Laws exist such as New Jersey's Athletic Code of Conduct that was established in 2002. It allows local official the authority to banish misbehaving adults from future games until they take a course in anger management; Arizona's establishment of a Class 1 misdemeanor for touching officials at kids' games.

■ Facility and program solutions include New Brunswick, NJ construction of a youth complex that is elevated 10 feet with bleachers located away from the foul line and spectators being separated by the dugouts; Jupiter, Florida's requirement of parents to take a class on sport conduct and sign a code of conduct; New Albany, Ohio's requirements for parents in the school district to take a 90-min class on sport conduct and ethics and sign a code of conduct; and, Los Angeles, California' letter home with athletes spelling out appropriate parental behavior for sidelines and distribution of yellow warning cards to fans who disrupt the event.

■ Crowd control aspects in facility are being replaced by a guest relations approach to those involved in the sport experience and stadia are being remodeled to provide protective tunnels, permanent canopies, and special designated "family" enclosures.

These are but a few of the many processes that must prevail when an organization assumes the responsibility for community sport development. Of course these solutions, when not coupled with a fully comprehensive set of approaches, merely serves as an immediate and superficial means to mitigate violence, because a single law or specific directive does not prevent issues that arise due to improper training, supervision, facility development, anger and frustration, and poor developmental practices.

Recommendations

The following recommendations are ways to address the problem more broadly:

■ High Performance Programs

1. Establish policies, procedures, and rules to account for the rights and interests of all participants.

2. Create less controlling environments designed to promote growth, development, and empowerment.

- Informal and Alternative Sports

    1. Make play spaces more safe and accessible to as many participants as possible being particularly sensitive to social class and gender patterns.

    2. Provide indirect guidance without being controlling.

    3. Treat these sports as worthwhile sites for facing challenges and developing competence.

    4. Develop youth leadership abilities to secure safety and programmatic satisfaction.

- Changing Organized Sports

    1. Increase action.

    2. Increase personal involvement.

    3. Facilitate close scores and realistic challenges.

    4. Facilitate friendship formation and maintenance.

With the above recommendations, restructuring of the way we see sport is essential – what exists today based on money and power, expands to be inclusive, accessible, affordable, and enjoyable. Nothing prevents someone from moving forward from beginning instruction to ever-advancing skill development that leads to an unbroken path to the ultimate success desired. Through international, national, regional, state, and local coordination, where the power to change rests primarily with the local sector, the dream envisioned by Pierre de Coubertin in the early 1900s is realized – sport and fitness for all who participate.

WHAT'S IN STORE? THE FUTURE OF SPORT

As we conclude this text, it is wise to prognosticate on the future trends that may impact cultures, countries and sport. It is suggested that the following 10 trends will affect how sport and violence is handled:

Trend #1 Privatization of sport: If the current trend toward public divestment of sport experiences continues, youth will be offered more and more options from sport organizations that are privately formed and affected by special interest. With this trend, sport sponsorship and elite programs at earlier ages will predominate, sport power structures may not be professionalized, adult-controlled structured sport will continue, and there will be earlier and earlier identification of talent for scholarships and sponsorships.

Trend # 2 Sport rage: With increased pressure on players and those involved in the sport environment it is expected that parents and adult role models will increasingly assume the role of "agent" for their charges due to increase in the financial investment in sport. In addition incidents within and outside of the playing environment will increase with the continued belief that the elusive scholarship or professional sponsorship is just around the corner. In addition, there will continue to be weak systems for enforcement that will fail to curtail excessive pressure or correct skirmishes that arise when anger takes over.

Trend # 3 Increase in sport-related injury at younger ages: Overuse issues will plague those not physically developed to contain stress of strain on muscles and bones. Under-training or failure to develop basic fitness such as balance, coordination, strength, cardiovascular capacity, flexibility, and endurance will delay readiness to engage in contact and stress sports. In addition, an increase in sport specialization will preclude participation in a variety of sports, and overall training will be sacrificed.

Trend#4 Increased technology keeping children at home in self-learning environments: With the establishment of the Wii system of sport, continuance of sedentary activities, social isolation preferred to intense pressure, and youth-created and continued activities will be favored over adult-controlled activities.

Trend # 5 Extended economic problems will force choices: The continued affordability issue of youth sports exacerbated by the need to curtail some activity is inevitable. Further, youth will choose to drop out earlier and engage in low-cost pursuits. Public agencies will continue to be pressured to provide more affordable options. With the continuance of this type of pressure, the more serious sport lobbies will increase as more compete for less resource.

Trend #6 There will be more attention paid to develop the positive role models in accomplished athletes as they become more popular as leaders who exhibit character and ethical development. The increased visibility of the National Collegiate Athletic Organization, sport-specific professional sport associations, national governmental associations, sport clubs, and the national high school activities association bodies in providing programs to boost respect for sport and for sport leaders is evident. This will also be coupled with overall health concerns in countries that target the elimination of obesity and illness through preventive measures. Targets toward all may lower disparities between haves and have-nots.

The most compelling evidence of this trend was the report developed by the Coalition on Intercollegiate Athletics and presented at a conference in 2005 (COIA, 2005). This report sent reverberations throughout all collegiate institutions when it documented issues regarding the role of intercollegiate sport on a college campus. Through this report, the NCAA and the National Association of Intercollegiate Athletics began reforms that highlighted more stringent eligibility requirements, recruiting standards, and the academic path of the athlete. In addition, the National High School Activities Association which regulates all state high school activities association responded with similar changes. These changes will have far-reaching appeal and will also affect how standards are set for other programs.

Trend #7 Increased concern over child health issues will shift the trend from sport to active living. The Play Act in the United States encourages one hour of play per day outside of the home in general activity endeavors. Community active living models across the life span are also encouraging less driving and more use of trails for cycling and walking. Increases in health partnerships are forming for preventive efforts at improving health behavior.

Trend #8 Increased development of national and state policy will focus on sport and health: With the already increasing role of Health and Human Services and specific Ministries of Health, Health, Promotion, and Active Living, greater influence exists for more effective program delivery at the local level. In addition, regulatory agencies will weigh in on some aspects of sport organizations through the provision of mandatory and permissive training, education, and certification on some aspects of all sport organizations. Will we see an international policy on sport, leisure, and health?

Trend #9 Sport specialization will continue: If current power structures continue to exert their will upon sport programming, a continued unidimensional approach to sport will continue. Youth athletes will continue to drop out of these environments at an increasing rate due to burnout, injury, and just not choosing the sport involvement. This will affect sport participation at all levels with earlier drop-out statistics and endangered high school, club, and college programs.

Trend # 10 All governmental organizations will be called upon to solve the problems inherent in the cycle of sport and violence. These organizations will be valued as the nexus that can structure a solution, rethink the role of sport for the greater good, and respond to a call to change the system (Tables 10.3 and 10.4).

Figure 10.1 shows a path that may be used in a community with relationship to a particular country to effect change in sport. In this table a comprehensive look at sport issues and their relationship to agencies and business is shown and points of needed contact is described.

Table 10.3	Famous Quotes
Charles Dickens	Institutionalised in sports, the military, acculturated sexuality, the history and mythology of heroism, violence is taught to boys until they becomes its advocates
Gordie Howe	All hockey players are bilingual. They know English and profanity.
Marcus Aurelius	How much more grievous are the consequences of anger than the causes of it.
Ernest Hemingway	Auto racing, bull fighting, and mountain climbing are the only real sports … all others are games.
George Orwell	People sleep peaceably in their beds at night only because rough men stand ready to do violence on their behalf.
Leo Buscaglia	Don't hold to anger, hurt or pain. They steal your energy and keep you from love.
David Barry	Violence and smut are of course everywhere on the airwaves. You cannot turn on your television without seeing them, although sometimes you have to hunt around.
Joyce Carol Oates	When people say there is too much violence in [my books], what they are saying is there is too much reality in life.
Booker T. Washington	I will permit no man to narrow and degrade my soul by making me hate him.
Quentin Tarantino	Violence is one of the most fun things to watch
Dennis Prager	How a society channels male aggression is one of the greatest questions as to whether that society will survive. That's why I am not against violence in the media, I am against the glorification of immoral violence.
Helen Douglas	Character isn't inherited. One builds it daily by the way one thinks and acts, thought by thought, action by action. If one lets fear or hate or anger take possession of the mind, they become self-forged chains.
Nikki Giovanni	Sacred cows make very poor gladiators.
Pierre Elliott Trudeau (Canadian Prime Minister)	Canada is a country whose main exports are hockey players and cold fronts. Our main imports are baseball players and acid rain.
Henry W. Longfellow	If we could read the secret history of our enemies, we should find in each man's life sorrow and suffering enough to disarm any hostility.
John Dryden	Beware of the fury of the patient man.
David Emerson	I have a background from my younger days in hockey. When somebody slammed you into the boards with undue force and aggression, you took their number.
Buddha	Holding on to anger is like grasping a hot coal with the intent of throwing it at someone else; you are the one who gets burned.
Rodney Dangerfield	I went to a fight the other night, and a hockey game broke out.
Unknown	Sticks and stones may break your bones when there's anger to impart. Spiteful words can hurt your feelings but silence breaks your heart.
Derric Rossy	I think [trash-talking and stunts] is a part of boxing that keeps people away; keeps away people who like golf and basketball and sports like that. Now, fight fans do like that there is violence, but Long Island is a different kind of crowd. So, with boxing here we need to be gentlemen and do our business in the ring.
Lord Halifax	Anger is seldom without an argument but seldom with a good one.

Table 10.3	Famous Quotes—*Cont'd*
Mel Angelstad	I know the only reason I made it anywhere in hockey was because I was a fighter. I know that was my role. I made it to the NHL doing that. If I don't fight again in my life that doesn't mean I'm not a tough guy.
Unknown	Anger is as a stone cast into a wasp's nest.
Sugar Ray Robinson	I ain't never liked violence.
Percy Bysshe Shelley	There is no sport in hate when all the rage is on one side
Chuck Norris	Men are like steel: when they lose their temper, they lose their worth.
Tryon Edwards	To rule one's anger is well; to prevent it is still better.
Marcus Antonius	Consider how much more you often suffer from your anger and grief, than from those very things for which you are angry and grieved.
Sepp Blatter	The only way to fight this is to do exactly what we have done when it came to violence. We have to take away the points because it happens in those leagues where the money is sufficient so, even if you gave a fine of $100,000, it would be paid the next day. That does not change the attitude, so you have to go into a sporting sanction.
Cato	An angry man opens his mouth and shuts up his eyes.
Jamie Levine	You pass by a car wreck and everybody looks. You may cover your face but you are looking through your fingers. Why do people go to NASCAR races? It's not to watch the cars go around in a circle. It's to see the crashes. Hockey is the same thing, fights. You don't go to a rodeo to watch a guy stay on a bull for eight seconds. You want to see that guy get thrown off and stomped. … Our sport is the only true sport, man versus man. This is for real. This is as real as it gets. People are trying to inflict some pain on their opponent.
W. R. Alger	Men often make up in wrath what they want in reason.
Lynn Jamieson	There is a fear of there being violence in any kind of a venue that has large numbers of people. And sports has always been one of the areas with the visibility and media attention that's given that it's always a logical and potential place for terrorist violence.
Golda Meir	You cannot shake hands with a clenched fist.
Adolf Hitler	The very first essential for success is a perpetually constant and regular employment of violence.
Noam Chomsky	You never need an argument against the use of violence, you need an argument for it.
Leigh Steinberg	In reality, we can prove that the incidents of drug, alcohol abuse and violence have dropped dramatically among professional athletes – but the problem is it would be impossible to convince than fans, because of what they read on the AP wire.
Theodore Roosevelt	There is a homely adage which runs: "Speak softly and carry a big stick; you will go far"
St. Francis De Sales	There was never an angry man that thought his anger unjust.
John Chaney	I'm sending a message, and I'm going to do what we used to do years ago – send in the goons.
Chinese Proverb	If you are patient in one moment of anger, you will escape a hundred days of sorrow.
Shakespeare	Men in rage strike those that wish them best.
Bill Cosby	The main goal of the future is to stop violence. The world is addicted to it.
Yogi Berra	I think Little League is wonderful. It keeps the kids out of the house.

Continued

Table 10.3	Famous Quotes—*Cont'd*
Elizabeth Kenny	He who angers you conquers you.
Greek	Those who the Gods would destroy First they would make angry
Pope John Paul II	Social justice cannot be attained by violence. Violence kills what it intends to create.
John Steinbeck	In the souls of the people the grapes of wrath are filling and growing heavy, growing heavy for the vintage.
Willard Gaylin	Expressing anger is a form of public littering.
Henry Beecher	Never forget what a man says to you when he is angry.
Bob Dylan	Democracy don't rule the world, You'd better get that in your head; this world is ruled by violence, But I guess that's better left unsaid.
Lawrence J. Peter	Speak when you're angry, and you'll make the best speech you'll ever regret.
Tamil proverb	Great anger is more destructive than the sword.
Jesse Ventura	Wrestling is ballet with violence.
Mark Twain	It's not the size of the dog in the fight, it's the size of the fight in the dog.
Pythagoras	Anger begins with folly and ends with repentance.
Oscar Wilde	America is the only country that went from barbarism to decadence without civilization in between.
Pasquier Quesnel	Anger causes us often to condemn in one what we approve in another.
Lucius Annaeus Seneca	It is the failing of youth not to be able to restrain its own violence.
Charles De Gaulle	When I am right, I get angry. Churchill gets angry when he is wrong. So we were often angry at each other.
Alfred Montapert	Every time you get angry, you poison your own system.
Martin Luther	Nothing good ever comes of violence.
Daniel Webster	Keep cool; anger is not an argument.
Jim Morrison	Violence isn't always evil. What's evil is the infatuation with violence.
Thomas Haliburton	When a man is wrong and won't admit it, he always gets angry.
Thomas Fuller	Two things a man should never be angry at: what he can help, and what he cannot help.
Jimmy Kimmel	What I said about Pistons fans during halftime was a joke, nothing more. If I offended anyone, I'm sorry. Clearly, over the past 10 years, we in L.A. have taken a commanding lead in post-game riots. If the Lakers win, I plan to overturn my own car.
Clarendon	Anger is the most impotent passion that accompanies the mind of man; it effects nothing it goes about; and hurts the man who is possessed by it more than any other against whom it is directed.
Newton N. Minow	Children will watch anything, and when a broadcaster uses crime and violence and other shoddy devices to monopolize a child's attention, it's worse than taking candy from a baby. It is taking precious time from the process of growing up.
George Will	You really don't want a president who is a football fan. Football combines the worst features of American life. It is violence punctuated by committee meetings.
Philip Stubbes	As concerning football, I protest unto you that it may rather be called a friendly kind of fight than a play or recreation – a bloody and murdering practise than a fellowly sport or pastime

Table 10.3 Famous Quotes—*Cont'd*

Elizabeth 1	Anger makes dull men witty, but it keeps them poor.
Thomas A. Kempis	Be not angry that you cannot make others as you wish them to be, since you cannot make yourself as you wish to be.
James Thurber	Let us not look back in anger or forward in fear, but around in awareness.
Aristotle (384–322 BC) – Greek philosopher	Anyone can become angry. That is easy. But to be angry with the right person, to the right degree, at the right time, for the right purpose and in the right way – that is not easy.
Proverbs 14:17a	He that is soon angry dealeth foolishly…
Benjamin Franklin	Whatever is begun in anger ends in shame.
Seneca	He is a fool who cannot be angry; but he is a wise man who will not.
Ralph Waldo Emerson	A man makes inferiors his superiors by heat; self control is the rule. Anger is an uncontrollable feeling that betrays what you are when you are not yourself. Anger is that powerful internal force that blows out the light of reason. Know this to be the enemy: it is anger, born of desire.
Dr. Robert Anthony	The angry people are those people who are most afraid.
Brooks Orpick	It's good to see guys sticking up for one another. Everyone gets along in this room, and if you see one of our guys take a cheap shot, we will go after him.
Tyron Edwards	To rule one's anger is well; to prevent it is still better.
David Bonier	This China trade deal is basically like the Bobby Knight of trade deals. You know, you abuse, you abuse, you abuse, and then they say 'Well, OK, we'll let you try one more time'.
Thomas Fuller	Anger is one of the sinews of the soul; he that lacks it has a maimed mind.
Joseph Brodsky	Life is a game with many rules but no referee. One learns how to play it more by watching it than by consulting any book, including the holy book. Small wonder, then, that so many play dirty, that so few win, that so many lose.
Horace	Anger is a momentary madness, so control your passion or it will control you.
Martina Navratilova	People in the States used to think that if girls were good at sports their sexuality would be affected. Being feminine meant being a cheerleader, not being an athlete. The image of women is changing now. You don't have to be pretty for people to come and see you play. At the same time, if you're a good athlete, it doesn't mean you're not a woman.
Walter S. Landor	The flame of anger, bright and brief, sharpens the barb of love.
John Wooden	Ability may get you to the top, but it takes character to keep you there.
George Jean Nathan	No man can think clearly when his fist are clenched.
Jesse Owens	I wanted no part of politics. And I wasn't in Berlin to compete against any one athlete. The purpose of the Olympics, anyway, was to do your best. As I'd learned long ago from Charles Riley, the only victory that counts is the one over yourself.
Arnold Schwarzenegger	Strength does not come from winning. Your struggles develop your strengths. When you go through hardships and decide not to surrender, that is strength.
William Shenstone	Think when you are enraged at anyone, what would probably become of your sentiments should he die during the dispute.
Bill Bradley	There has never been a great athlete who died not knowing what pain is.
Elizabeth Kenny	My mother used to say, "He who angers you, conquers you!" But my mother was a saint.

Continued

Table 10.3	Famous Quotes—*Cont'd*
Al McGuire	I don't know why people question the academic training of an athlete. Fifty percent of the doctors in this country graduated in the bottom half of their classes.
Eric Hoffer	The remarkable thing is that we really love our neighbor as ourselves: we do unto others as we do unto ourselves. We hate others when we hate ourselves. We are tolerant toward others when we tolerate ourselves. We forgive others when we forgive ourselves. We are prone to sacrifice others when we are ready to sacrifice ourselves.
Frederick Buechner	Of the Seven Deadly Sins, anger is possibly the most fun. To lick your wounds, to smack your lips over grievances long past, to roll over your tongue the prospect of bitter confrontations still to come, to savor to the last toothsome morsel both the pain you are given and the pain you are giving back – in many ways it is a feast fit for a king. The chief drawback is that what you are wolfing down is yourself. The skeleton at the feast is you.
Napoleon Bonaparte	There are only two forces in the world, the sword and the spirit. In the long run the sword will always be conquered by the spirit.
James Thurber	Let us not look back in anger or forward in fear, but around in awareness.
Thomas a Kempis	Be not angry that you cannot make others as you wish them to be, since you cannot make yourself as you wish to be.
William Blake	I was angry with my friend I told my wrath, my wrath did end. I was angry with my foe: I told it not, my wrath did grow. A Poison Tree
Theodore Roosevelt	If you could kick the person in the pants responsible for most of your trouble, you wouldn't sit for a month.

SUMMARY

Through a number a coordinated efforts the future of sport is bright. It is imperative that all organizations band together and effect policy changes that mitigate violence. Those best in a position to do so include governmental agencies, the schools, and law enforcement. Those who can effect change from the grass roots level include those involved in sport and the general citizenry. Ideally, it is important to have an atmosphere for all who participate that leaves them with the feeling that they improved, met a personal goal and said: "That was fun!"

Table 10.4	Ten Trends to Mitigate Sport Violence

Trend #1 Privatization of sport

Trend # 2 Sport rage

Trend # 3 Increase in sport-related injury at younger ages

Trend#4 Increased technology keeping children at home in self-learning environments

Trend # 5 Extended economic problems will force choices

Trend #6 There will be more attention paid to the develop of positive role models in accomplished athletes as they become more popular as leaders who exhibit character and ethical development

Trend #7 Increased concern over child health issues will shift the trend from sport to active living

Trend #8 Increased development of national and state policy toward sport and health

Trend #9 Sport specialization will continue

Trend # 10 All governmental organizations will be called upon to solve the problems inherent in the cycle of sport and violence

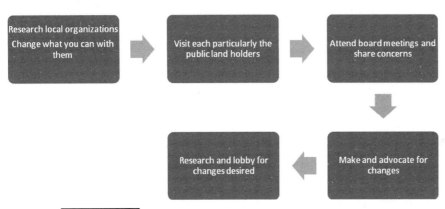

FIGURE 10.1 *The advocate's path through sport organizations.*

REFERENCES

Australian Capital Territory Health, 2000. Physical Education and Sport Policy: Implementation Guidelines. Canberra, AU: Australian Sport Commission.

Brewer, J., Hunter, A., 1989. Multi-method Research; a Synthesis of Styles. Sage, Newbury Park, CA.

CPRS' youth development policy and strategies, 2000. California Parks and Recreation 56 (1), 42–44.

Carson, J., 2009. Personal account of violence in sport, February 2.

Council on Intercollegiate Athletics, 2005. Academic Integrity in Intercollegiate Athletics: Principles, Rules, and Best Practices. Vanderbilt, Nashville, Tennessee.

Dromgoole, W., 1900. The Bridge Builder. The Builder, Boston.

Houlihan, B., 2005. Public sector sport policy. International Review for the Sociology of Sport 40 (20), 163–185.

Heinzmann, G., 2002. Facts, myths and videotape. Parks & Recreation 37 (3), 66–72.

Hootman, J.M., Dick, R., Agel, J., 2007. Epidemiology of collegiate injuries for 15 sports: summary and recommendations for injury prevention initiatives. Journal of Athletic Training 42 (2), 311–319.

Hoover, J.H., Olsen, G.W., 2001. Teasing and Harassment: the Frames and Scripts Approach for Teachers and Parents. National Educational Service, Bloomington, IN, 132 pp.

Insight on the News, 2001. New penalties for being a bad sport 17 (15), 35–38.

Jamieson, Betty, Mother of Lynn Jamieson 2009. Personal account of violence in sport, February 4.

Karlander, D., 2009. Personal account of violence in sport, February 4.

Ministry of Sport, 2002. The Canadian Sport Policy. Ministry of Sport, Ottawa, CA.

Trochim, W., 2001. The Research Methods Knowledge Base. Atomic Dog, Cincinnati, OH.

FEEL GOOD 10.1

Yogi Berra's Speech to the St. Louis University Graduation on May 19, 2007:

"Thank you all for being here tonight. I know this is a busy time of year, and if you weren't here, you could probably be somewhere else. I especially want to thank the administration of St. Louis University for making this day necessary. It is an honor to receive this honorary degree. It is wonderful to be here in St. Louis and to visit the old neighborhood. I haven't been back since the last time I was here. Everything looks the same, only different. Of course, things in the past are never as they used to be. Before I speak, I have something to say. As you may know, I never went to college, or high school for that matter. To be honest, I'm not much of a public speaker, so I will try to keep this short as long as I can. As I look out upon all of the young people here tonight, there are a number of words of wisdom I might impart. But I think the more irrelevant piece of advice I can pass along is this: 'The most important things in life are the things that are least important'. I could have gone a number of directions in my life. Growing up on the Hill, I could have opened a restaurant or a bakery. But the more time I spent in places like that, the less time I wanted to spend there. I knew that if I wanted to play baseball, I was going to have to play baseball. My childhood friend, Joe Garagiola, also became a big-league ballplayer, as did my son, Dale. I think you'll find the similarities in our careers are quite different. You're probably wondering, how does a kid from the Hill become a New York Yankee and get in the Hall of Fame? Well, let me tell you something, if it was easy nobody would do it. Nothing is impossible until you make it possible. Of course, times were different. To be honest, I was born at an early age. Things are much more confiscated now. It seems like a nickel ain't worth a dime anymore. But let me tell you, if the world was perfect, it wouldn't be. Even Napoleon had his Watergate. You'll make some wrong mistakes along the way, but only the wrong survive. Never put off until tomorrow what you can't do today. Denial isn't just a river in Europe. Strive for success and remember you won't get what you want unless you want what you get. Remember, none are so kind as those who will not see. Keep the faith and follow the Commandments: Do not covet thy neighbor's wife, unless she has nothing else to wear. Treat others before you treat yourself. As Franklin Eleanor Roosevelt once said: 'The only thing to fear is fear itself.' Hold onto your integrity, ladies and gentlemen. It's the one thing you really need to have; if you don't have it, that's why you need it. Work hard to reach your goals, and if you can't reach them, use a ladder. There may come a day when you get hurt and have to miss work. Don't worry, it won't hurt to miss work. Over the years, I have realized that baseball is really just a menopause for life. We all have limitations, but we also know limitation is the greatest form of flattery. Beauty is in the eyes of Jim Holder. Half the lies you hear won't be true, and half the things you say, you won't ever say. As parents you'll want to give your children all the things you didn't have. But don't buy them an encyclopedia, make them walk to school like you did. Teach them to have respect for others, especially the police. They are not here to create disorder, they are here to preserve it. Throughout my career, I found good things always came in pairs of three. There will be times when you are an overwhelming underdog. Give 100 percent to everything you do, and then that's not enough, give everything you have left. "Winning isn't everything, but it's better than rheumatism.' I think Guy Lombardo said that. Finally, dear graduates and friends, cherish this moment; it is a memory you will never forget. You have your entire future ahead of you.

Good luck and Bob's speed."

(Carson, 2007)

SPORT STORIES 10.1

As you know, your father and I have been staunch Giants fans, and when we were recently attending a Giants game, we noticed an extremely drunk fan nearby. He was yelling and drinking, and suddenly he started throwing beer all over the place, and it was hitting nearby fans. Shortly, he was escorted out by personnel.

Betty Jamieson, Mother of Lynn Jamieson, (2009).

SPORT STORIES 10.2

In the NAHL, I was playing for the Central Texas Black-hawks. We were playing our third to last game of the regular season and we were not going to make the playoffs. We were playing the Fort Worth Calvary, whom had been knockedout of the playoffs the night before, this was their last game of the season. Our coach allowed us to pick our starting line up, we started all our tough guys and told the other team to be ready to fight at the drop of the puck, they didn't take us seriously. Right off the opening face-off, ourright winger sucker punched the guy he was lined up against. Immediately our defensemen went after their defensemen and both sets of wingers started fighting. Wasn't long before the goalies met and fought as well. The refs couldn't do much since there was three of them and five separate fights going on. After the game our coach was suspended indefinitely.

Karlander, D. (2009).

Bibliography

Ajzen, I., Fishbein, M., 1980. Understanding Attitudes and Predicting Social Behavior. Prentice Hall, Englewood-Cliffs, NJ.

Ajzen, I., Madden, T., 1986. Prediction of goal orientated behavior: Attitudes, intentions, and perceived behavioral control. Journal of Experimental Social Psychology 22, 453–474.

Ajzen, I., 1989. Benefits of Leisure: A Social Psychological Perspective. University of Massachusetts at Amherst (paper provided by Dr. Ajzen), pp. 1–12.

Amateur Softball Association. (2005, July). What is the Amateur Softball Association? Retrieved July 12, 2005, from the Amateur Softball Association Website: http://www.asasoftball.com/default.asp.

Ambah, F.S., 2008. A drive toward the goal of greater freedom: Women's team fights Saudi restrictions on female athletes. The Washington Post Tuesday, April 15, 2008, A9.

Archdiocese of Indianapolis, 2003. To be safe and secure. Report. Archdiocese, Indianapolis, IN.

Arms, R., Russell, G., Sandilands, M., 1979. Effects on the hostility of spectators of viewing aggressive sports. Social Psychology Quarterly 42 (3), 275–279.

Austin, D., 1973. The Effects of Insult and Approval on Aggressive Behavior. Unpublished doctoral dissertation. University of Illinois, Champaign.

Austin, D., 1999. Therapeutic Recreation Processes and Techniques, fourth ed. Sagamore, Champaign, IL.

Australian Capital Territory, 2000. Health, Physical Education and Sport Policy: Implementation Guidelines. Australian Sport Commission, Canberra, AU.

Baggett, C. (2008, November). Football Dispute Leaves 2 Dead. Retrieved November 10, 2008, from the All Alabama Website: http://www.al.com/news/pressregister/metro.ssf?/base/news/122631213873770.x ml&coll=3.

Baron, R., Byrne, D., 1994. Social Psychology: Understanding Human Interactions, seventh ed. Allyn & Bacon, Boston.

Bandura, A., Walters, R., 1963. Social Learning and Personality Development. Holt, Rinehart & Winston, New York.

Bandura, A., 1986. Social Foundations of Thought and Action: A Social Cognitive Theory. New Jersey, Englewood Cliffs.

Barthes, R., 1967. Elements of Semiology. Jonathan Cape, London.

Beam, J.W., Serwatka, T.S., Wilson, W.J., 2004. Preferred leadership of NCAA Division I and II intercollegiate student-athletes. Journal of Sport Behavior 27 (1), 3–17.

Bearison, D., Bain, J., Daniele, R., 1982. Developmental changes in how children understand television. Social Behaviors and Personalities 10 (2), 133–144.

Berkowitz, L., 1978. Sports competition and aggression. In: Staub, W. (Ed.), An Analysis of Athlete Behavior. Movement Publications, Ithaca.

Bloor, M., 1997. Techniques of validation in qualitative research; a critical commentary. In: Miller, G., Dingwall, R. (Eds.), Context & Method in Qualitative Research. Sage, Thousand Oaks, CA.

Bonnano, J., 2009. Due process, free speech, and New Jersey's Athletic Code of Conduct: An evaluation of potential constitutional challenges to a good idea. Seton Hall Journal of Sports and Entertainment Law 14 (2), 397–440.

Bredemeier, B.J., Weiss, M.R., Shields, D.L., Cooper, Bruce A.B., 1987. The relationship between children's legitimacy judgments and their moral reasoning: aggression tendencies, and sport involvement. Sociology of Sport Journal 4, 48–60.

Brekken, Chris, 2009. Personal account of violence in sport, February 2.

Brekken, Ted K.A., 2009. Personal account of violence in sport, February 2.

Brewer, J., Hunter, A., 1989. Multi-method Research; A Synthesis of Styles. Sage, Newbury Park, CA.

Brock-Utne, B., 1987. Sports, Masculinity and Education for Violence. International Peace Research Institute, Oslo.

Bryant, J., Comisky, P., Zillmann, D., 1981. The appeal of rough and tumble play in televised professional football. Communication Quarterly 29 (4), 256–262.

Buss, A., 1961. The Psychology of Aggression. Wiley, New York.

Calhoun, R., 2007. Interview with R354 Sport and Violence class students, Indiana University.

Campo, S., Poulos, B., Sipple, J., 2005. Prevalence and profiling: hazing among college students and points of intervention. American Journal of Health Behavior 29 (2), 137–149.

Carlson, J., 2009. Personal account of violence in sport. February 2.

Carroll, R., 1980. Football hooliganism in England. International Review of Sport Sociology 15 (2), 77–92.

Carson, J., 2009. Personal account of violence in sport. February 2.

Chavez, V.N., 2007. Youth development: creating a framework for action. California Parks and Recreation 63 (2), 26–43.

Coffey, A., Atkinson, P., 1996. Making Sense of Qualitative Data. Sage, Thousand Oaks, CA.

Colburn, K., 1986. Deviance and legitimacy in ice hockey: a microstructural theory of violence. The Sociological Quarterly, 27(1), 63–74.

Coakley, J., 1986. Sport in Society; Issues & Controversies, seventh ed. McGraw-Hill, Boston.

Coakley, J., Dunning, E., 2000. Handbook of Sports Studies. Sage, London. 570 pp.

Coakley, J.J., 2007. Sports in Society: Issues and controversies, ninth ed. McGraw Hill Higher Education, Hightstown, NJ, 676 pp.

Corbin, J., Strauss, A., 1990. Grounded theory research: procedures, canons, and evaluative criteria. Qualitative Sociology 13 (1), 3–21.

Council on Intercollegiate Athletics, 2005. Academic integrity in intercollegiate athletics: Principles, rules, and best practices. Vanderbilt, Nashville, Tennessee.

CPRS' Youth Development Policy and Strategies, 2000. California Parks and Recreation 56 (1), 42–44.

Crawford, D., Jackson, E., Godbey, G., 1991. A hierarchical model of leisure constraints. Leisure Sciences 13, 309–320.

Crow, B., Rosner, S., 2002. Institutional and organizational liability for hazing in intercollegiate and professional team sports. St. John's Law Review 76, 87–114.

Cudney, S.R., 2000. Heroes,hoboes, and the question of ethics. Journal of Sport and Social Issues 24 (4), 370–379.

Dalrymple, T., 2002. Rages of the ages. National Review 54 (2), 22–25.

DaCosta, L., Miragova, A. (Eds.), 2002. Worldwide experiences and trends in Sport for All. Meyer & Meyer Sport Ltd., UK, p. 792.

Davidson, P. (2007). Research review: research into sport events. Australasian Parks and Leisure, (March/April, 2007), 61, pp. 10–11.

Deffenbacher, J., Petrilli, R., Lynch, R., Oetting, E., Swaim, R., 2003. The driver's angry thoughts questionnaire: a measure of angry cognitions when driving. Cognitive Therapy and Research 27 (4), 383–402.

Docheff, D.M., 2004. It's no longer a spectator sport: eight ways to get involved and help fight parental violence in youth sports. Parks and Recreation 39 (3), 63–70.

Dromgoole, W., 1900. The Bridge Builder. The Builder. Boston.

Dunning, E., Maguire, J., Murphy, P., Williams, J., 1982. The social roots of football hooligan violence. Leisure Studies 1, 2, 139–156.

Dupuis, M., Bloom, G.A., Loughead, T.M., 2006. Team captains' perceptions of athlete leadership. Journal of Sport Behavior 29 (1), 60–78.

Duquette, B., Tragis, J., 2009. Veteran youth hockey coach Wolter to be honored. Retrieved at http://newsminer.com/news/2009/feb13 2/15/2009.

Elloitt, H., 1997. Speak softly and carry a big stick. Ambassador, 24–29.

Engelhardt, G.M., 1995. Fighting behavior and winning national hockey league games: A paradox. Perceptual and Motor Skills 80, 416–418.

ESPN, 2006. Kids are all Right: Vikings Ban Hazing of Rookies. Retrieved January 10, 2009. From the ESPN website: http://sports.espn.go.com/nfl/news/story?id=2547145.

ESPN, 2009. Providence Friars Fan who Rushed Court Held Without Bail. Retrieved January 27, 2009, from the ESPN website: http://sports.espn.go.com/ncb/news/story?id=3864193.

Evans, T., Thamel, P., 2009. Barely Teenagers, already Groomed for Stardom. The New York Times, 1. Sunday January 4, 2009 Sport Sunday.

Farber, M., 2006. Tiny happy people (Holding Sticks). Sports Illustrated, May 15, 2006, 140 (18), 51–58.

Farry, T., 2002. Sports Hazing Incidents. ESPN Online. Path: http://espn.go.com/otl/hazing/list.html Retrieved December, 28, 2006.

Feldman, R., 1995. Social Psychology. Prentice Hall, Englewood Cliffs, NJ.

Fellman, G., 1998. Rambo and the Dalai Lama; The Compulsion to Win and Its Threat to Human Survival. State University of New York Press, Albany.

Ferguson, A., 1999. Inside the crazy culture of kids sports. Time 154 (2), 52–60.

Fishbein, M., Ajzen, I., 1975. Belief, Attitude, Intention, and Behavior: An Introduction to Theory and Research. Addison-Wesley, Reading, MA.

Flexner, S.B. (Ed.), 1987. The Random House Dictionary of the English Language, second ed. Random House, New York, NY.

Foley, D., 2001. The great American sport ritual: Reproducing race, class, and gender inequality. In: Yiannakis, Andrew, Melnick, Merrill J. (Eds.), Contemporary Issues in Sociology of Sport. Human Kinetics, Champaign, IL, p. 478.

Foster, P., Rayner, G., 2008. England Rugby Rape Claim; Sex Ban for Players. Telegraph. Retrieved February 1, 2008 from http://www.telegraph.co.uk/news/worldnews/australiaandthepacific/newzealand/2 164911/England-rugby-rape-claim-Sex-ban-for-players.html.

The Four Faces of Anger. www.stressdoc.com/anger3.htm. Retrieved 1/28/09.

Freud, S., 1933. Introductory Lectures on Psychoanalysis. W.W. Norton, New York.

Freud, S., 1950. Why War? Hogarth Press, London.

Garland, J., Rowe, M., 2000. The hooligan's fear of the penalty. Soccer and Society 1 (1), pp. 144–157.

Gibbs, N., 2001. "It's only me". Time 157 (11), 22–23.

Gough, R., 1998. Moral development research in sports and its quest for objectivity. In: McNamee, M., Parry, S. (Eds.), Ethics & Sport. E & FN Spon, London.

Guivernau, M., Duda, J., 2002. Moral atmosphere and athletic aggressive tendencies in young soccer players. The Journal of Moral Education 31 (1), 67–85.

Gussen, J., 1967. The psychodynamics of leisure. In: P. Martin (Ed.), Leisure and Mental Health: A Psychiatric Viewpoint. A.P.A., Washington.

Hardcastle, J., 2008. Sports Violence. Ezine articles. http://ezinearticles.com/?Sports-Violence&id=290850&opt=print. Retrieved 8/26/08.

Harmon, L.K. Get out and stay out. Parks and Recreation, 43(6), 50–55.

Harrell, W., 1981. Verbal aggressiveness in spectators at professional hockey games: The effects of tolerance of violence and amount of exposure to hockey. Human Relations 34 (8), 643–655.

Hartley, G., 1990. Athletic Footwear Association. American Youth and Sports Participation. Athletic Footwear Association, North Palm Beach, FL.

Heinzmann, G., 2002. Facts, myths and videotape. Parks & Recreation 37 (3), 66–72.

Hirschhorn, L., 1994. Leading and planning in loosely coupled systems. cFAR, Philadelphia, PA.

Hobson, K., 2006. Baby, work out!. U.S. News and World Report. 140 (24), 56–70.

Hockeyfighter.com, 2009. The Man Behind the Legendary Film Character. Path: http://www.hockeyfighters.com/Forum/phpBB2/viewtopic.php?p=32282 &highlig ht=zealot Retrieved January, 18, 2009.

Holowchak, M., 2003. Aggression, gender, and sport: reflections on sport as a means of moral education. Journal of Social Philosophy 34 (3), 387–399.

Hootman, J., Dick, R., Agel, J., 2007. Epidemiology of collegiate injuries for 15 sports: summary and recommendations for injury preventive initiatives. Journal of Athletic Training 42 (2), 311–319.

Hoover, J.H., Olsen, G.W., 2001. Teasing and Harassment: The Frames and Scripts Approach for Teachers and Parents. National Educational Serviuce, Bloomington, IN, 132 pp.

Hoover, N., 1999. National Survey: Initiation rites and athletics for NCAA sports teams'. Path: http://www.Alfred.edu/news/html/hazing.html. Retrieved December, 20, 2006.

Houlihan, B., 1997. Sport, Policy, and Politics. Routledge, London, 313 pp.

Houlihan, B., 2005. Public sector sport policy. International Review for the Sociology of Sport 40 (20), 163–185.

Hughes, R., Coakley, J., 1991. Positive deviance among athletes: The implications of overconformity to the sport ethic. Sociology of Sport Journal 8, 307–325.

Hyman, M., 2009. Young bodies under pressure. Youth Sports Network: Suny Youth Sports Institute. http://www.youthsportsny.org. Retrieved 1/22/2009.

Insight on the News, 2001. New penalties for being a bad sport. Washington Times 17 (15), 35–38.

Jamieson, Betty, Mother of Lynn Jamieson, 2009. Personal account of violence in sport, February 4.

Jamieson, David L., 2009. Personal account of violence in sport, February 2.

Jamieson, J., 2009. Personal written statement.

Jamieson, L.M., 2004. Value of government policy in sport and leisure. Proceedings for the World Leisure Congress, Brisbane, AU, October 2–4, 2004.

Jamieson, L.M., Pan, Z., 2000. Government policy on sport for all: developed and developing countries. Journal of the International Council for Physical Education, Recreation, Sport and Dance XXXVI (4), 16–20.

Jones, H., Stewart, K., Sunderman, R., 1996. From the arena into the streets: hockey violence, economic incentives and public policy. American Journal of Economics and Sociology 55 (2), 231–243.

Karlander, D., 2009. Personal account of violence in sport. February 4.

Karns, J. Myers-Walls, J.A., 2009. Ages and stages of child and youth development: A guide for 4-H leaders. http://www.ces.purdue/extmedia/NCR/NCR-292.html.

Kelly, B., McCarthy, J., 1979. Personality dimensions of aggression: its relationship to time and place of action in ice hockey. Human Relations 32 (3), 219–225.

Kelly, J., 1990. Leisure, second ed. Prentice Hall, Englewood Cliffs, NJ.

Keown, T., 2001. If at first.... ESPN, 4(11), 82–87.

Kidman, L., McKenzie, A., McKenzie, B., 1999. The nature and target of parent's comments during youth sport competitions. The Journal of Sport Behavior 22 (1), 54–68.

King, A., 2001. Abstract and engaged critique in sociology: On football hooliganism. British Journal of Sociology 52 (4), 707–712.

Lance, L., Ross, C., Houck, T., 1998. Violence in sports: perceptions of intramural sport participants. NIRSA Journal, Spring, 145–148.

Lance, L., Ross, C., 2000. Views of violence in american sports: a study of college students. College Student Journal 34 (2), 191–200.

Lawton, R., Nutter, A., 2002. A comparison of reported levels and expression of anger in everyday and driving situations. British Journal of Psychology 93 (3), 407–427.

Linbos, M.A., Peek-Asa, C., 2003. Comparing unintentional injuries in a school setting. Journal for School Health 73 (3), 101–106.

Luhmann, N., 1995. Social Systems. Stanford University Press, Stanford, California.

Malcom, N.L., 2003. Constructing female athleticism. American Behavioral Scientist 46 (10), 1387–1404.

Maraniss, D., 2008. When worlds collided. Sports Illustrated 108 (22), 53–60.

Maxwell, J., 2005. Qualitative Research Design; An Interactive Approach, second ed. Sage, Thousand Oaks, CA.

McCarthy, M., 2008. Sports also paying a price amid struggling economy. USA Today 1–2B, October 17, 2008, B1–2.

McCarthy, T., 2001. Warning: The legacy of Columbine. Time 157 (11), 23–25.

McCallum, J., 2004. The ugliest game; an NBA brawl exposes the worst in player and fan behavior and serves as a frightening wakeup call. Sports Illustrated 101 (21), 44–51.

McCaw, S.T., Walker, J.D., 1999. Winning the Stanley Cup Final Series is related to incurring fewer penalties for violent behavior. Texas Medicine 85, 66–69.

Menninger, W., 1960. Recreation & Mental Health. Recreation & Psychiatry. National Recreation Association, New York.

Michiana High School League. (2008). Zero Tolerance: Verbal and physical abuse of officials. (Pamphlet).

Midnight basketball and beyond…Sports in youth development. Profile, Fall 1999, 35 (5), 5–7.

Miller, A.G., 2004. The Social Psychology of Good and Evil. The Guilford Press, New York.

Ministry of Sport, 2002. The Canadian Sport Policy. Ministry of Sport, Ottawa, CA.

Morin, S., 2009. Play like a girl. USA Hockey Magazine 31 (1), 30–33.

Morra, N., Smith, M., 1996. Interpersonal Sources of Violence in Hockey: The Influence of the Media, Parents, Coaches, and Game Officials. In: Smoll, F., Smith, R. (Eds.), Children and Youth in Sport: A Biopsychosocial Perspective. McGraw-Hill, Boston.

Mosher, C., Miethe, T., Phillips, D., 2002. The Mismeasure of Crime. Sage, Thousand Oaks.

Moz, J-M., 1999. Boiling Point: The High Cost of Unhealthy Anger to Individuals and Society. Heath Communications, Florida.

Mundy, J., 1997. Developing anger and aggression control in youth in recreation and park systems. Parks and Recreation 32 (3), 63–69.

Mull, R.F., Bayless, K.G., Ross, C.R., Jamieson, L.M., 1997. Recreational sport management, third ed. Human Kinetics, Champaign, IL, 334 pp.

Mull, R.F., Bayless, K.G., Jamieson, L.M., 2005. Recreational sport management, fourth ed. Human Kinetics, Champaign, IL, 354 pp.

Nathanson, K., 2007. Turn it around, team. Indiana Daily Student 140 (70), 5.

National Alliance for Youth Sports, 2009. Time Out! for better sports and kids. Retrieved from www.tomeforbettersportsforkids.org, 2/9/2009.

NBC6, 2003. Streaker Stalks U.S. Open Champ: Jim Furyk Calls Incident An 'Embarrassing Situation'. Online. Path: http://www.nbc6.net/sports/2272724/detail.html Retrieved December, 28, 2009.

Newman, I., Benz, C., 1998. Qualitative-Quantitative Research Methodology; Exploring the Interactive Continuum. Southern Illinois University Press, Carbondale, IL.

NHL, 2007. Making Sense of the NHL's New Uniforms, What's Changed, What's the Same. Retrieved January 21, 2007, at the official NHL website: http://www.nhl.com/nhl/app/?service=page&page=NewsPage&articleid=287803.

Nichols, G., 2004. Crime and punishment and sports development. Leisure Studies 23 (2), 177–194.

Nixon II, H.L., 1997. Gender, sport, and aggressive behavior outside sport. Journal of Sport and Social Issues 21 (4), 379–391.

Norton, P., Burns, J., Hope, D., Bauer, B., 2000. Generalizations of Social Anxiety to Sporting and Athletic Situations: Gender, Sports Involvement, and Parental Pressure. Depression and Anxiety 12, 193–202.

Office of Juvenile Justice and Delinquency Prevention, 2008. Fact sheet highlights youth gang survey. Juvjust https://www.exchange.iu.edu/owa.

Oloffson, K., 2008. Long live the swimmer. Inside 3 (2), 12–14, 20–21.

Ommundsen, Y., Lemyre, P., Roberts, G., Miller, B., 2005. Peer relationships in adolescent competitive soccer: associations to perceived motivational climate, achievement goals, and perfectionism. Journal of Sports Sciences 23 (9), 977–989.

O'Morrow, G., 1971. The whys of recreation activities for psychiatric patients. Therapeutic Recreation Journal 5 (3), 97–103.

Onofrietti, T., 1996. The recreation-education model: A philosophy of youth sports. NIRSA Journal 20 (3), 18–19.

Orr, T.J., 2007. Interview with Richard Mull. Former Director Indiana University Tennis Center. February 13, 2007, Unpublished, Bloomington.

Orr, T., 2008. Personal interview with Mark Baltz, NFL Referee, Indianapolis, Indiana, October 24, 2007.

Owczarski, J., 2008. Specialization can be detrimental to young athletes. Beacon News. Retrieved from www.suburbanchicagonews.com/beaconnews/sports, 1/22/2009.

Parry, J., 1998. Violence and Aggression in Contemporary Sport. In: Parry, J., McNamee, M. (Eds.), Ethics in Sport. E&FN Spon, London.

Pasquarelli, L., 2008. Williams Killed When Limo Sprayed with Bullets. Retrieved December 10, 2008, from the ESPN Website: http://sports.espn.go.com/nfl/news/story?id=2716385.

Paul, R.J., 2003. Variations in NHL attendance: The impact of violence, scoring, and regional rivalries-Discrimination and the NHL. Journal of Economics and Sociology 62 (2).

Price, S.L., 2008. Eight is not enough. Sports Illustrated 109 (7), 96.

Pronger, B., 1999. Outta my endzone: sport and the territorial anus. Journal of Sport & Social Issues 23 (4), 373–389.

Providence Journal, 2002. Hockey Dad gets 6 Years in Jail. January 25, 1.

Quanty, M., 1976. Aggression Catharsis: Experimental Investigations and Implications. In: Green, R., O'Neil, E. (Eds.), Perspectives on Aggression. Academic Press, New York.

Rainey, D.W., Hardy, L., 1999. Assaults on rugby union referees: A three union survey. Journal of Sport Behavior 22 (1), 105–1132.

Ramsey, G., Rank, B., 1997. Rethinking youth sports. Parks and Recreation 32 (12), 30–34.

Rebellion Hockey. (February 3, 2005). Hooligans Assault Official in Norway's Top League. Retrieved February 4, 2005, from http://www.hockeyrefs.com/intheheadlines/02032005,2.htm.

Reilly, R., 2007. School for the uncool. Sports Illustrated 107 (11), 98.

Reshef, N., Paltiel, J., 1989. Partisanship and sport: The unique case of politics and sport in Israel. Sociology of Sport Journal 6, 305–318.

Roberts, S., 2008. For the U.S., a new red alert. Sports Illustrated 109 (6), 88.

Roberts, S., 2008. The prying game. Sports Illustrated 109 (11), 76.

Roddy, D., 2004. This sporting life. Pittsburgh Post-Gazette. http://pittsburgh post-gazette.com/pg/04340/421600.stm.

Rowland, C., Stewart, W., 2008. Research Update: Vying for volunteers. Parks and Recreation 43 (10), 28–29.

Schaak, Brad, Orr, T.J., 2009. Interview with Brad Schaak. Current and Long time Youth Hockey Coach, February 1.

Schneider, A., Butcher, R., 2001. Ethics, Sports and Boxing. In: Morgan, W., Meier, K., Schneider, A. (Eds.), Ethics in Sport. Human Kinetics, Champaign.

Schwarz, E., Tait, 2006. All together now. Australasian Leisure Management (July/August, 2005), 51, 48–50.

Scraton, P., 2004. Death on the terraces: The contexts and injustices of the 1989 Hillsborough disaster. Soccer and Society 5 (2), 183–200.

Sen, A., 2006. Identity and Violence: The Illusion of Destiny. W.W. Norton and Company, New York, 215 pp.

Shalter, P. Raising Your Champion. Champion Athletic Consulting, Dayton, OH.

Sharkin, B., 2004. Road rage: risk factors, assessment, and intervention strategies. Journal of Counseling & Development 82 (2), 191–199.

Shaughnessy, J., 2008. Living her dream. The Criterion XLVIII (36), 1.

Sherman, L.W., 1997. Preventing Crimes: What Works, What Doesn't, What's Promising. National Institute of Justice, Washington, D.C.

Sherman, R., 1997. Fighting for Women. Athletic Business 21 (1), 53–59.

Singer, R., 2008. Policing Dietary Do's and Doughnuts. U.S. News & World Report *144* (18), 29.

Seff, M., Gecas, V., Frey, J., 1993. Birth order, selfconcept, and participation in dangerous sports. The Journal of Psychology 127 (2), 221–232.

Shields, E., 1999. Intimidation and violence by males in high school athletics. Adolescence 34, 135, 503–521.

Shillito, P., 2004. Violence: A Rising Sports Trend. The Orion online. California State University, Chico.

Shipnuck, A. (June, 2003). The Week: Bad Boy Makes Good. Golf online. Retrieved January 21, 2009, at the Sports Illustrated website:http://sportsillustrated.cnn.com/golf/plus/2003/06/30/.

Silva, J., 1983. The perceived legitimacy of ruleviolating behavior in sport. Journal of Sport Psychology 5 (4), 438–448.

Silverman, D., 1993. Interpreting qualitative data: methods for analyzing talk. In: Text and Interaction. Sage, London.

Simon, P., 2001. Violence in Sports. In: Morgan, W., Meier, K., Schneider, A. (Eds.), Ethics in Sport. Human Kinetics, Champaign.

Slife, B., Williams, R., 1995. What's Behind The Research? Discovering Hidden Assumptions in the Behavioral Sciences. Sage, Thousand Oaks, CA.

Smart, R., Ashbridge, M., Mann, R., Adlaf, E., 2003. Psychiatric distress among road rage victims and perpetrators. Canadian Journal of Psychiatry 48 (10), 681–688.

Smith, D., 1998. Recreation as a Strategy to Prevent Juvenile Delinquency: A Case Study Examination of the Role of Recreation in Facilitating Primary and Secondary Social Institutions. Unpublished doctoral dissertation. Indiana University Libraries, Bloomington.

Smith, D., Stewart, S., 2003. Sexual aggression and sports participation. Journal of Sport Behavior 26 (4), 384–395.

Smith, M., 1979. Hockey violence: A test of the violent subculture hypothesis. Social Problems 27 (2), 235–247.

Smith, M., 1983. Violence and Sport. Butterworths, Toronto.

Smith, M., 2003. What is Sports Violence? In: Boxill, J. (Ed.), Sports Ethics; An Anthology. Blackwell Publishing, Oxford.

Smith, S., Carron, M., 1990. Comparison of competition and cooperation in intramural sport. NIRSA Journal, Fall, 44–47.

Smith, S., 2009. Dead Athletes' Brains Show Damage from Concussions. CNN Retrieved January 21, 2009, at the CNN website: http://www.cnn.com/2009/HEALTH/01/26/athlete.brains/index.html.

Sorek, T., 2005. Between football and martyrdom: the bi-focal localism of an Arab-Palestinian town in Israel. The British Journal of Sociology 56 (4), 635–661.

Spinrad, L., T (Eds.), 1979, Speakers Lifetime Library, Vol. 1. Parker, West Nyack, NY, p. 256.

Steelman, T., 1995. Enhancing the youth sports experience through coaching. Parks and Recreation 30 (11), 14–18.

Steinbach, P. (May, 2007). Face offerings, Athletic Business, 31 (5), 48–49.

Stewart, K.G., Ferguson, D.G., Jones, J.C.H., 1992. On violence in professional team sport as the endogenous result of profit maximization. Atlantic Economic Journal 20 (4), 55–65.

Storch, E., Werner, N., Storch, J., 2003. Relational aggression and psychosocial adjustment in intercollegiate athletes. Journal of Sport Behavior 26 (2), 155–167.

Sulloway, F., 1996. Born to Rebel: Birth Order, Family Dynamics, and Creative Lives. Pantheon Books, London.

Theberge, N., 1989. A feminist analysis of responses to sports violence: Media coverage of the 1987 World Junior Hockey Championship. Sociology of Sport Journal 6, 247–256.

Therber, F., 2009. A Hawkeye turned Hoosier, Goldman has built IU's wrestling program. *Herald Times*, February 3, B1.

Thing, L.F., 2001. The female warrior. International Review for the Sociology of Sport 36 (3), 275–288.

Thompson, H., 2007. Mothers know best. USA Hockey 29 (9), 40–45.

Tomlinson, A., 2007. The Sport Studies Reader. Routledge, London, 470 pp.

Trochim, W., 2001. The Research Methods Knowledge Base. Atomic Dog, Cincinnati, OH.

van der Dennen, Johan M.G., 2000. "Problems in the Concepts and Definitions of Aggression, Violence, and Some Related Terms." Retrieved January 21, 2009, at Wiley website: http://rint.rechten.tug.nl/rth/dennen/problem1.htmlÒ.

Vandewater, E., 2005. Family conflict and violent electronic media use in school aged children. Media Psychology 7 (1), 73–87.

VonRoenn, S., Zhang, J., Bennett, G., 2004. Dimensions of ethical misconduct in contemporary sports and their association association with the backgrounds of stakeholders. International Sport Journal 3 (1), 37–54.

Weems, R., 2009. Personal account of violence in sport. February 18.

Weinstein, M.D., 1995. Masculinity and hockey violence. Sex roles: A journal of research. Plenum Publishing, Santa Monica, CA.

Welch, M., 1997. Violence against women by professional football players. Journal of Sport and Social Issues 21 (4), 392–412.

Wells, B., 2008. How much competition is too much for kids? The Repblican sports Desk.http://www.mass.live.com/sports/index.ssf/2008/12.

Wenthe, D., 1997. Kool kids: corporate-sponsored free swim. Parks and Recreation 32 (11), 58–61.

Whannel, G., 2000. Sport and the media. In: Coakley, J. (Ed.), Handbook of Sports Studies. Sage, London.

Wilsey, S., 2006. The beautiful games: Why soccer rules the world. National Geographic 209 (6), 42–69.

Wilcox, R. (Ed.), 1994. Of fungos and fumbles Explaining the cultural uniqueness of American sport, or a paradoxical peek at sport: American style. Fitness Information Technology, Inc, Morgantown, WVA, p. 521. Ralph C. Wilcox, Ed. Sport in the global village.

Wilkins, N., 1997. Overtime is better than sudden death. Parks and Recreation 32 (3), 54–61.

Witt, P.A., Crompton, J., Baker, D., 1995. Evaluating youth recreation programs. Leisure Today, 3–6.

Wolff, R., 2001. Give the heave-ho to outrageous behavior. Time 95 (23).

Wolff, R., 2001. Don't turn your child into a sports specialist. Time 95 (23).

Wood, R., 1992. Physical Aggression As A Function of Anger In Men and Women. Unpublished doctoral dissertation. Indiana University Libraries, Bloomington.

Worrell, G., Harris, D., 1986. The relationship of perceived and observed aggression of ice hockey players. International Journal of Sport Psychology 17 (1), 34–40.

www.stophazing.com.

www.nays.com.

www.nrpa.org.

www.ncaa.com.

Yaeger, D., 2003. Son of Saddam: As Iraq's Top Olympic Official, Uday Hussein is accused of the torture and Murder of Athletes Who Fail to Win. Sports Illustrated Online. Path: http://sportsillustrated.cnn.com/si_online/news/2003/03/24/son_of_saddam/ Retrieved May 22, 2006.

Yin, R., 2003. Case Study Research: Design Methods, third ed. Sage, Thousand Oaks, CA.

Young, K., White, P., 1995. Sport, physical danger, and injury: The experiences of elite women athletes. Journal of Sport and Social Issues 19 (1), 45–62.

Young, S., Ross, C.M., 2000. Recreational sports rrends for the 21st Century: Results of a Delphi Study. NIRSA Journal 24 (2), 24–37.

Zani, B., Kirchler, E., 1991. When violence overshadows the spirit of sporting competition: italian football fans and their clubs. Journal of Community & Applied Social Psychology 1, 5–21.

INDEX